SHETLAND'S NORTHERN LINKS
LANGUAGE AND HISTORY

SHETLAND'S NORTHERN LINKS
LANGUAGE AND HISTORY

Edited by
Doreen J. Waugh

Associate Editor
Brian Smith

Scottish Society for Northern Studies
1996

Published in Scotland by:
The Scottish Society for Northern Studies
c/o School of Scottish Studies
University of Edinburgh
27 George Square
Edinburgh EH8 9LD

The printing of this book is made possible by a gift to the University of
Cambridge in memory of Dorothea Coke, Skjaeret, 1951

ISBN 0-950599-49-2

Cover designed by Richard Stafford from a photograph, by John Coutts,
of St Mary's Kirk, Sand.

Text set throughout in Times New Roman

Printed by:
Shetland Litho
Prince Alfred Street
Lerwick
Shetland ZE1 0EP

To the memory of
Thomas Mortimer Yule Manson
1904-1996

CONTENTS

CONTRIBUTORS

PETER ANDERSON is Deputy Keeper, Scottish Record Office, Edinburgh.

JOHN R. BALDWIN is an independent historical researcher with particular interests in the Northern Isles and the Faroes. He is also editor of several volumes in the Scottish Society for Northern Studies monograph series.

MICHAEL P. BARNES is Professor of Scandinavian Studies, University of London.

RONALD G. CANT is now retired from his post as Reader in Scottish History, University of St Andrews.

JAMES R. COULL is Senior Lecturer in the Geography Department, University of Aberdeen.

BARBARA E. CRAWFORD is Lecturer in Medieval History, University of St Andrews and former President of the Scottish Society for Northern Studies (1981-84).

GILLIAN FELLOWS-JENSEN is Reader in the Institute of Name Research, University of Copenhagen.

ALEXANDER FENTON is Director of the European Ethnological Research Centre, Edinburgh and former Professor of Scottish Ethnology, School of Scottish Studies, University of Edinburgh.

NOEL FOJUT is Principal Inspector of Ancient Monuments with Historic Scotland, Edinburgh.

LAURENCE GRAHAM is a retired headmaster, writer of Shetland dialect material and joint editor of *The New Shetlander*.

STEFFEN STUMMANN HANSEN is a Research Fellow in the Institute of Archaeology and Ethnology, University of Copenhagen.

MICHAEL R. H. JONES is Professor of Geography, University of Trondheim.

GUNNEL MELCHERS is Reader in the Department of English, University of Stockholm.

IAN A. MORRISON is Fellow of the University of Edinburgh, Honorary Senior Lecturer, University of St Andrews and current President of the Scottish Society for Northern Studies.

BRIAN SMITH is Archivist for the Shetland Islands Council, Lerwick.

DOREEN J. WAUGH is an independent place-name researcher and former President of the Scottish Society for Northern Studies (1990-93).

GRAEME WHITTINGTON is Professor of Geography, University of St Andrews.

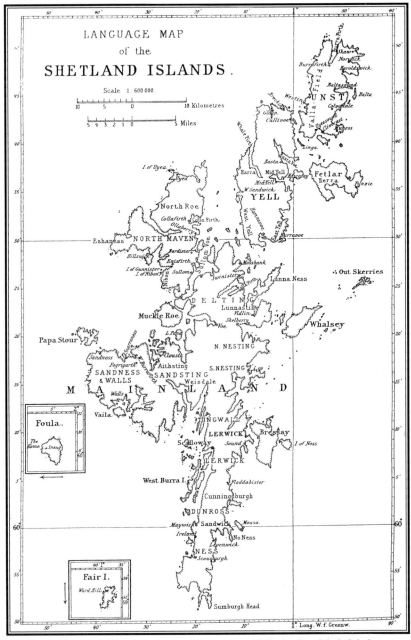

Reproduced from the 1993 reprint of *The Place-Names of Shetland* by Jakob Jakobsen.

PREFACE

Shetland's Northern Links: Language and History is one in a series of publications by the Scottish Society for Northern Studies. The conference which gave rise to the publication was held in Lerwick, Shetland, in July 1993, and it marked two special occasions: the quarter-centenary of the Society's existence and the centenary of the arrival of the Faroese philologist Jakob Jakobsen in Shetland at the start of his three-year period of place-name and dialect field work in the islands. As President of the Society at the time, I was particularly pleased to be able to organise a conference in my native Shetland, in conjunction with the locally-based Jakob Jakobsen Centenary Committee whose members planned to mark the event by reprinting Jakobsen's *The Place-Names of Shetland*, with a new introduction by Dr Gillian Fellows-Jensen of the University of Copenhagen, written against the background of her own work on Scandinavian place-names in England, and by inviting Professor Michael Barnes of the Scandinavian Studies Department, University of London, to give a public lecture.

Professor Barnes is interested in Scandinavian languages in general and, in particular, those of the Norse colonies of the west. He has written extensively on Faroese and on the varieties of Scandinavian spoken in the Northern Isles and elsewhere in the British Isles. The public lecture by Professor Barnes, on the topic of Jakobsen and the Norn language of Shetland, is now published as the opening chapter of this volume and the ensuing four chapters, plus the final chapter by the editor, also relate specifically to aspects of language use in Shetland; hence the title *Shetland's Northern Links: Language and History*. The remaining eleven chapters range over a variety of disciplines and periods in time but all contribute in some way to a greater understanding of Shetland's history.

Immediately prior to the launch of the reprint of Jakobsen's volume and the public lecture in the Garrison Theatre, Lerwick, conference delegates were privileged to be invited to a reception by the Shetland Islands Council and its Convener at the time, Edward Thomason, and I should like to thank the members of the council for their generosity. I owe thanks to many other people in Shetland who contributed to and attended the conference and have since shown interest in publication of the present volume but, above all, I owe a great deal to Brian Smith, my associate editor, who has been a constant source of encouragement and information. Robert Wishart, Managing Director of The Shetland Times Ltd and Shetland Litho has also been enormously helpful. He introduced me to Richard Stafford who produced the attractive cover design based on a photograph, by the Lerwick photographer John Coutts, of St Mary's Kirk at Sand.

Finally, I should express thanks to all the contributors to this volume whose enthusiasm for and knowledge of Shetland has made it possible to produce a second Society monograph on the topic. The first, *Scandinavian Shetland: An Ongoing Tradition?*, which appeared in 1978 and was edited by John R. Baldwin, is now out of print but it is pleasing to note that some of the contributors to the original volume are making a reappearance in *Shetland's Northern Links: Language and History.*

Doreen J. Waugh

At the Jakob Jakobsen Centenary celebrations are — from left — Jakobsen Committee member, John Graham; President of the Scottish Society for Northern Studies, Doreen Waugh; Jakobsen Committee member, Brian Smith; Gillian Fellows-Jensen, Copenhagen, who wrote the new introduction for the reprint of Jakobsen's *The Place-Names of Shetland*; Michael Barnes, London, who gave the Jakobsen Centenary Lecture at the Garrison Theatre, Lerwick; Jakobsen Committee member, Laurence Graham.

Photo: Malcolm Younger. July 1993.

JAKOB JAKOBSEN AND THE NORN LANGUAGE
OF SHETLAND

Michael P. Barnes

For Shetlanders, the name of the scholar in whose memory this centenary lecture is being given carries strong connotations of a Scandinavian linguistic heritage. Jakob Jakobsen and Norn, to quote the words of the popular song (though forsaking the benefit of rhyme) 'go together like a horse and carriage'. This juxtaposition of scholar and phenomenon therefore seems a natural choice for today's lecture topic. But as well as summarising Jakobsen's achievements in Shetland, and in a modest way attempting a revaluation of his work on Norn, I shall try to take a slightly broader view of the man and a more critical one of Shetland's linguistic heritage. What images does the name Jakobsen conjure up outside these islands, and what is, or was, Norn?

It is perhaps worth reminding ourselves at the outset that Jakobsen was a Faroeman. Brief accounts of his life and work have been furnished by Matras (1957; 1973) and Grønneberg (1981). What neither of these scholars do, however, is to make clear how widely perceptions of Jakobsen differ depending on one's perspective.

To the academic community at large he is a Norse philologist who contributed valuable material of particular help in understanding the origins and development of large numbers of individual Scandinavian words. The pages of etymological dictionaries such as Torp 1919 and de Vries 1962 bear ample testimony to the impact of his research in this area.

In Faroe, Jakobsen, or 'Jákup doktari' as the Faroese themselves often say, is a figure of enormous stature, held in great esteem and affection. And this is scarcely surprising when one reviews the contribution he made to the study of his native language and culture. At a time when Faroese was almost exclusively an oral medium, he performed several prodigious feats of composition and publishing — indeed in some respects it would not be inappropriate to call Jakobsen 'the father of modern written Faroese'. He was the compiler of the vocabulary volume of *Færøsk Anthologi* (Hammershaimb 1891) — an extensive collection of ballads, legends and related material — and it is that vocabulary which forms the basis of the current Faroese-Danish dictionary (Jacobsen and Matras 1961), of which the recent Faroese-English dictionary (Young and Clewer 1985) is in large part a translation. Jakobsen also collected and edited a vast corpus of Faroese legends and folk-tales (Jakobsen 1898-1901), published a volume of pre-Reformation documents relating to Faroe (Jakobsen 1907), and wrote a historical and literary study of the legendary Faroese character Páll Nólsoy (Jakobsen 1908-12). For this last work, considered by some to be his greatest, he was obliged to create single-handed a Faroese scholarly idiom; previously the language of scholarship in the islands had been exclusively Danish. Further contributions Jakobsen made to Faroese studies were in the fields of place-names and orthography. As a champion of orthographic reform, it must be said, he achieved very little, but that is a fate he shares with many, including no less a controversialist than Bernard Shaw. For both practical and pedagogical reasons Jakobsen wanted to remove the Icelandic and etymological garb in which written Faroese had been clothed since the middle of the nineteenth century and bring spelling more into line with pronunciation. However, his proposals, first made in 1889, met with vehement opposition, and although he adapted his own spelling in various ways, few of his fellow-countrymen were in the end prepared to follow him. In spite of this set-back, Jakobsen was and remains a towering intellectual figure in his native Faroe — best known there, understandably, as the scholar who strengthened respect for the Faroese language and played an important part in equipping it to deal with the demands of the modern world.

Jakobsen, then, is a man with a considerable and varied reputation. Naturally enough, it is his work on 'the Norn language of Shetland' that looms largest in the minds of the people of the Northern Isles, but before proceeding to consider that aspect of his career, it was fitting, I felt, that I should place on record here a brief acknowledgement of his many other achievements and offer thereby some indication of his considerable scholarly versatility.

As is well known, Jakobsen first arrived in Shetland in the summer of 1893. Here he remained for almost two years, working with single-mindedness and dedication to record every remnant of Norn he could find. Words, phrases, snatches of conversation, proverbs, rhymes, riddles, place-names — as well as other, less conspicuous items — all were carefully noted down and discussed. Although he made two further brief visits to Shetland, in 1905 and 1912, it was in the years 1893-5 that the bulk of the work of collection was accomplished. (An account of Jakobsen's activities in Shetland can be found in Grønneberg 1981.)

Following this initial stay, Jakobsen began to issue the results of his research in both learned and popular form. More or less complete bibliographies of his published works can be found in Jakobsen 1957 (251-3) and Joensen *et al.* 1964 (265-7), while Grønneberg 1981 (87-9) separates from the rest those items that deal with Shetland and Orkney. Here it will be sufficient to mention his doctoral thesis, *Det norrøne sprog på Shetland* (1897a), the two popular lectures, *The Dialect and Place Names of Shetland* (1897b), the pioneering *Shetlandsøernes stednavne* (1901) — the English-language version of which (*The Place-Names of Shetland*, 1936) is now happily reprinted as part of the centenary celebrations — and the monumental two-volume *Etymologisk ordbog over det norrøne sprog på Shetland* (1908-21) and its English translation *An Etymological Dictionary of the Norn Language in Shetland* (1928-32, reprinted 1985 by the Shetland Folk

2

Society). The doctoral thesis, the place-name volume and the dictionary can without doubt be classed as landmarks in the history of Scandinavian philology; the two popular lectures, for their part, provide entertaining and lucid summaries of the author's most important discoveries for the lay reader.

In casting round for a fair measure of Jakobsen's achievement I have found comparison of the post-language-shift documentation of Norn with that of Cornish particularly illuminating. Both languages appear to have died — in the sense of losing their last native speakers — in the final quarter of the eighteenth century. Insofar as one can assume that elements of a language will live on for a while after the disappearance of native competence, one would have expected nineteenth-century Cornwall and Shetland to have yielded roughly equal amounts of material. In fact, the data we have about Norn from the late nineteenth century exceed by far, both in variety and volume, the information available to us about Cornish from the whole of the century — notwithstanding the fact that there seems to have been a more widespread interest in Cornish than in Norn. Jakobsen's *Etymological Dictionary*, in addition to listing approximately 10,000 individual words, a quite staggering number, contains a great many 'fragments of Norn'. Seekers after remnants of Cornish could only find 'odd words and phrases, the basic numerals, the Lord's Prayer' (Price 1984: 137). It is not impossible, of course, that — for whatever reason — there was simply less Cornish to discover than there was Norn, but it also seems clear that there was no one in the far west of Cornwall at the relevant period with Jakobsens's energy, dedication and persistence.

Jakob Jakobsen is thus plainly a man who deserves our gratitude and praise. Because of this, however, there is a danger when we try to assess his contribution that we may descend into eulogy and clothe him in a mantle of perfection. That does neither him nor us a service because it masks reality, and prevents a true appreciation of merit. Meticulous and critical scholar that Jakobsen was, it is hardly an approach that would have commended itself to him. The greatest service we can do Jakobsen, I believe, is to cast a critical eye on his work and weigh up its advantages and shortcomings dispassion-ately, because only when we uncover the solid core of his achievement can we (a) properly understand his worth and (b) identify those areas where further study needs to be undertaken. Jakobsen himself would surely have wished for nothing less.

Insofar as each age has its own preoccupations and sensibilities, its own ways of looking at things, there can never be a 'proper' or 'definitive' assessment of the achievements of earlier scholars. One generation may re-discover and exalt what an earlier one has decried. Our task in attempting a revaluation of works of the past can thus only be to judge them in the light of what we think important, giving reasons for our judgement at appropriate points.

How well, then, has Jakobsen's work on Norn stood the test of time? How far does it address the concerns of modern philologists and linguists and make sense to them?

It is perhaps as well to begin by emphasising what Jakobsen actually did. When he arrived in Shetland in 1893, his concern was to rescue from oblivion as much of the Norn language as possible. He was driven partly by feeling for his native Faroese, which he seems to have thought in danger of suffering the same fate as Norn, and partly by the appetite of the philologists of his day for comparative linguistic material. It should not be forgotten that nineteenth-century linguistics and comparative philology were one and the same thing; the focus was entirely historical and the main aim was to trace languages, in particular the Indo-European languages, back to common ancestors and thus demonstrate their relationships. True to his purpose, Jakobsen set about finding as many informants as possible and interviewing them. All the information they were able to give him — continuous pieces of Norn, isolated phrases, individual words, and variant pronunciations — he noted down in meticulous detail.

Unfortunately neither Jakobsen himself nor anyone else seems to have left a detailed record of his interviewing techniques. A basic outline is offered in the introduction to the *Etymological Dictionary* (1928-32: xxvii-xxix), but it cannot be said that one emerges from this account with a very clear picture of the manner in which he operated. How much of his material did he obtain from informal conversation, for example, how much from urging his informants to recall Norn words and phrases, and how much as a result of repeated prompting? Did he talk to informants of 'Norn' or of 'Shetland dialect' — or just of old words and phrases? If we had a clearer idea of the way in which individual pieces of information were elicited, we would be in a better position to evaluate them as source material.

Having amassed a huge amount of data, Jakobsen left Shetland in 1895 and spent the next fifteen to twenty years organising and publishing it. His return visits in 1905 and 1912 appear to have yielded a few significant additions, but nothing to compare with what he obtained in the 1890s.

The publishing of the Norn material naturally involved not just the sifting and organisation of the data and notes Jakobsen had obtained in the course of his fieldwork, but also detailed analysis and comment. *Det norrøne sprog på Shetland* deals mainly with individual words: it classifies them according to their areas of application, adduces cognates from other forms of Scandinavian, and offers brief discussion as appropriate; in addition we find a short section on grammar ('grammar' in this context being virtually synonymous with inflexions), a longer section on sounds and sound changes, and a collection of Norn fragments, some with comments, some without. *The Dialect and Place Names of Shetland* consists, as already noted, of two separate papers: the one on the dialect once again deals chiefly with individual words and their derivation, while that on the place-names explains the meaning of the more common kinds of name and endeavours 'to suggest general rules, according to which the place-names have been given' (p.120); in both cases items are loosely arranged according to areas of application and/or sense. *Shetlandsøernes stednavne/The Place-Names of Shetland* explains the origins of some 2,800 names, arranged according to topographical elements, farm-names, natural features etc. The *Etymological Dictionary*, naturally enough, is mainly taken up with individual articles on the thousands of words Jakobsen collected, but these are preceded by a lengthy introduction and, in the later, English-language version of the work, by a great many 'fragments of Norn' — some, but by no means all of which, had previously been published in *Det norrøne sprog på Shetland*. The introduction, which itself is fuller in the English than in the Danish-language version (mainly because of the inclusion of other parts of *Det norrøne sprog på Shetland*), and also somewhat reorganised, treats among other things the following: the history of Orkney and Shetland; the language shift in which Norn was replaced by Scots; Jakobsen's movements in Shetland and the principal informants he met on his various journeys (as well as in Lerwick); the relationship of Norn to other forms of Scandinavian; and indications in Shetland dialect of influence from non-Scandinavian languages.

My main aim in outlining the contents of Jakobsen's principal works on Norn in what must appear tedious detail has not been to show what the reader will find there. That is surely well enough known. Rather, my concern has been to underline what he will not find. Words there are a-plenty, also sounds and sound changes, comparisons with other languages and a strong historical perspective. But what of the systems of Norn?

During the years Jakobsen was working with the Shetland material, a Swiss linguist, Ferdinand de Saussure, was worrying about the state of his discipline. Linguists, he felt, had failed to think seriously about what they were doing and to identify properly the object of their study. It was all very well comparing languages and tracing their ancestry, but what was language? The answer he gave was simple enough. Language is a collection of signs. The signs are arbitrary in the sense not only that there is no intrinsic connection between a sign and what it denotes but also that each language has its own way of organising the world into concepts and categories. This implies that to be meaningful both the linguistic signs and the things signified must be part of a system, since neither can be defined except by their relations to other members of the same system. Language thus essentially consists of systems of oppositions in which each element is defined negatively; it is what the other elements are not. That means that the elements of which language is made up are abstract units whose actual realisation may vary — but only insofar as their realisation does not become confused with that of a contrasting unit. The primary task of the linguist must therefore be to identify and describe the various systems that underlie actual language performance.

5

Although concerns and methodologies have changed radically since Saussure's day, his thinking profoundly influenced the development of linguistics. Indeed, the claim is often made that he laid the foundations of the modern discipline. Since Saussure and Jakobsen were contemporaries, and Saussure's most influential treatise was only published posthumously in 1916, it would of course be foolish to criticise Jakobsen for not having adapted his approach to take account of ideas that were still in embryo during most of the period in which he was collecting and writing. Criticism is certainly not my purpose in introducing Saussure and Saussurean concepts at this point. What I want rather to emphasise is that a linguist or even an interested layman looking back at Jakobsen's work today must regret that the priorities of linguistic enquiry in the late nineteenth and early twentieth century did not extend to the establishing of basic systems. Very possibly, this could not have been done for Norn in any case, for it is far from clear that the information available to Jakobsen would have been sufficient to have allowed the identification of even the crudest oppositions. Nevertheless, one cannot but feel frustrated when reading Jakobsen's works by his failure to look for the wood because of his constant and overriding concern with the individual trees.

I will give an example to illustrate what I mean. Each language or dialect has a set number of distinctive speech sounds. It is their existence that enables us to distinguish one word from another. Thus English *pin* is not confused with *bin* unless a speaker should confuse /p/ with the contrasting unit /b/. The number of distinctive speech sounds varies considerably from language to language, but the average is said to be about thirty-five. It is clearly of far greater importance to identify these basic units of opposition than to describe every shade of sound one encounters. Some speakers of English pronounce *pin* [pʰɪn], others [pɪn], but in neither case will the word be confused with *bin*, because the basic opposition /p/:/b/ has been maintained. In the light of this, what are we to make of the myriad of variant pronunciations Jakobsen offers us in his *Etymological Dictionary*? In a rare outburst of criticism, Stewart (1964: 172) describes the listing in the dictionary of twenty-five variant pronunciations of the word *gopn* 'the hollow of the hand, a handful' (1928-32: 253) as 'phonetics run riot', and it is hard to disagree with this verdict. The question we would wish Jakobsen had addressed is: how did speakers distinguish *gopn* from other words — that is, what were the distinctive units of which his twenty-five variant pronunciations were the realisations? Had he been able to establish, however tentatively, a system (or systems in the case of significant dialectal variation) of distinctive speech sounds, we would not only have known more about Norn in its last years as a living language, but also have been able to trace more easily the lines of its development from Old Norse. In the case of Faroese, for example, we can for the most part predict with certainty what the present-day reflexes of an Old Norse word will be. That is in no way true of Norn.

6

The point I have made by reference to sounds and sound systems applies equally to other levels of linguistic analysis. Few answers are provided by Jakobsen for the person with questions about the morphological, syntactic or semantic systems of Norn.

Viewed from the modern perspective, then, Jakobsen's Norn studies leave many gaps. We must regret that he did not fill them, but we can well understand that he, like us, was limited by the intellectual climate of the times in which he lived and worked. If we consider him simply as a philologist of his day, and perhaps more than anything as an antiquarian, his achievements must in most respects be judged both wide-ranging and solid. Muted criticism has, it is true, been offered of some of Jakobsen's etymologies. Svavar Sigmundsson (1984), for example, quotes detailed evidence to support the assertion that 'it is easy to find omissions of Icelandic cognates, and of [sic] errors in etymology [arising therefrom]' (pp.285-6), and further notes that Scandinavian ancestry was falsely attributed to a number of words that were in fact of Dutch or Scots origin. But such mild correctives hardly constitute a challenge to Jakobsen's authority as the custodian and interpreter of Norn. There is, however, one area in which he has been subject to more serious criticism. His views on the Norn-Scots language shift in Shetland, for long taken as more or less axiomatic, have recently been declared by more than one scholar to be untenable.

As we have seen, the nineteenth-century philologist and the modern linguist differ greatly in their approaches to language. They also differ in the rigour of argument they require in the practitioners of their respective disciplines. While modern linguistics eschews the imprecise formulation and the arbitrary claim, and offers few hiding places for the fuzzy thinker, comparative philology is rife with intuitive responses, impressionistic accounts and ad-hoc solutions. The comparative philologist seldom worked within an explicit theoretical framework and was relatively unconstrained by the need to give definitions and adhere to them once given. This left him free to advance ideas for no better reason than that that was the way he felt things must surely have been.

Jakobsen's views on the shift from Norn to Scots in Shetland typify this nineteenth-century approach. Without ever formulating a clear hypothesis, he manages to leave the reader with the impression that the shift was effected by a gradual but increasingly Scots dominated intermixture of the two languages. This development had not even reached its end by the time he arrived in Shetland, he appears to suggest, but was at a stage where the grammatical structure of the language was entirely Scots while large areas of the vocabulary were still of Scandinavian origin. How or why Jakobsen came to think along these lines is unclear, but it is possible that he was to some extent influenced by prevailing attitudes in Shetland. To many Shetlanders the distinction between a Scandinavian language and a form of Scots heavily impregnated with Scandinavian words appears to have been blurred. In the

7

preface to his *An Etymological Glossary of the Shetland and Orkney Dialect* (1866: vi), Edmondston offers the following view:

> From more frequent business and social intercourse with their southern neighbours, the people of Shetland are rapidly losing, or rather have already lost, a distinctive dialect; and when the present old inhabitants have passed away, most of the old *Norn* will be buried with them.

What seems to be revealed here is an inability to distinguish between Scots and Norn, though much hangs on the precise meaning of 'a distinctive dialect'. Lack of clear thinking on the matter is certainly reflected in the works of later Shetlandic writers, who have often tended to see Shetland dialect as something quite distinct from Scots, several assuming it to be in some way a direct descendant of Scandinavian or at the very least to have arisen from an amalgamation of Scandinavian and Scots (e.g., Saxby 1907-8: 65-9; Sandison 1953: ix-xii). Graham (1984: xiii) declares without further ado: 'The Shetland dialect is an amalgam of Norse, Lowland Scots and English.' Stewart (1964: 170) draws attention to confused thinking on the issue among the general population:

> They could give him [Jakobsen] their age-old words, whose meanings they knew well-enough, fondly imagining that they, in their Scots context, were a Norse language, their Norn.

It is obvious that Jakobsen with his vast experience clearly understood the difference between a language and a substratum, and indeed he regularly refers to Norse or Norn as a language quite distinct from any form of nineteenth-century Shetland speech. Nevertheless, he may have been sufficiently influenced by the notion that Norn somehow lived on in the Scots and English of Shetland to consider that the only plausible explanation for the linguistic state of affairs in the islands was that there had been some kind of fusion of Norn and Scots.

For the sake of directness and clarity I have so far been summarising what I perceive to have been Jakobsen's view. It is only just, however, to let the man speak for himself. Here are the essentials of what he has to say about the shift from Norn to Scots (1928-32: xix-xx).

> The last man in Unst who is said to have been able to speak Norn, Walter Sutherland from Skaw, died about 1850. In Foula, on the other hand, men who were living much later than the middle of the present (19th) century are said to have been able to speak Norn. The Norn spoken towards the middle of the century and later can hardly have been of much account. The difference between it and the dialect of the oldest people of the present generation probably consisted in little more than the fact that the former contained a greater sprinkling of Norn words which the younger people did not understand...
> The statement that the Norn died out in the previous [eighteenth] century must not, however, be taken too literally. The process has been a steady and gradual one, which is still continuing even at the present day. One must

certainly suppose that even at the beginning of the 18th century the dialect was hard hit, and after that time it seems to have degenerated very rapidly...

The first portions of the old language to be affected, as one can easily imagine, and as appears from the fragments preserved, were the inflections, the grammatical endings...next the minor words frequently recurring in speech, such as: conjunctions, prepositions, pronouns, numerals, and common adverbs; likewise adjectives and verbs in general use, as well as abstract nouns.

As a rule the substantives, denoting visible things, inanimate objects and living beings, have lasted longer...names of implements, household utensils; and this, of course, naturally applies to such things as stand in close connection with the daily life and activities of the people.

One aspect of this account strikes the reader immediately: there is in it a kind of prediction after the event. Jakobsen appears to be suggesting that the sequence of linguistic losses and replacements he assumes for Shetland is generally to be expected in cases of language death ('as one can easily imagine'), but he offers no evidence in support of such a contention. His method is simply to analyse the Norn elements that were extant in his day and extrapolate backwards in time. Thus, numerals ('minor words frequently recurring in speech') would, he reckons, be lost relatively early. But if we once more turn our gaze to the south-west of Britain, we find that in the century and a half that followed the death of Cornish it was the numerals which were remembered better than anything else (Ellis 1974: 125-9).

Recalling the quotation from Edmondston, with its apparent vagueness about the status of Norn, we can also note Jakobsen's loose use of the term 'dialect', which is allowed to denote both eighteenth-century Norn and the speech of 'the oldest people of the present generation'.

The strongest message to emerge from what Jakobsen says, however, is that the language shift in Shetland was a very gradual process by which elements of Norn vocabulary and grammar had been, and were still being, replaced, one by one, by Scots and/or English equivalents. This was a message that seems to have found widespread favour. By some it was not only accepted, but elaborated and refined. Flom (1928-9: 145), for example, gives the following account of early twentieth-century Shetland dialect:

Its grammar is in the main Scotch, but with a few Norse forms; its accent is West Norwegian; its phonology a mixture of the two. In its phraseology the Norse element would seem to be the dominant one; but yielding slowly to Lowland and Standard English. In its vocabulary it is part Norse and part Lowland Scotch (and English), with less important other elements... On the semantic side, Norse and Scotch uses are found side by side in well-nigh every sentence spoken; its compound words very frequently combine one stem from the one language with one from the other. This unusual example of mixed speech, with its exceedingly irregular forms, is the outgrowth of the complete union of two languages.

Flom also writes of 'the progressive disintegration of Norse', of 'the fusion between the two languages' which is 'intimate', and of 'the last stages of the

9

decay of the ancient Norn in Shetland' (1928-9: 153, 158-9). He even goes so far as to offer an estimate of the changing ratio of Norn and Scots words in 'the total word-stock of the Shetlands' (1928-9: 150). Although Flom adduces reasons of his own to support his thesis of a mixed language, and even contradicts Jakobsen's dictum that 'minor words frequently recurring in speech' were among the first to go, there can be little doubt that in its main thrust his account is strongly influenced by the views of his predecessor. Indeed, there are copious references to Jakobsen's works throughout the article.

For over half a century no challenge was offered to this notion of a gradual change from Norn to Scots and/or English accomplished via the partial or total fusion of the two languages. That is odd, because in its roots the notion seems to be purely intuitive — though there is, of course, nothing to say that intuitive ideas may not be right. The reason for the lack of critical discussion seems to have been threefold: (1) the stature of Jakobsen, (2) a falling off of interest in Norn and (3) the absence of a general theoretical framework in which questions of language death and language shift could be discussed. Fortunately, none of these three factors is any longer a barrier. Jakobsen still enjoys a high reputation, but we feel free to draw attention to and if necessary criticise those aspects of his work that advances in linguistic science have shown to be wanting; Norn is now once more the subject of lively scholarly debate; and an increasing body of knowledge about language contact and language death enables us to place the shift from Norn to Scots in a much wider context.

Debate was joined in 1984 when Laurits Rendboe and I independently (but see Barnes 1984b: 40-41) published brief papers on Norn. Mine was an encyclopaedic article, which perhaps explains why I transmitted the views of earlier scholars on the language shift somewhat uncritically; I did nevertheless find it prudent to add the following rider (1984a: 355-6):

> Although what we appear to see is a gradual change from pure Norn to Scots (and more recently English), it is unlikely that there were ever speakers who mixed the two languages up so inextricably that a trained linguistic observer would have been unable to determine which language they were speaking. If an individual's grammatical, and, above all, phonological structure were Scots, that person was no longer speaking Norn, however many Norn words or phrases his or her language contained.

My view was based partly on the fact that no one, to my knowledge, has produced a documented example of a truly mixed language, and partly on the idea that phonological and grammatical structure is primary. English, after all, is classified as a Germanic language, even though less than half its vocabulary is of Germanic origin.

Rendboe's approach was far more radical. He dismissed the mixed language idea entirely and argued on the basis of a re-interpretation both of

10

the testimony of seventeenth and eighteenth-century writers and of the eighteenth and nineteenth-century fragments that have survived that Norn remained a pure Scandinavian language more or less until the death of the last native speakers. His conclusion was (1984: 80):

> As long as the Norn was spoken by the Shetlanders 'amongst themselves', it did not deteriorate in the manner thought by some, neither by being inextricably mixed up with Scots, nor by a breakdown of the grammatical system. As far as the available evidence shows, Norn stood firm to the end.

In subsequent publications, especially *Det gamle shetlandske sprog* (1987), Rendboe has continued to urge this view.

In the two principal contributions I have made to the debate (1989; 1991) I have tried to set out an alternative hypothesis that takes account not just of literary and language-internal evidence, but also of social and political history and of what we know of language shifts elsewhere. My quarrel with Rendboe is twofold. (1) He is not a dispassionate investigator; one sometimes has the impression when reading his treatises that he allows the desired conclusion to form the starting point and assembles and interprets evidence with the sole aim of supporting his conclusion. (2) In ignoring the wider context of language contact and language death Rendboe too easily falls prey to the lure of the *ad-hoc* explanation, and to that extent has not moved on from the position of the nineteenth-century philologists. Often I can think of other interpretations of his data than the ones he provides, but in the absence of any theoretical framework or external body of evidence to which appeal can be made, there is no way in which the validity of such competing interpretations can be ascertained. It is only, I believe, by looking at the Shetland data — historical, literary and linguistic — in the light of other cases of language shift that we can hope both to offer plausible explanations of individual problems and also to suggest a total interpretation of the change from Norn to Scots that has the power to persuade.

This is not the place to rehearse the accumulated wisdom about language decline and death (see, for example, Dressler and Wodak-Leodolter 1977), but the essentials are these. Language fusion is a very sparsely documented process indeed, and the development envisaged by some, in which Shetland Norn is supposed gradually to have adopted more and more Scots features until it became more Scots than Norn, is, as far as I know, unparalleled. What regularly happens in language shift is that the dying language exhibits symptoms of interference and decay. It loses functions, often ending up purely as a language of the home. It also loses structures, in part at least because the usual regulatory mechanisms that help preserve language structure — institutional norms, literary tradition, correction by elders — are breaking down or are non-existent. As a language decays, so its speakers desert it for the higher-prestige alternative. This is usually accomplished in the course of three generations. The first generation are native speakers of the decaying language who learn the new tongue for reasons of necessity, but mostly remain more proficient in the old. The next generation, largely because of greater exposure at a younger age — often from their own parents — become truly bilingual, or in some cases more proficient in the new language. The children of these bilinguals are seldom exposed to the old language even in the home, and end up at best with only a very imperfect or passive knowledge of it. (The last stages of this process can be observed at the present time in, for example, parts of the far west of Ireland.)

What we have to ask ourselves in the case of Shetland is whether there is any evidence to suggest that the language shift which displaced Norn might have taken a different course from that documented so frequently elsewhere. The answer, as far as I can see, is no. Unless and until such evidence is discovered, I therefore think we have to conclude that both Jakobsen's and Rendboe's interpretations of the shift are wrong. To believe either in language fusion or in a Norn that 'stood firm to the end' we would need far stronger historical, literary and linguistic indications than those which up to now have been shown to exist. It is, of course, surprising that so many items of Norn vocabulary were preserved in Shetland Scots, but that is not in itself an argument for language fusion. The large substratum, for whose preservation we have first and foremost to thank Jakobsen, seems rather to reflect Norn in its dying stages when it was probably little more than the language of fishing, farming and the home. In certain areas of usage, for example the taboo language of fishermen, special factors were probably at play; in others, such as the denotation of different shades of colour in sheep or cows, Scots will have had few words with which to replace the familiar Norn terms; and sometimes, doubtless, Norn words and phrases were simply too firmly associated with the Shetland way of life to be easily lost — as long as that way of life continued.

These in part theoretical and abstract considerations have brought us to the point where it is possible to sketch the linguistic history of Shetland since the Viking Age and thus to clear up some of the terminological confusion I have commented on earlier.

The Viking invaders, who appear to have begun settling in Shetland about AD 800, rapidly imposed their language on the islands. Since the majority appear to have come from Norway, probably western Norway, we must assume that their speech was a form of west Scandinavian. For some seven to eight hundred years this language remained dominant in Shetland. We have only the haziest notion of how it developed because of the extreme scarcity of relevant data, but in the absence of any normative influences aberrant forms were doubtless legion. In some respects the development of Shetland Scandinavian seems to have paralleled that of Faroese. In Faroe, where Danish was for so long the official medium, the indigenous tongue was certainly free to go off at every conceivable tangent. For political, economic and social reasons which are too well known to need rehearsing here, Scandinavian was eventually replaced by Scots in Shetland. From what we know of the history of the islands after their pledging to Scotland, it seems probable, but not certain, that the fundamental shift took place in the seventeenth century (cf. Barnes 1991: 449-56). Following the shift, it is no longer appropriate to speak of the language of Shetland as Scandinavian, although, as has earlier been stressed, the newly acquired Scots contained a considerable Scandinavian substratum. Today, English is replacing Scots and the Scandinavian element is vastly reduced.

What, then, of 'Norn' and of 'the dialect'? Norn, as we have seen, has meant different things to different people. Such semantic elasticity is of course only tolerable if each user defines what he means by the term, but explicitness is not a virtue that has commended itself to the majority of contributors to the discussion. To me it seems obvious that in a Shetland context Norn should be employed to denote the form of Scandinavian once spoken in the islands, and nothing else. That is in keeping with its etymology; the term, after all, comes from ON *norrœnn* 'of northern origin, Norse' and/or *norrœna* 'Northern language, Norse language'. Dialect is probably best defined as a regionally distinctive variety of speech within a speech community. Under that definition Norn was hardly a dialect since its speakers appear to have considered that they formed their own speech community in the same way as speakers of Faroese (cf. Rendboe 1987: 2-4). Shetland Scots or Shetland English, on the other hand, seem eminently well qualified for dialect status, since both Scots and English embrace much wider speech communities than Shetland.

It is interesting to speculate on what might have been. Had Norn managed to survive in one or two outlying areas as has Gaelic in the Hebrides and in Ireland, we would presumably now be seeing a Shetland struggling to maintain its native tongue. We can visualise evening classes in Norn for the Scots or English-speaking majority seeking to rediscover their roots. And we can imagine many of the participants slowly giving up as they discover that language learning is not all fun, but involves long hours of steady toil as well. Perhaps there would be dual-language road signs, Norn television, even Norn soap operas. Alas, all this must remain in the realm of fantasy, for Norn, like Cornish, is dead.

But could it be revived? Cornish has its revivalist zealots, although the language they speak and teach has recently been dubbed 'Cornic' and dismissed as largely bogus (Price 1984: 141-4). Unfortunately, or perhaps fortunately, Shetland Norn is in a much worse state of preservation than Cornish. Much of the basic vocabulary and grammar is missing as are most of the form words, and we have little idea of how it might have been pronounced in its final years. The revivalist would have to begin by re-inventing the phonological system on the basis of eighteenth-century spellings (very limited in scope and by no means fully elucidated), nineteenth and twentieth-century dialect pronunciation and the systems of the most closely related forms of Scandinavian. This does not sound to me like a realistic or a sensible proposition.

So Shetland will have to think of Norn in the same terms as the Brochs, Jarlshof and other icons of the past. It forms an important but broken link with distant generations and is thus part of the islands' multi-faceted cultural heritage. Like many of the more physical remains, Norn is now only imperfectly understood, but the remnants are still there for us to gaze at — thanks in large measure to Jakob Jakobsen, Faroeman and scholar.

Bibliography

Barnes, Michael, 1984a: 'Orkney and Shetland Norn'. In: Peter Trudgill (ed.), *Language in the British Isles*, Cambridge, 352-66.

Barnes, Michael, 1984b: 'Norn', *Scripta Islandica* 35, 23-42.

Barnes, Michael P., 1989: 'The death of Norn'. In: Heinrich Beck (ed.), *Germanische Rest- und Trümmersprachen*, Berlin, 21-43.

Barnes, Michael P., 1991: 'Reflections on the structure and the demise of Orkney and Shetland Norn'. In: P. Sture Ureland and George Broderick (eds.), *Language Contact in the British Isles*, Tübingen, 429-60.

Dressler, Wolfgang and Wodak-Leodolter, Ruth (eds.), 1977: *Language Death (International Journal of the Sociology of Language* 12).

Edmondston, Thos., 1866: *An Etymological Glossary of the Shetland and Orkney Dialect.* London.

Ellis, P. Berresford, 1974: *The Cornish Language and its Literature.* London.

Flom, George T., 1928-9: 'The transition from Norse to Lowland Scotch in Shetland, 1600-1850', *Saga-Book* X, 145-64.

Graham, John J., 1984: *The Shetland Dictionary* (2nd ed.). Lerwick.

Grønneberg, Roy, 1981: *Jakobsen and Shetland.* Lerwick.

Hammershaimb, V.U. (ed.), 1891: *Færøsk Anthologi* I-II. København.

Jacobsen, M.A. and Matras, Chr., 1961: *Føroysk-donsk orðabók* (2nd ed.). Tórshavn.

Jakobsen, Jakob, 1897a: *Det norrøne sprog på Shetland.* København.

Jakobsen, Jakob, 1897b: *The Dialect and Place Names of Shetland.* Lerwick.

Jakobsen, Jakob (ed.), 1898-1901: *Færøske folkesagn og æventyr.* København.

Jakobsen, Jakob, 1901: 'Shetlandsøernes stednavne', *Aarbøger for nordisk oldkyndighed og historie* II. række: 16, 55-258.

Jakobsen, Jakob (ed.), 1907: *Diplomatarium Færoense* I. Tórshavn.

Jakobsen, Jakob, 1908-12: *Poul Nolsøe. Lívssøga og irkingar.* Tórshavn.

Jakobsen, Jakob, 1908-21: *Etymologisk ordbog over det norrøne sprog på Shetland.* København.

Jakobsen, Jakob, 1928-32: *An Etymological Dictionary of the Norn Language in Shetland* (reprinted 1985). London.

Jakobsen, Jakob, 1936: *The Place-Names of Shetland* (reprinted 1993). London.

Jakobsen, Jakob, 1957: *Greinir og ritgerðir.* Tórshavn.

Joensen, Hans Debes et al. (eds.), 1964: *Fróðskaparrit* 13.

Matras, Chr., 1957: 'Dr. Jakob Jakobsen, føroyingurin, granskarin'. In: *Jakob Jakobsen, Greinir og ritgerðir,* Tórshavn, 7-21.

Matras, Chr., 1973: *Nøkur mentafólk.* Tórshavn.

Price, Glanville, 1984: *The Languages of Britain.* London.

Rendboe, Laurits, 1984: 'How "worn out" or "corrupted" was Shetland Norn in its final stage?', *NOWELE* 3, 53-88.

Rendboe, Laurits, 1987: *Det gamle shetlandske sprog. NOWELE* Supplement vol. 3. Odense.

Sandison, William (ed.), 1953: *Shetland Verse: Remnants of the Norn.* Shrewsbury.

Saxby, Jessie M.E., 1907-8: 'Notes on the Shetland dialect', *Saga-Book* V, 65-9.

Stewart, John, 1964: 'Norn in Shetland', *Fróðskaparrit* 13, 158-75.

Svavar Sigmundsson, 1984: 'A critical review of the work of Jakob Jakobsen and Hugh Marwick'. In: Alexander Fenton and Hermann Pálsson (eds.), *The Northern and Western Isles in the Viking World*, Edinburgh, 280-91.

Torp, Alf, 1919: *Nynorsk etymologisk ordbok.* Kristiania.

de Vries, Jan, 1962: *Altnordisches etymologisches Wörterbuch* (2nd ed.). Leiden.

Young, G.V.C. and Clewer, Cynthia R., 1985: *Faroese-English Dictionary.* Peel.

TINGWALL: THE SIGNIFICANCE OF THE NAME

Gillian Fellows-Jensen

Introduction: *thing and ting*[1]

In present-day English the word *thing* means 'an entity of any kind', concrete or abstract, as in the pronouns *anything, something* or *nothing*. It can even be used as a term of endearment, at least to those not in a position to remonstrate, for example Alice in Wonderland, into whose arm the Duchess tucked her arm affectionately, saying 'You can't think how glad I am to see you again, you dear old thing!' In the modern Scandinavian languages, too, the cognate word *ting* has the same all-embracing kind of meaning and is found in pronouns such as Danish *nogenting* 'anything' and *ingenting* 'nothing'. When used of a person, however, it is generally in a derogatory sense, referring mainly to women who are old, ugly or loose-living or perhaps all three at once (ODS s.v. *ting*).

As a place-name specific or generic, it is clear that *thing* must have a concrete significance. There are a number of field-names recorded in Middle English and early Modern English sources in which it is compounded with a personal name or a term denoting a human-being and seems to have the sense 'possession'. The earliest example I have noted is *Aynolfesthyng* 1356 in Ash in Surrey (Gover et al. 1933: 270) but the vast majority of occurrences date from the 15th to the 17th centuries.

In Old English and the other early Germanic languages, however, the word thing and its cognates, which were all of neuter gender, had the meaning 'assembly, meeting' and it is from this meaning that the modern, more general meaning has developed. In a language such as Danish in which a modified form of grammatical gender has survived to the present day, *ting* in its original sense retains its neuter gender, while *ting* in the wider sense has acquired common gender so that we have *et ting* 'an assembly' and *en ting* 'a thing'. When a Danish newspaper headline today uses the term *Tinget* with the suffixed definite article, it is referring to *Folketinget*, the Danish parliament, but this term only dates back to the nineteenth century. It was the renown of the Icelandic parliament, the *Alþingi*, that inspired Norway, after secession from Denmark in 1814, to employ the term *ting* for the three chambers of the Norwegian parliament (*Lagting, Odelsting* and *Storting*), while Denmark, after the abolition of absolute monarchy and its replacement

---

1. For their generous response to my requests for information, I should like to express my warmest thanks to Richard Cox, Barbara Crawford, Ian Fraser, William Gillies, Ann Harrison, Bill Nicolaisen, Brian Smith, John Kousgård Sørensen, Þórhallur Vilmundarson and Doreen Waugh.

16

by the new constitution of 1849, followed the same inspiration and chose to call the two divisions of the Danish parliament *Landsting* and *Folketing*. In the Faroes, the *Løgting* or 'law assembly' has borne this name from at least 1400, although it was earlier known as *Alþing*.

Thing and *ting* in place-names

As well as of legislative assemblies, the word *ting* has also been used through the centuries in Scandinavia of judicial assemblies and it is in this sense that it normally occurs in major and minor place-names in both Scandinavia and the British Isles. The Danish parish known as *Ting Jellinge*, for example, has since 1480 been distinguished from the neighbouring village of *Sønder Jellinge* by the prefixing of *Ting*, referring to the fact that the hundred *ting* or assembly was held here (Jørgensen 1977: 100, 298).

It is comparatively rare for *thing* in the sense 'assembly' to occur as a place-name generic. The village and district name *Morthen* in the West Riding of Yorkshire has early forms such as *Mordinges* 1164-81, *Morthinges* 1202-08, *Morthyng* 13th century and can only be explained as a compound of Old English (OE) *mōr* or Scandinavian (Scand) *mór* 'moorland' with OE or Scand *þing* and A.H. Smith has argued very plausibly that it is probably a vestige of some early Viking organisation in this moorland area (Smith 1961-63: 1. 101-02, 141, 168-69; 7. 54 n.3). The name of the assembly would seem to have been transferred both to a village and to the district subject to the *thing*, which apparently embraced the area between Rotherham and the southern boundary of the Riding. A name identical in origin with *Morthen* may once have been found in Berwickshire. The place-name *Mordington* there has been tentatively explained as an original OE *morð-hring* 'murder ring' with subsequent addition of OE *tūn* 'settlement' (Williamson 1942: 30; Nicolaisen 1976: 28). This explanation of the name, which is based on an isolated form *Morttringtonam* 1095, as opposed to the other forms such as *Morðintun* c.1095, *Morthinton* 1095x1100, seems rather far-fetched and Nicolaisen has suggested in the addenda in the reprint of his book an alternative derivation of the first part of the name as OE *mōr-þing* 'moorland assembly'. Mordington House stands on the moors to the north of Berwick-on-Tweed, just on the Scottish side of the border. It may once have been the meeting-place for an assembly of the inhabitants of this moorland area.

Assembly names in *-thing*

In Iceland a number of district assemblies with names such as *Sunnudalsþing* and *Skaftafellsþing* were established in the course of the tenth century (Thorsteinsson 1985: 26-27). There is a small group of names in Shetland ending in *ting*. Five of these are now parish names: *Delting, Lunnasting, Nesting, Aithsting* and *Sandsting* (Jakobsen 1936: 126; Stewart 1987: 300). The word *ting* has been compounded with the name for, or a description of,

17

the locality at which the local assembly met: Dale, Lunna, the ness called Neep, Aith and Sand. These parish-names are not recorded in written sources until 1490 or later and they may well be comparatively late formations. The two remaining names in *-ting* in Shetland are recorded in a document from 1321 as *Rauðarþing* and *Thveitaþing* but it is not known for certain to which localities they refer. It has been suggested by John Stewart that *Rauðarþing* was an early assembly held in the area now referred to as North Roe and that this latter name, which is not recorded until 1660, may originally have been **rauð-eið* 'red isthmus' (Stewart 1987: 79), while P.A. Munch considered that *Rauðarþing* was identical with the parish of North Mavine, in which there are several places with names containing the element *rauðr* 'red' (Andersen 1984: 30). *Thveitaþing* has been identified by John Stewart with *Twatt* in Aithsting and by Jakob Jakobsen as an area embracing all the places with names containing the element *þveit*. Of the five names in *-þveit* recorded by Stewart, four are borne by localities in the parish of Walls, situated at no great distance from each other, and none is recorded in a document earlier than 1507 so it is possible that the area was earlier known as *Thveitaþing* and that the generic in their names refers to this area rather than to a localised clearing.

T(h)ing as a place-name specific

In southern England there are a number of place-names which contain as specific OE *þing* in the sense 'assembly'. *Fingest* in Buckinghamshire (*Tingeherst* 1163; Mawer & Stenton 1925: 176)) and *Thinghill* in Herefordshire (*Tingehele* 1086; Ekwall 1960: 466) would both seem to mean 'assembly hill', while *Finedon* in Northamptonshire (*Tingdene* 1086; Gover et al. 1933: 181) means 'assembly valley'. All three localities presumably received their names because they were the sites for local meeting-places.

Þing-haugr

Place-names containing *þing* are of quite common occurrence in northern and eastern England and the coining of most of these names has been ascribed to settlers of Scandinavian origin, who would have been familiar with the word *þing* in the sense 'assembly' from their homelands. In Denmark, the commonly occurring name *Tinghøj* 'assembly mound' denotes the meeting-place of a 'hundred assembly', although it normally survives as the name of a farm (Hald 1969: 37). The name *Tinghøj* is not of course to be analysed as a compound place-name with the generic *-høj* but as a simplex appellatival name, that is an appellative which has assumed the function of a place-name.

The cognate Scandinavian appellative **þing-haugr* functions quite frequently as a place-name in England. Of particular significance are names such as *Thingoe* in Suffolk, which is borne by an administrative hundred, and

Þinghou in Lincolnshire and *Thinghou* in Norfolk, which apparently denote hundred meeting-places (Anderson 1934: 60, 68, 95). *Fingay Hill* in the North Riding of Yorkshire, recorded as *Thynghou* c.1250, seems likely to have been the meeting-place of the judicial assembly for the whole riding (Smith 1925: 213). In theory, these various English names could be reflexes of an English compound of *þing* and *hōh* but the fact that the names occur in areas of marked Danish settlement, combined with the fact that the Danish compound occurs frequently as a place-name in Denmark, while there are no certain examples of *þing-hōh in southern England, make it reasonable to assume a Danish origin for *Thingoe, Fingay* etc.

The Scandinavian compound *þing-haugr* is not, of course, specifically Danish but it is in Denmark that it would seem to have achieved greatest popularity. *Þinghaugr*-names do occur in Norway, for example *Tinghaugen* in the parish of Hedrum in Vestfold (*Thinghouffuen* 1664; NG 6. 342), as well as in areas of Norwegian settlement in the British Isles, for example the mound known as *Dingishowe* which stands on the isthmus joining the parish of Deerness to the Orkney Mainland (Marwick 1952: 79).

Þing-staðr

Another compound appellative which functions as a place-name in Denmark is *þing-staðr 'assembly place'. This word is current in the form *tingsted* in modern Danish as the term for the place where a judicial court sits. The appellative *tingsted* occurs as a parish name *Tingsted* on the island of Falster, while a conglomeration of farms and houses in the parish of Vester Marie in Bornholm also bears the name *Tingsted* (Kousgård Sørensen 1958: 122). This appellative is of much more common occurrence as a place-name in Sweden, where it is found as the name of several parishes and hamlets (Linde 1951: 62-64). It does not seem to have been carried as a place-name to the British Isles but the English appellative *thingstead* is used of some presumed assembly-sites.

Þing-vellir in Scandinavia

Whereas the *Tinghøj-* and *Tingsted*-names occur most frequently in eastern Scandinavia and in areas where Danish vikings settled, another group of names, those in *þing-vellir 'assembly plains', for example the Shetland *Tingwall*, have a markedly western distribution. It is *Þingvellir* in Árnessýsla in Iceland that is the most well-known of them. The role played by this locality and the *Alþingi* held there as the scene for dramatic events in the Icelandic family sagas has meant that its fame has spread worldwide. There is an account of its early history in *Íslendingabók* (Benediktsson 1986: 8-9). The *Alþingi* was established about the year 930. It met for two weeks at midsummer each year. It was on a hill known as *Lögberg* or 'law-rock', standing on the northern bank of a lake later known as *Þingvallavatn*, that the laws were pronounced. The *lögrétta* or legislative assembly, which consisted

19

of the *goðar* or priest-chiefs from the various districts, met on the other side of the river Öxará and the *holmgangur* or institutionalised duels were fought on the *Holmur* in the river until this practice was abolished by law in about 1010. The delegates to the *Alþingi* put up their booths and grazed their horses on the surrounding plain, which had become public property as a result of confiscation after a murder. This plain became known as *Þingvellir*. Land on which to pitch tents and graze horses would of course have been a prerequisite for the holding of any assembly to which delegates had to travel from far afield. Even the more local things whose authority extended over small districts needed to be held at sites where open land was available and which lay on convenient routes of communication. *Þingvǫllr* in Helgafellssveit in Snæfellsnessýsla is named in a document from about 1274 (*þijng vallar holmur*; DI II. 116) and the farm of this name is recorded as *Þingvollur* in a document from 1377-78 (DI III. 326). Later the place became known as *Þingvellir*, presumably as a result of the loss of -r- in the genitive singular form *þingvallar-* and the subsequent misinterpretation of the name as a plural form, perhaps by association with the name of the site of the *Alþingi*. It is claimed that Þorsteinn Þorskabítr's farm on the coastal promontory near Helgafell, which is described in *Eyrbyggja saga* chap. 11, is to be identified with *Þingvellir* (Sveinsson & Þórðarson 1935: 18 n.3). There are other *Þingvellir*-type names in Iceland but they are not recorded in early sources.[2]

The Norwegian vikings who settled in Iceland must have taken the concept of the *þing* or legal assembly with them. The question is whether they also brought the name **Þingvǫllr* or **Þingvellir* ready coined for the land surrounding the assembly-place or whether the name *Þingvellir* arose naturally as a fitting description of the locality around the Icelandic meeting-place. There are a few *Þingvellir*-names in continental Scandinavia that are recorded in early sources. The earliest record of such a name is *de Thingwaldum* 1290, which refers to a parish that is now the central part of the town which was granted its charter under the name Karlstad in 1584, situated on Lake Vänern in Värmlands län, Sweden (SOV I. 41; VII. 17). Other records of this name are as *par. Thingwalli* 1291, *de Thynguallum* 1305. The site can be easily reached by land and water from far around and it is at no great distance from the frontier with Norway. The cathedral now stands on the mound which was earlier known as *Lagberget* (*a lagberghe* 1411). The village called *Tingvall* in Naverstad parish, Bullarens härad, Bohuslän, Sweden, is first recorded as *j Þinguollum* in a charter dated 1334 (OGB XVIII. 129). This Tingvall was originally the site of the assembly-place of the härad. Like Tingvalla (Karlstad), it is situated fairly close to the frontier with Norway. A farm called *Tingvalla* in Dals-Eds parish, Vedsbo härad,

---

2. For a discussion of *þingvellir*-names recorded in younger sources in Scandinavia see Gillian Fellows-Jensen, 'Tingwall, Dingwall and Thingwall', *NOWELE* 21/22 (1993), 53-67. The present paper incorporates much of this earlier work.

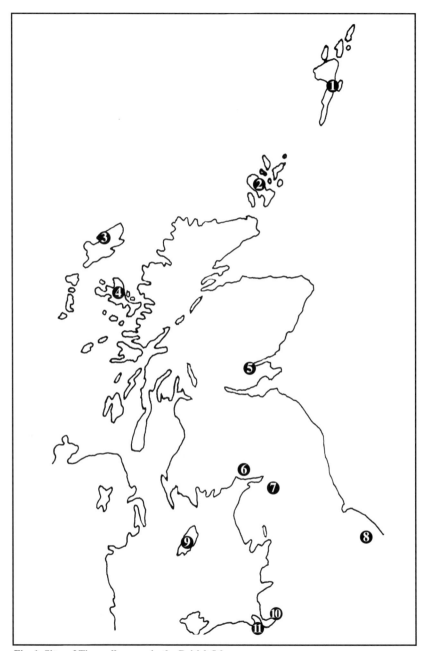

Fig. 1. Sites of Tingwall-names in the British Isles.

21

Älvsborgs län (*SOÄ* XIX. 26) is first recorded in the 16th century but it is uniquely well situated from the point of view of communications on a direct route into Norway (Rosell 1983: 18).

Almost exactly contemporary with the first record of Tingvall in Bohuslän is that of *Tingvoll* parish and herred in Møre and Romsdal, Norway, *a Þingwelli* 1333, *a Thingwallom* c.1430 (NG 13. 370). The parish church here stands on level ground near the shore of the Tingvoll fiord.

There is no way of knowing whether or not *Tingvalla* in Värmland, *Tingvalla* in Bohuslän and *Tingvoll* in Norway antedate the naming of the famous *Þingvellir* in Iceland. It is striking that at Tingvalla (Karlstad) there is also a *Lagberget*, corresponding to the *Lögberg* in Iceland, but it was, of course, to be expected that there would be a name for the locality at which the laws were actually promulgated as well as a name for the surrounding land.

Þing-vellir in the British Isles

The Norwegians who settled in Shetland, Orkney, the Hebrides, Man and mainland Scotland brought with them both the concept of the thing and the idea that a thing needed to be held at a site with good communication-routes by land or sea and where there was suitable accommodation on level ground for the tents and horses of those attending the thing. They sometimes called this level ground *þingvǫllr* or *þingvellir*. There are no fewer than eleven names in the British Isles which may be reflexes of these Scandinavian terms and the localities denoted by eight of these can still be identified. I shall discuss these names briefly here in topographical order from north to south.

1. Tingwall, a parish about 6 km to the north-west of Lerwick, Mainland, Shetland (HU 4143). *a Þinga velle* 19/5 1307 (DN I. 98), *Tyngvale* 1389 (DN II. 396), *Tyngvell* 1467x1507, *Tyngwall* 1525, *Tingwale* 1576 (Stewart 1987: 298). Initial /þ/ is replaced by /t/ in the Shetland dialect. The annual chief assize in Shetland is said to have been held here. Late in the 13th century this assembly was referred to as the *loghþing* (DN I. 89). At the beginning of the 18th century, John Brand described the site and the way in which the court was conducted as follows:

> It was in this Parish in a small Holm [HU 4143], within a Lake nigh to this Church, where the Principal Feud or Judge of the Country used to sit and give Judgment, hence the Holm to this day is called the *Law-Ting* (from which probably the Parish of *Tingwal* had its name) we go into this Holm by steping stones, where three or four great Stones are to be seen, upon which the Judge, Clerk and other Officers of the Court did sit: All the Country concerned to be there stood at some distance from the Holm on the side of the Loch, and when any of their Causes was to be Judged or Determined, or the judge found it necessary that any Person should compear before him, he was called upon by the Officer, and went in by these steping stones, who when heard, returned the same way he came: And tho now this place be not the Seat of Judgement, there is yet

22

something among them to this day, which keepeth up the Memory of their old Practice, for at every end of the Loch there is a House, upon whose Grass the Country Men coming to the Court did leave their Horses, and by reason the Masters of these Houses did suffer a loss this way, they were declared to be Scat-free (Brand 1701: 121-22).

According to Thomas Gifford's description of the site, the causeway leading to the holm was known as the *Lawtainy* (Gifford 1786: 9-10). Brian Smith has suggested to me that the lawthing holm at Tingwall might originally have been a duelling-holm rather than the site of the *thing* itself. No artificial features have been found on the holm and it must be admitted that the procedure described by John Brand would have slowed down the business of the *thing* immensely. It is, however, unlikely to be possible to determine with certainty whether the holm was ever used for duels or whether the judge had his seat there from the very beginning.

2. Tingwall, a farm in Rendall parish, Mainland, Orkney (HY 4022). *Á Þingavoll* [anno 1154] c.1700 (*Orkneyinga saga*, chap. 95), *Tyngwell* 1492 (Marwick 1952: 121). Initial /þ/ is replaced by /t/ in the Orkney dialect. There is a broch near the site and a green mound at the farm which may have marked the place of assembly. There are no records of meetings here, however, and it may merely have been the site of a local or district thing, although its location is fairly central for the island group as a whole.

3. *Tiongal*, whose name survives in Cnoc an Tiongalairidh < *Cnocan Tiongalairidh*, the name of a hillock in the township of Tolsta Chaolais, Isle of Lewis (NB 1937). The specific of the name *Tiongalairidh* is probably either **þingvǫllr* in stem-form or **þingvellir* in its genitive form *þingvalla*. The generic is Gaelic *áirge* 'milking-place', perhaps as the Gaelic loanword in Scandinavian *ærgi* (Cox 1990: 96; 1991: 484-86). Initial /þ/ was replaced by /t/ in Gaelic. The presence of an assembly-place here in the heartland of Norse settlement in Lewis is not surprising but the site may only have had local significance. The lower-lying land on the coast of East Loch Roag would have been well suited for grazing the horses of delegates attending an assembly.

4. *Tinwhil*, a place that cannot be localised but whose site was probably at approximately NG 415583, where Glen Hinnisdal, the valley of the river Hinnisdal, broadens out somewhat, Isle of Skye. *Glen Tinwhill* 1733, *Glen Tinesdale* 1804, *Amhainn Hinisdil* 1824 (Gordon 1963: 88-91). The generic in the name *Hinnisdal* is Scandinavian *dalr* 'valley'. The first element of the Gaelic name which is its specific is probably Scandinavian *þings-*. To judge from the form Tinwhill recorded in 1733, *þings-* would seem to be an elliptical form of this, which in turn would be a reflex of a Scandinavian place-name or appellative **þingvǫllr* or *-vellir*. Initial /þ/ was replaced by /t/ in Gaelic. In the modern name the initial has been aspirated after Gaelic *Gleann*. There is no record of an assembly's being held here but, as noted by

23

Bridget Gordon, the Glen would have been easily accessible by land or by sea from the whole of the western side of Trotternish.

5. Dingwall, a town and parish on the north-western shore of the Cromarty Firth, where this is joined by the river Peffer, Ross-shire, Scotland (NH 5458). Its Gaelic name is now *Inbhir Pheofharan* (*Inver-Peffrey*). *Dingwell in Ross* 1227, *Dignewall* 1263, *Dingenale* c.1275, *Dingwal* 1308, *Dingwall* 1382 (Watson 1904: 93). The Scandinavian name was originally adopted by Gaelic speakers, who replaced initial /þ/ by /t/. The initial *D-* in all the recorded forms of Dingwall probably reflects the fact that the Gaelic starting-point for the subsequent adoption of the name into English was the dative case, probably dependent on the preposition *in* (later *ann, an*[(n)]) 'in'. The *n* of the preposition would have had the effect of voicing the initial /t/ of the Gaelic form of the name to /d/. William Gillies informs me that nasal mutation is also reflected, for example, in the Scots-English form *Dam-* of a few Gaelic place-names in *Tom-* 'hillock'. Dingwall lies at some distance from the main concentration of Scandinavian place-names in north-eastern Scotland but the town would seem to have been the meeting-place for the Norse settlers and their Gaelic neighbours in Easter Ross (Crawford 1986: 43). Its survival as the name of an administrative centre in the upper part of the Cromarty Firth suggests that it must have persisted as an assembly-place long after these Norse settlers had been absorbed into the local Gaelic population and the Orkney earls had lost control of the province. In 1503 there was still a moot-hill (*montem*) of Dingwall close to the town and this may well have marked the meeting-place of the thing.

6. Tinwald, a parish situated on gently rising ground in Nithsdale north of Dumfries, Dumfriesshire, Scotland (NY 0081). *Tynwald* 1335-36, *Tynualde* 1477, *Tynwald* 1522 (Williamson 1942: 20). Initial /þ/ was replaced by /t/ in Gaelic. The spelling of the second element of the name shows confusion with Old English (Anglian) *wald* m. 'high land covered with wood'. Tinwald lies close to the river Nith, which marks the western boundary of the part of Dumfriesshire where Scandinavian names are of fairly common occurrence. To the west of the river, place-names are predominantly Gaelic. The Mote of Tinwald is known to have been a site at which sasine of lands was ceremoniously granted.

7. Dingbell Hill in Whitfield parish, Northumberland, England (NY 7758). *Vingvell hill* 1386, *Dingbell Hill* 1613 (Mawer 1920: 63). If the form *Vingvell* really does represent an older *þingvellir, the initial consonant must be erratic, just possibly resulting from a confusion of the letters *þorn* and *wen* in an Old English record. The later *Dingbell*-spellings would seem to represent confusion of *-vell* with the common noun *bell*, which is used in the local dialect of a hill, and subsequent reinterpretation of *Thing-* as *Ding-*, an onomatopoeic word imitating the sound of a bell. There is no phonological explanation for a development of Scandinavian initial /þ/ to /d/ in the

24

Northumberland dialect. Sir Allen Mawer doubted whether a Scandinavian assembly would ever have been held in Whitfield and thought Dingbell Hill might have been so called because it reminded some Scandinavian settler of 'the hill in some far-distant place of assembly in his own homeland'. There is certainly little evidence for Scandinavian settlement to be derived from the place-names in the neighbourhood of Dingbell, although it is not far from Ouston (*Ulfs-tūn) and lies on the main route from Alston (originally *Halfdanar-bý) to Corbridge and Newcastle. It is just conceivable that Dingbell may have marked the easternmost limit of Scandinavian penetration from Cumberland but the inexplicable initial D- rather suggests that the name has nothing whatsoever to do with the Scandinavians and their thing-sites.

8. *Thingwala*, a place that cannot be localised more closely than to the parish of Whitby, Yorkshire North Riding, England (c.NZ 8910). *Thingwala* [c.1077] late 12th century, *Tingwal* [1145x1148] c.1240 (Atkinson 1879: xxii, 3, 118; Smith 1925: 128). Initial /þ/ survives in English. The exact site of *Thingwala* cannot be located but it seems likely that it was the meeting-place for Norse settlers in Eskdale or perhaps in the whole of Cleveland. The area is rich in Scandinavian place-names. It is of particular interest that Normanby (*Norðmanna-bý) (NZ 9206) and Airy Hill (*ærgjum 'at the shielings') (NZ 8909) are not far from Whitby and both their names point to settlers who had come to the Danelaw from the west, where Norwegians and Gaelic-speakers had been brought into contact with each other.

9. Tynwald Hill, in the treen of Balladoyne, in the parish of Kirk German, sheading of Glenfaba, Isle of Man (SV 2781). *Tyngualla* [anno 1237] c.1376 (Broderick 1979: f. 44r), *Tynwald* 1515 (Kneen 1927: 416). Initial /þ/ is replaced by /t/ in Manx Gaelic. In a central position and easily accessible from all points of the compass, Tynwald Hill would have been a convenient meeting-place. It stands on the site of a Bronze Age burial-mound and would thus seem to have been established as a place of assembly long before the arrival of the Vikings on Man. The Manx name of the hill, *Cronk Keeill Eoin* 'the hill of the church of St John', shows that the site has also had a religious significance.

The Manx parliament is still known as *Tynwald*. It now meets in the Tynwald Chamber in Douglas. The old tradition of an annual open-air assembly at Tynwald Hill survives to the present day, however. It is held on old midsummer day, July 5th, for the purpose of promulgating the Acts passed during the last session of Tynwald and for transacting other business.

10. Thingwall, a township in Childwall parish, West Derby hundred, Lancashire, England (SJ 4190). *Tingwella* 1177, *Thingwalle* 1212, *Thingwell* 1226 (Ekwall 1922: 112). Initial /þ/ survives in English. Thingwall Hall stands on a round, gently sloping hill between Roby (*rá-bý or 'boundary village') and West Derby (*djúra-bý 'deer village' or perhaps 'deer-park', the centre of West Derby hundred). There is a concentration of place-names of

25

Scandinavian origin in this hundred.

11. Thingwall, a township in the ancient parish of Woodchurch, Wirral hundred, Cheshire, England (SJ 2784). *Tuiguelle sic* for *Tinguelle* 1086 (Domesday Book), *Tingewella* 1249x1265, *Thingwelle* 1278 (Dodgson 1972: 273). *Thingwall* is on high ground which commands an extensive view but the actual site of the assembly cannot be located. To judge from the many place-names of Scandinavian origin there, the northern part of the Wirral peninsula must have been densely settled by Scandinavians. It has been suggested that the southern boundary of the territory of the Norse community was marked by Raby (**rábý* 'boundary village') and that Thingwall was its centre of administration.

The dating of the *Þingvellir*-names

It will be noted that the *Þingvellir*-names in the British Isles are not recorded in very early sources. The oldest original record is of the Cheshire *Thingwall* in Domesday Book of 1086, while the lost Yorkshire *Thingwala* is named in a late twelfth-century transcript of a document from about 1077. It is clear, however, that many of the names must have been coined much earlier than their first written records. The Scandinavian territories in Yorkshire, Lancashire and Cheshire, for example, had passed under the control of the English king well before the middle of the tenth century. The thing-sites in Shetland, Orkney, the Hebrides and Man must have been taken into use in the course of the ninth century. When settlers from Man or from south-west Scotland later landed in Wirral and south-west Lancashire, they established their local assemblies at localities they called *Thingwall*, even though the characteristic feature of these English sites was a hill and not a plain. It is not possible to date the arrival of these settlers in Cheshire and Lancashire with any certainty but it seems most likely to have taken place early in the tenth century. In the second decade of this century the English were busy fortifying Cheshire townships, apparently in an effort to contain the Vikings in Wirral, while Amounderness in Lancashire, which may still have been under Scandinavian rule at this time, was back in the hands of the English king Athelstan by 934. It seems unlikely that new Scandinavian settlement can have continued to take place in Lancashire and Cheshire much later than about 920. Conditions in the north-west of England were certainly still very unsettled throughout the first half of the tenth century, however, and enclaves of autonomous Vikings may have continued to live there and govern themselves. All in all, however, it seems most likely that Thingwall in Wirral and Thingwall in Lancashire were brought into use and named before the establishment of the Icelandic *Alþingi* on *Þingvellir* in 930. The immediate inspiration for these two names was probably Tynwald on Man. Tynwald in its turn, like most of the *þingvellir*-names in the Kingdom of the Isles, may have received its inspiration from *Tingwall* in Shetland but there would seem to be no way in which this can be determined.

Tingwall in Shetland, *Tinwald* in Dumfriesshire and *Tynwald* in Man are borne by localities where legal assemblies continued to be held for centuries, even after the Scandinavian language had dropped out of use. *Tingwall* in Orkney is in an area of dense and lasting Norse settlement and the name probably only dropped out of use because the seat of judgment was moved eastwards to Kirkwall, and *Tiongal* in Lewis is in the heartland of Norse settlement here. Several of the other seven *þingvellir*-localities, however, are found on the outskirts of, or at some distance from, the major areas of Norse settlement. This fact was already noted by Sir Walter Scott, who wrote after visiting the Shetland *Tingwall* in 1814, 'It seems odd that in Dumfries-shire and even in the Isle of Man, where the race and laws were surely Celtic, we have this Gothic word Ting and Tingwald applied in the same way' (Ash 1984: 203). *Dingwall* and *Dingbell* in particular lie well away from areas rich in Scandinavian place-names. *Tinwhil* in Skye is geographically isolated from the marked cluster of Scandinavian names in the Outer Hebrides. *Thingwala* in Yorkshire was in an area of mainly Danish settlement, while the two English *Thingwalls* are found in Scandinavian enclaves that are well away from the major areas of Scandinavian settlement in England in the Danelaw and Cumbria. It would seem that in order to survive it was not necessary for a *þingvellir*-name to be borne by a place of assembly which continued in use as such for centuries. In areas removed from the main concentrations of Norse settlement the name might survive the abandonment of the assembly-place with a new function as the name of a farm or hamlet.

Abbreviations and Bibliography

Andersen, Per Sveaas, 1984: 'Peter Andreas Munch and the beginning of Shetland Place-name Research'. In: Crawford 1984: 18-32.

Anderson, O.S., 1934: *The English Hundred-Names* 1. Lund.

Ash, Marinell, 1984: ' "So much that was new to me": Scott and Shetland'. In: Crawford 1984: 193-207.

Atkinson, J.C. (ed.), 1879: *Cartularium Abbathiæ de Whiteby* I. Durham: Publications of the Surtees Society Vol. LXIX.

Benediktsson, Jakob (ed.), 1986: *Íslendingabók. Landnámabók.* Íslenzk Fornrit I. Reykjavík.

Brand, John, 1701: *A Brief Description of Orkney, Zetland, Pightland Firth and Caithness.* Edinburgh.

Broderick, George (ed.), 1979: *Cronica Regum Mannie & Insularum.* Douglas.

Cox, R.A.V., 1990: 'The Origin and Relative Chronology of *Shader*-Names in the Hebrides'. *Scottish Gaelic Studies* XVI, 95-113.

Cox, R.A.V., 1991: 'Norse-Gaelic Contact in the West of Lewis: The Place-Name Evidence'. In: P.S. Ureland and G. Broderick (eds.), *Language Contact in the British Isles*, Tübingen, 479-94.

Crawford, Barbara E. (ed.), 1984: *Essays in Shetland History.* Lerwick.

Crawford, Barbara E., 1986: 'The Making of a Frontier: The Firthlands from the Ninth to Twelfth Centuries'. In: J.R. Baldwin (ed.), *Firthlands of Ross and Sutherland*, Edinburgh, 33-46.

DI = *Diplomatarium Islandicum* Iff. Kaupmannahöfn/Reykjavík. 1857ff.

DN = *Diplomatarium Norvegicum* Iff. Christiania. 1849ff.

Dodgson, J.McN., 1972: *The Place-Names of Cheshire* Part IV. English Place-Name Society Vol. XLVII. Cambridge.

Ekwall, E., 1922: *The Place-Names of Lancashire.* Manchester.

Ekwall, E., 1960: *The Concise Oxford Dictionary of English Place-Names.* 4th ed., Oxford.

Gifford, Thomas, 1786: *An Historical Description of the Zetland Islands.* London.

Gordon, Bridget, 1963: 'Some Norse Place-Names in Trotternish, Isle of Skye'. *Scottish Gaelic Studies* X, 82-112.

Gover, J.E.B. et al., 1933: *The Place-Names of Northamptonshire.* English Place-Name Society Vol. X. Cambridge.

Hald, Kristian, 1969: *Stednavne og Kulturhistorie.* Copenhagen.

Jakobsen, Jakob, 1936: *The Place-Names of Shetland.* London & Copenhagen. Reprint 1993, Lerwick.

Jørgensen, Bent, 1977: *Reciprokering.* Navnestudier 14. Copenhagen.

Kneen, J.J., 1927: *The Place-Names of the Isle of Man* IV. Douglas.

Linde, Gunnar, 1951: *Studier över de svenska sta-namnen.* Uppsala.

Marwick, Hugh, 1951: *Orkney.* London.

Marwick, Hugh, 1952: *Orkney Farm-Names.* Kirkwall.

Mawer, A., 1920: *The Place-Names of Northumberland and Durham.* Cambridge.

Mawer, A. & Stenton, F.M., 1925: *The Place-Names of Buckinghamshire.* English Place-Name Society Vol. II. Cambridge.

Nicolaisen, W.F.H., 1976: *Scottish Place-Names.* London. Reprint 1986.

NG = *Norske Gaardnavne* 1-19 (Kristiania/Oslo, 1897-1936).

ODS = *Ordbog over det danske Sprog* 1-28 (Copenhagen, 1918-56).

OGB = *Ortnamnen i Göteborgs och Bohus län* Iff. (Göteborg, 1923ff.).

Rosell, E., 1983: *Ortnamn i Dalsland.* Stockholm.

Smith, A.H., 1925: *The Place-Names of the North Riding of Yorkshire.* English Place-Name Society Vol. V. Cambridge.

Smith, A.H., 1961-63: *The Place-Names of the West Riding of Yorkshire* 1-8. English Place-Name Society Vols. XXX-XXXVII. Cambridge.

SOV = *Sveriges ortnamn. Ortnamen i Värmlands län* I-XVI (Uppsala, 1922-84).

SOÄ = *Sverges ortnamn. Ortnamn i Älvsborgs län* 1-20 (Stockholm, 1906-48).

Stewart, J., 1987: *Shetland Place-Names*. Lerwick.

Sveinsson, Einar Ól. & Þórðarson, Matthías (eds.), 1935: *Eyrbyggja Saga*. Íslenzk Fornrit IV. Reykjavík.

Thorsteinsson, Björn, 1985: *Island*. Copenhagen.

Watson, W.J., 1904: *Place-Names of Ross and Cromarty*. Inverness.

Williamson, May Gordon, 1942: *The non-Celtic place-names of the Scottish Border counties*. Unpublished Ph.D. thesis, University of Edinburgh.

THE DEVELOPMENT OF THE
SPOKEN AND WRITTEN SHETLAND DIALECT:
A HISTORIAN'S VIEW

Brian Smith

I am having the temerity to write about the Shetland dialect and its history because I believe that we can't altogether leave the subject to linguists. I say so because we have an example of the havoc that a linguist can play with the subject. I'm speaking about Laurits Rendboe's prolific work on Shetland Norn and the modern Shetland dialect. Rendboe isn't typical, but I'm afraid that some of his predilections and obsessions, and in particular the way that he deploys what he imagines is history, are paralleled in work by other linguists, even that of the revered Jakob Jakobsen.

For Rendboe, and Jakobsen, the death of Norn was tragic, the result of brutal oppression by Scotsmen. That oppression, involving the manipulation of weights and measures by Scottish incomers, especially between the 1560s and 1611, turned Shetland society 'topsy-turvy', in Jakobsen's phrase (Jakobsen 1928-32: xiv-xv). By some unexplained development these oppressions persuaded Shetlanders that, and I quote Jakobsen again, it was 'genteel to adopt Scottish words and modes of expression' (Jakobsen 1928-32: xvi). That was the first nail in Norn's coffin, exacerbated much later by the 'steamer service and penny papers' (cited in Grönneberg 1981: 18). By the time that Jakobsen arrived here, in 1893, there were only what the Nornophiles regard as the 'pitiful remains' of a great language.

According to Rendboe, in a new twist to the story, Norn actually survived, under the hated but mimicked new regime, for a very long time. It lingered here far longer than in Orkney, presumably because Orkney was much nearer the continent of Scotland. People had told Jakobsen that there were Norn-speakers in Foula as late as the second half of the nineteenth century, but Jakobsen was sceptical. That so-called Norn, he said, 'can hardly have been of much account'. It simply 'contained a greater sprinking of Norn words which the younger people did not understand' (Jakobsen 1928-32: xix). Jakobsen was one of the world's great *pessimists*: he was interested in the dead language, not the living one which had replaced it. He was so pessimistic that he predicted that Shetland's Norn vocabulary would disappear 'in the near future' (Jakobsen 1928-32: xx).

Rendboe makes much of Jakobsen's late-19th century Norn-speakers, but he doesn't quote Jakobsen's words of caution. He implies that there were secret Norn-speakers in the late eighteenth and even the nineteenth century, people who displayed great cunning in hiding their language from landlords and ministers (Rendboe 1984; 1985a). These linguistic rebels spoke 'pure'

Norn, uncontaminated by Scots. But all good things come to an end. Even Rendboe has to admit that there's no Norn around today. But he imagines that we're still dreaming about it, and that it is lurking around in our psyche.

As I said, we can't leave the history of our language to the linguists. I'm going to argue that Jakobsen and Rendboe — especially Rendboe — got it wrong. I suggest that Norn died for very complex reasons, and that the modern Shetland dialect established itself at a rather earlier date than the linguists sometimes imagine. I'll argue that much the same process, at much the same speed, happened in Orkney. Finally, I believe that the modern Shetland dialect is far more flexible, and its speakers and writers far more sophisticated, than the Nornophiles imagine.

The life and death of Norn

Before we understand the modern Shetland dialect we have to get Norn out of the way. I have rather a lot to say about that.

One of the most cherished old chestnuts about Shetland Norn is a belief that Shetlanders were writing documents in a Norse language until the first decade of the seventeenth century. The pundits contrast this remarkable situation with that in Orkney, where Scots documents are said to appear much earlier, and where Norse documents undoubtedly disappear at an early date. The Shetland antiquary Gilbert Goudie hunted down many of these Norse documents, 'waifs and strays' as he affectionately called them, and wrote a long and enormously influential article about them (Goudie 1904: 78-131).

There are several points to make about Goudie's documents. First, almost all of them were written in Norway. As a result they were naturally written in Norwegian, or rather in Danish. During the sixteenth and early seventeenth centuries Shetland still had strong commercial links with Norway, and strong landowning connexions, links which Orkney had lost many years previously (Smith 1990: 25-37). It was inevitable that Shetlanders and Norwegians, from time to time, would write down details of their mutual transactions. However, these documents tell us little or nothing about the language spoken in Shetland at the time. Only one of them can be said with certainty to have been written in Shetland, by Shetlanders. It was written in 1545.

Having said that, I have little doubt — although there's precious little information on the subject — that Shetlanders of the sixteenth century spoke a Norse language. However, I have little doubt either that, especially during the second half of the century, they were proficient in other languages as well. The most extraordinary feature of the documentary record of Shetland history, from the moment when we have lots of documents, is the fact that no-one ever refers to language *problems*. We only need to contrast that with the situation in Gaelic Scotland to smell a rat immediately. The first substantial record of public affairs in Shetland, the complaint against Laurence Bruce of

31

Cultmalindie in February 1577, is a fine example of mutual communication between Shetlanders, who are said to have spoken 'all in ane voice', and the men who wrote the Shetlanders' complaints down. Seven hundred male Shetlanders attended an assembly at Tingwall where two visiting Scots commissioners, Messrs Mudy and Henderson, transcribed their intricate grievances (Balfour 1859: 15-92). Those of us who have read that lengthy record not once but a hundred times marvel at how thoroughly Mudy and Henderson did their job, without any apparent howlers.

Similarly, there is no indication that the Shetlanders had had any difficulty in communicating with the main object of their complaint, Laurence Bruce of Cultmalindie, or with his Scots creatures — at least at the level of language. Furthermore, in one passage the Shetlanders describe how they overheard some German merchants discussing complex arrangements concerning commercial matters, and again they seem to have had no difficulty in understanding them (Balfour 1859: 41). I have a strong impression, from looking at these and other sources, that many late sixteenth century Shetlanders were good at languages.

To understand that proficiency we don't need to investigate the Shetlanders' genes, but their society. Shetland in the late sixteenth century had emerged in good shape from the long late medieval depression. Her population was rising, and she was participating in a lively trade with merchants from Germany, Scotland, Holland and England. Until 1611 there was a vigorous local government here which, among many other things, kept the visiting merchants in check. This society wasn't, as Jakobsen and others have put it, 'topsy-turvy', whatever that means. It was a healthy and relatively prosperous society, whose inhabitants, as far as we can tell, were noted for linguistic virtuosity.

The situation concerning the Scots language is relatively complex, but not impossible to reconstruct. Scots was of course the language of churchmen. As Sir Thomas Craig wrote about 1605, 'in the Orkneys and Shetland, where in the course of [the 16th] century nothing but Norse was spoken, the ministers of God's word now use English in church and are well enough understood' (Terry 1909: 288-9). Once again there's no evidence of language problems. Scots was also the language of the law courts, but, as readers of Earl Patrick's court book of 1602-4 will know (Donaldson 1954), the officials of that court frequently used and were perfectly familiar with the lexicon of Shetland institutions. In fact those officials were often Shetlanders.

And it would be wrong to argue that Scots who set up shop in Shetland in the sixteenth and seventeenth centuries were themselves monoglot. In 1624, for instance, the bishop of Orkney visited Shetland to adjudicate in a dispute between the Neven and Mouat families. One morning John Neven, brother of one of the main protagonists in the case, arrived to speak with Ninian Neven, and, to the bishop's annoyance, 'conferit with him secreitlie in ane unknowen language' (*Register of the Privy Council of Scotland*, xiv:

760). We don't know what language Neven was speaking: it may have been Norn, or, perhaps more likely, German, or even Dutch. There's evidence from a later source that Ninian Neven could speak Dutch. The point is that the ruling class in Shetland was just as capable as the natives of linguistic ingenuity.

Of course, this situation didn't remain stable. During the seventeenth century Shetland, like societies throughout Europe, became crisis-ridden. I have no space to discuss the details here, but, in a nutshell, the local government collapsed after the departure of Earl Patrick, and, for a variety of reasons, the Shetlanders' contacts with German, Dutch and Norwegian merchants and fishermen, especially the Norwegians, diminished. These events naturally had an effect on the Shetlanders' proficiency with languages, although the new town of Lerwick remained a keyhole, so to speak, where foreign influences could enter.

By the late seventeenth and early eighteenth century the situation is crystal clear. Norn was still alive, probably very much alive in some areas, but most of the commentators adopt a slightly negative tone about its prospects. One cleric says that the Shetlanders 'speak among themselves a corrupt Nords tongue (called Norn) *but not so much now as formerly*' (Bruce 1908: 4). Robert Sibbald, writing in the early eighteenth century, and apparently basing his remarks on information from Shetland friends, says that 'many of them speak a Norse Tongue, corrupted (they call Norn) amongst themselves, *which is now much worn out*' (Sibbald 1845: 15-16). (My italics.) John Brand, visiting Shetland in 1700, turns the equation the other way round: 'English is the Common Language among them, yet many of the People speak Norse or corrupt Danish, especially such as live in the more Northern Isles, yea so ordinary is it in some places, that it is the first Language their Children speak' (Brand 1701: 69).

Nearly everybody (except Rendboe) agrees that Norn disappeared during the eighteenth century, but there is disagreement about the tempo of that disappearance. Once again we find little or no reference to difficulties of communication between different social classes in the islands — not surprisingly, because we didn't find such references a century and a half earlier. According to Thomas Gifford, writing about 1733, many Shetlanders still spoke Norn among themselves, but everyone, he said, spoke English by that time, 'which they pronounce with a very good accent' (Gifford 1976: 31-2). The only hint of a problem appears not in Shetland but in Orkney, in 1725, when the minister of the remote parish of Sandwick said that his flock needed a charity school, because, as he put it, 'the old broken Danish language is used among many of the people, which occasions ignorance in the place' (Campbell 1953: 175). But that minister wasn't, strictly speaking, complaining about difficulties in communication; his main concern was the desirability of genteel speech. As the century progressed more schools were established throughout the islands; significantly, there are no references at all to language problems in Shetland among the minutes of the Society for Propagating Christian Knowledge.

Once again we have to keep in mind the social and economic background to these accounts. The main difference between seventeenth and eighteenth century Shetland was the fact that, in the later period, local merchant-lairds controlled commerce with the continent. In the earlier period German merchants had had semi-permanent bases in many parts of the islands, Dutch fishermen had fraternised with Shetlanders, and ordinary Shetlanders had sailed to Norway to trade in wood. As the Earl of Rothes had written in the 1660s, as a result of 'the constant uninterrupted trade they have ever had with the Hollander, Hamburger, Luebecker and Bremeners ... there is none in that island of six or seven years of age, but they can speak Hollands or Norse' (Ball 1965: 6-7). That situation had changed fundamentally by 1750. Eighteenth century Shetlanders had fewer opportunities to hear or practise foreign languages than their grandfathers. On the other hand, many of them now had the opportunity to hear English lessons at school. James Mackenzie, writing in Orkney in 1750, said that the S.P.C.K. schools had been the death of Norn (Mackenzie 1836: 12); I see no reason to doubt that the same thing happened in Shetland, at exactly the same time.

Our best source of information about the eighteenth century is the journal of George Low, a young minister from Orkney who visited Shetland in 1774. Low only mentions Norn in the section of his journal dealing with Foula. Jakobsen thought that Low's account proved that Norn was still a 'living language' in Foula at that late date (Jakobsen 1928-32: xvii). Low's account actually proves the opposite. Low said that 'there are some who know a few words of Norn' in the island, and that 'nothing remains but a few names of things and two or three remnants of songs which one old man can repeat, and that but indistinctly' (Low 1879: 104ff.). Low's most knowledgeable informant recited a Norn ballad to him, but couldn't translate it. Low didn't describe a living language; he described a dead one.

There's an interesting parallel account from Orkney. Walter Scott, in a note to *The Pirate*, tells us about a clergyman in North Ronaldsay who had recited Thomas Gray's 'The fatal sisters' to an island audience, presumably in the early 1770s, shortly after Gray's collected *Poems* appeared. The islanders interrupted him to say that they knew the poem well in Norse, and had often sung it to him. This story deserves more attention than it has received. Gray had translated 'The fatal sisters' not from Norse but from a Latin text of the poem. The people of North Ronaldsay, unlike Low's informant in Foula, must have been very alive to the meaning of their Norse original if they could immediately recognise what was strictly speaking a paraphrase of it. It's a great pity that Low didn't turn his attention to North Ronaldsay as well as Foula.

Of course, I don't know how 'pure' Shetland Norn was in its last lustre, or precisely how it co-existed with or broke down in the face of Scots. No-one knows. Rendboe lays great stress on the famous rhyme, recorded by Jakobsen, where the author praises or mercilessly scolds — you take your choice — a Shetlander who has been to Caithness and learned to speak Scots. If I were a philologist I wouldn't lay a lot of stress on that verse: Jakobsen doesn't explain where he got it. He merely says that it is 'said' to come from Unst, and that it is 'said' to date from the eighteenth century. Not very satisfactory. And if I were Laurits Rendboe I wouldn't cite it at all. As Michael Barnes has hinted, it suggests that, contrary to Rendboe's whole argument, Norn was becoming contaminated by Scots during its last days (Barnes 1984: 41).

Summing up the situation about Norn, then, I look at the problem like this. Norn remained a living language until the crisis years of the late seventeenth century, although many people who spoke it could cope with Scots and other languages as well. By the early eighteenth century, however, Norn was on the way out: not because of oppression, but because the Shetlanders, especially younger Shetlanders, chose not to speak it. They turned their attention elsewhere. It's as simple as that. I now turn to the language they chose to speak, and still speak.

Early Shetland dialect texts

Our earliest Shetland dialect text was published, or at least printed, in 1817. It has a strange history. It was the work of Archibald Barclay, who was then about 30. Barclay was a son of an eighteenth century minister of Unst, and eventually became secretary to the Hudson's Bay Company. He was exactly the kind of person who, according to Laurits Rendboe, would have paid no attention to and had no knowledge of what ordinary Shetlanders were saying.

Around 1816 Barclay wrote a humorous letter in Shetland dialect to his friend John Sands in Liverpool. Sands was tickled, and passed a copy to a third Shetlander, Thomas Irvine of Midbrake in North Yell. Irvine was working at a Deaf and Dumb School in Bermondsey in London, and he thought it would be a good wheeze to print a dozen copies of the piece on the school printing press, for distribution to friends (Shetland Archives: D.16/294/3).

A glance at Barclay's letter reveals that he was a very accomplished Shetland dialect speaker. There are several things to say about this enormously interesting production. First, if we pass over the wild spelling and the extremely rich vocabulary, a modern Shetlander would be able to stumble through it without much difficulty. It's a piece of slapstick, built around the adventures and misfortunes of about a dozen no doubt well-known inhabitants of Unst.

Barclay's production became a set-piece in nineteenth century expositions of the Shetland dialect. In 1836 an anonymous contributor from Morpeth published it in the *Gentleman's Magazine*, with a not too-inaccurate translation. 'I have procured from the Shetland islands', he wrote, 'a specimen of the language still spoken among the common people there. ... The narrative, it is plain, has been contrived to embody in it as many words and phrases peculiar to the vulgar language of the district as its compass would admit of.' The tone of this description is interesting. The anonymous expositor regards Barclay's piece as slightly amusing — as indeed it was meant to be. There's a faint implication that the 'vulgar language of the district' was a debased language. In 1861 W.R. Duncan published a rather better-spelled but incomplete version of Barclay's piece in the second edition of his *Zetland Directory and Guide*. In a footnote he wrote: 'the common language is fast yielding to a purer English, but well educated men are still much amused at the conversation of the labouring classes in the country'.

These commentators weren't prepared to take the Shetland dialect seriously. Ironically, the tone they adopt is similar to that adopted by the Norn fanatics, who regard the dialect as the 'pitiful remains' of a great language. Duncan and Co. regarded it as a pitiful shadow of the genteel *English* language. On the other hand, there were those who took it more seriously, or at least took it at face value. Samuel Hibbert, who visited Shetland in 1818, published what he calls 'a tolerable specimen of the modern Shetland dialect', a straightforward account of a bad day at the fishing narrated, presumably to Hibbert himself, by a fisherman at Fedeland in Northmavine (Hibbert 1822: 512-13). Almost simultaneously the Methodist missionaries who had started coming to Shetland after the Napoleonic wars began to take an interest in the way their Shetland flocks spoke. One of them, Sammy Dunn, wrote to Adam Clarke in 1822: 'Would you wish a glossary of Shetland words, which I am picking up? I have already about four hundred' (Clarke 1837: 154).

There were few local scholars of the language spoken in Shetland. Part of the reason for that was the lack of any urban culture in the islands: there were few libraries or schools worth the name, and intellectuals were few and far between. There were three exceptions: William Alexander Grant, Arthur Laurenson and Robert Sinclair, all Lerwick merchants in the mid-nineteenth century. Grant's career was promising. In his thirties he began a Shetland dictionary, with shrewd etymologies derived from Scandinavian dictionaries. Unfortunately he had a strange private life. In the early 1860s he struck up a disastrous love-hate relationship with a visiting Roman Catholic spy from Russia, and began to smear tar over the houses and offices of local dignitaries. As a result he had to leave Shetland suddenly. What remains of his work is in archives in Bilbao and Bergen, and much of it was posthumously incorporated in Thomas Edmondston's Shetland dialect dictionary of 1866 (Smith 1987).

Arthur Laurenson was a different kind of scholar. Withdrawn and ascetic, he read widely in Old Norse literature, and took an interest in the Shetland dialect. His little article 'Om sproget paa Shetlandsöerne' is an interesting early treatment of the subject (Laurenson 1860). But Laurenson agonised over his written work, and as a result only left fragments.

The third scholar, Robert Sinclair, a native of Aithsting, was in many ways the most accomplished; but, like Laurenson, he suffered from the Shetland complaint of not committing things to print. His only work is an enormous novel, with large sections in Shetland dialect, published serially in the *Shetland Times* in 1879. He emigrated to New Zealand shortly afterwards.

In the absence of linguistic work, or even detailed accounts of everyday speech, it's difficult to assess the Shetland dialect of this period on its own terms. I suspect, given what we do know, that Shetlanders hadn't lost the linguistic virtuosity of their ancestors; in other words, that they weren't speaking a debased version of either Norn or English. Jakobsen and others have painted a picture of a language under threat from schools and modern civilization. By the nature of things it's not usually feasible to find out precisely what was happening in schools, other than through the clipped written remarks of teachers or inspectors. Certainly we know that in late nineteenth century France there was a national war against the use of dialect in schools, following revelations in 1863 that a quarter of the country's population couldn't speak French (Weber 1979: 67ff.).

Fortunately we can get a glimpse of what was happening in at least one school in Shetland, in the early 1870s, thanks to Laurence Williamson, a scholar in the island of Yell. Williamson was a compulsive transcriber of discussions, and around 1875 he filled up the space at the end of a page of notes by recording a scene that had taken place in the classroom at East Yell, his old school (Shetland Archives: D.7/43/1). Williamson had a prodigious memory, and we can be fairly sure that his account is accurate. The interesting thing about it is the way that both the teacher, the larger than life local character Andrew Dishington Mathewson, and his pupils, switch from English to Shetland dialect in an extremely sophisticated way.

Here's a brief extract, with responses by the pupils in italics. 'William Johnson. *Absent.* He'll be firing the telegraph cups again. They say there are some of the stays missing. I saw een awa atween da deks o Gossabrough and Otterswick - I saw een hingin dirlin. Lowrie Henry Robertson. *Absent.* He's been all winter. *He's fishing pluckers.*' And so on.

Now, I don't want to suggest that dialogue like this was typical in Victorian schools in Shetland. A.D. Mathewson was an unusual man. But in these exchanges I can recognise features of the flexibility of contemporary Shetland dialect. Shetlanders of the seventeenth century were multilingual in Norn, Scots and Dutch; I can well imagine that their descendants in the nineteenth century were equally inventive in switching between dialect and standard English. As an aside I should mention that many Lerwegians of the 1860s could speak fluent Dutch (Laurenson 1860: 193). I don't suggest for a moment that this kind of bilingualism is a special Shetland characteristic; it's typical of many lively communities. To take an example from farther afield:

D.H. Lawrence's father, whose Nottinghamshire dialect is portrayed in *Sons and Lovers*, was capable of speaking the most flawless King's English, sometimes, when he wanted to annoy his son, with a ludicrously affected accent (Worthen 1991: 62).

As a result I believe we should look rather differently at Jakob Jakobsen's visit to Shetland in the early 1890s. We usually see his arrival as the advent of a saviour, poised to rescue our language from extinction. There's no doubt, of course, that Jakobsen's visit was important, not merely because of his prodigious collection of words, but because he encouraged people, especially young people, to take an interest in the history of their language and place-names. As one Shetlander said in 1894, 'Mr Jakobsen's visit ... must have an interest even for the most ignorant Shetlanders. How he makes our places alive with intelligence!' (Anderson 1894). On the other hand, there had been an efflorescence of Shetland dialect writing here before Jakobsen arrived. In the mid-eighties Haldane Burgess, L.J. Nicolson and Basil Ramsay Anderson had begun to feature in the local press as fine dialect poets, following the examples of James Stout Angus and George Stewart, who inaugurated modern Shetland dialect writing in 1879. Burgess and Nicolson were especially inventive: Nicolson wrote atheist verse, and Burgess explored radical and eventually socialist ideas in the dialect. They were irreverent. Both Nicolson and Burgess wrote hilarious pastiches of Tennyson's gruesome jubilee ode of 1887, Nicolson from a socialist and Burgess from a rumbustiously anti-monarchist point of view. This was the period when Lerwick began to come alive as a centre of Shetland's intellectual life: precisely the moment when Jakobsen was striding around in the outer isles.

Jakobsen was friendly with some of the Shetland dialect writers, especially Burgess, but there isn't much evidence that he took an interest in what they were trying to do. This is partly because he was a linguist through and through, and had little or no time for anything else (except singing Scandinavian songs). Jakobsen's obsession with Shetland's Norn and alleged Celtic vocabulary, to the complete exclusion of Scots, made his work excessively antiquarian, as Gunnel Melchers has pointed out. And there's also a certain philistinism in Jakobsen's remark, in the introduction to his dictionary (Jakobsen 1928-32: xx), that:

> compulsory education ... in which the use of English is impressed upon the children, and the use of such words and phrases as are peculiar to the Shetland dialect is not permitted in the schools, will involve, in the near future, the Anglicising of practically the whole speech.

This statement, as well as being grossly pessimistic, was, as I said before, an entirely inaccurate prediction. Jakobsen could only make such a statement because he believed that Shetlanders were passive *victims* of various kinds of linguistic oppression. Subconsciously he must have regarded their language, and hence their literature, as poverty-stricken. In that sense Jakobsen's visit and influence was not liberating at all.

The modern Shetland dialect

In the third and final part of this paper I want to look at the Shetland dialect from the point of view of the 1990s. Today we have problems and opportunities. There's no doubt that Shetlanders have forgotten or never encountered many thousands of the words recorded in Jakobsen's dictionary, although I sometimes get a surprise when I hear a gem. This is hardly surprising. The late 19th century economy and society of Shetland has disappeared forever, and as a result large parts of its lexicon have gone into oblivion.

As I said at the outset, Laurits Rendboe imagines that we still dream about Norn and the society where it flourished. I want to illustrate Rendboe's psychodrama of Shetland history and culture by looking at what he says about three well-known Shetland dialect poems.

First, T.A. Robertson's 'A Skyinbow a Tammie's'. Based thematically and metrically on Browning's poem of 1855, 'A tocatta of Galuppi's' , Robertson's poem is a meditation on the Shetland dialect. It contains the sweet lines: 'Trowe wir minds wir ain auld language/Still keeps rinnin laek a tön'. 'Wir ain auld language' is of course the Shetland dialect, of which Tammy Alex Robertson was one of the greatest modern proponents. However, Rendboe has a different interpretation. '"Our own old language",' he tells us, 'is not Mod[ern] Sh[etlandic], which is a comparatively recent formation, being Low Scots with a peculiar Shetland pronunciation, and many old Shetland words from Norn, the language which the poet has in mind, the original language of Shetland' (Rendboe 1985b: 46) In other words, the language running through T.A. Robertson's mind like a tune was a language he couldn't speak, and which no Shetlander has been able to speak since the eighteenth century: a language without written texts which is only known to us by name and reputation.

My second example of Rendboe's critical method is his treatment of James Stout Angus's 'Lad at wis taen in voar', a delicate poem narrated by a woman whose lover has been captured by the press gang. Other, more affluent men are pursuing her, but she vows never to forget her first love. Rendboe's exposition is as follows: 'When the flower of Shetland's male youth was taken away [by the press gang], the field was open for "the incomers" to get at the now defenceless weaker sex, to try to "Scotticize" Shetland in a very permanent way' (Rendboe 1985a: 19).

Finally, Haldane Burgess's epic 'Skranna', about a Shetlander, Rasmie, who is tempted by the devil: a poem about faith and ideals versus material temptations. The key word in the poem is 'feft'. 'Rasmie is "feft"', says the hero to the Devil — committed to Christianity — and the Devil disappears. But for Rendboe, unlike Rasmie and all other commentators, 'feft' refers to the constitutional arrangements between Denmark and Scotland concerning Shetland of 1469. 'Being the Old Norse Shetlander', he explains, '... whose land has only been temporarily impignorated, [Rasmie] ... cannot give in to such sweet talk' (Rendboe 1985a: 21-2)

What I find distressing about these contributions is their notion that Shetlanders are obsessed with narrow and mythical historical matters. The three poems I've mentioned aren't works of genius, but they make a stab at discussing important modern themes. Those themes aren't parochial, or pathological, like the attitudes described in Rendboe's work. Rendboe isn't prepared to treat Shetland poems as poems; for him they are sociology.

The period between Burgess's best work, produced in the 1890s, and the 1940s, when the poets associated with the *New Shetlander* magazine began to write, was bleak in Shetland, both from an economic and a cultural point of view. Shetlanders of that era certainly weren't thinking about Norn. An expatriate Shetland scholar, writing in the 1940s, guessed that only one Shetlander by then was knowledgeable enough to explain Shetland place-names from their Old Norse roots — and that Shetlander, William Ratter, had just died (Stewart 1948: 4). However, the appearance of the *New Shetlander* in 1947 inaugurated major change. The new developments weren't in the field of scholarship, but in letters, and in particular Shetland dialect verse. These events are truly contemporary: many of the protagonists are still with us.

I want to take a closer look at one of the *New Shetlander* poets: Billy Tait, who died in 1992. Billy Tait wasn't obsessed by Norn, but as a teacher in Lerwick he became deeply interested in Jakobsen's dictionary as a quarry for poetic words. (The school jotter where he transcribed his discoveries is now in the Shetland Archives.) Shetlanders, Billy wrote in the fourth *New Shetlander*, should follow Hugh MacDiarmid and Burns:

> not in the sense of imitating an alien though allied tradition, but in constructing an eclectic literary language, based on, but not bounded by the speech of the people. They must be afraid neither of experimenting, nor of judicious borrowing, but aware of the underlying genius of the language. ... They must look on it as their duty to restore to general currency by imaginative usage many of the fine old words now known only by a few.

'The underlying genius of the language.' This is a metaphysical idea, but I note that, when I reviewed Billy Tait's *Collected Poems* in the *New Shetlander* ten years ago, I referred to the Shetland dialect as 'a peculiarly poetic language'. A glance at Tait's work is enough to show that the modern Shetland dialect, far from being debased, or moribund, is almost incredibly flexible. For instance, I'd go as far as to suggest that Billy's translation of Ronsard's famous sonnet 'Quand vous serez bien vieille' is at least as great a poem as Yeats's 'When you are old', which was based on the same original.

40

Tait's translations of Villon, still partly unpublished, are another example of his virtuosity; they have been praised to the skies by scholars of medieval French.

This is not to say that the future of the Shetland dialect, as a written and spoken language, will be plain sailing. There still lingers a feeling, faint now, but still irritating, that the dialect is a good medium for farce: that it's not something for polite company. On Radio Shetland, for instance, they read the weather forecast and some of the more frivolous news items in dialect, but reserve standard English for solemn announcements. I remember overhearing two Shetlanders discuss Rosie Gibson's splendid film on the Shetland hosiery industry, which abounded with Shetland dialect, the day after it had been broadcast. They were affronted. 'Wha does du think wid a understood yun?' one of them said. They were worried about the national audience, and pre-sumably the scorn that national viewers would bestow on the unfashionable Shetlanders portrayed in the film.

Related to this, in my opinion, is a certain uneasiness Shetlanders still have about accepting their language as a literary language. Verse is all very well, but there is a great dearth of continuous Shetland prose. Shetlanders often find dense dialect prose difficult to read, and they seem to think that others will have even more difficulty. I can understand this fear, but I don't take it seriously. D.H. Lawrence's play *The Daughter-in-Law*, written in 1911, is entirely written in dialect, and hasn't been neglected; I heard it on the radio a year or two ago. I find it difficult to understand the dialect in *Wuthering Heights*, but it doesn't stop me from reading the book. In fact, when I come to think about it, English literature is full of dialect, of one kind or another: Elizabeth Gaskell, Tennyson, Dickens, even Hopkins. Three years ago I heard my favourite critic, Tom Paulin, deal with another critic, who had complained about dialect words in Paulin's own poetry. 'I can see it would be difficult if you thought you had to go off and consult a dictionary,' said Paulin, unrepentantly, 'but it *can't* be helped!' (Radio 3, 2 February 1992).

There is no difficulty now, as there is difficulty in some dialects, about spelling. John Graham saw to that three decades ago, in an almost single-handed revolution. His predecessor as editor of the *New Shetlander* had had an extremely flexible attitude to Shetland spelling: leave it to the author. As a result his contributors came up with some astonishing renderings of perfectly common local words. John put his foot and his blue pencil down, and as a result the *New Shetlander* is a living testimonial of how to spell Shetland dialect words. Occasionally a picturesque exception slips through, but the *New Shetlander* orthography is almost always logical and avoids confusing variants.

To conclude. I've never had a reputation for admiring Shetland shibboleths. I do, however, find much to admire in the contemporary results of Shetland's linguistic and literary history. I'm not obsessed, you may have gathered, with the death of Norn, or with the disappearance of words with Old

Norse roots. I'm concerned with the modern Shetland dialect and the poetry and prose written in it.

We must get away — and I hope that we have got away — from the idea that standard English, and standard Norn (whatever that was), are norms or essences from which the Shetland dialect diverges. As my favourite biologist, Stephen Jay Gould, puts it, 'variation is the raw material of evolutionary change. It represents the fundamental of nature, not an accident about a created norm. Variation is primary; essences are illusory.' The modern Shetland dialect is a fine, flexible variant, still full of life and potential.

Bibliography

Anderson, R., 1894: 'Old Norse intelligence — as seen in our place names', *Shetland News*, 25 August.

Ball, R.G., 1965: 'The Shetland garrison, 1665-1668', *Journal of the Society of Army Historical Research* 43.

Balfour, D. (ed.), 1859: *Oppressions of the Sixteenth Century in the Islands of Orkney and Shetland*. Edinburgh.

Barnes, M., 1984: 'Norn', *Scripta Islandica*, xxxv.

Brand, J., 1701: *A Brief Description of Orkney, Shetland, Pightland Firth and Caithness*. Edinburgh.

Bruce, J. (ed.), 1908: *Description of ye Island of Zetland*. Edinburgh.

Campbell, J.L., 1953: 'The Norse language in Orkney in 1725', *Scottish Historical Review* 32.

Clarke, A., 1837: *The Miscellaneous Works of Adam Clarke*, xii, London.

Donaldson, G. (ed.), 1954: *The Court Book of Shetland 1602-1604*. Edinburgh.

Gifford, T., 1976: *Historical Description of the Zetland Islands*. Sandwick.

Goudie, G., 1904: *The Celtic and Scandinavian Antiquities of the Shetland Islands*. Edinburgh etc.

Grönneberg, R., 1981: *Jakobsen in Shetland*. Lerwick.

Hibbert, S., 1822: *A Description of the Shetland Islands*. Edinburgh.

Jakobsen, J., 1928-32: *An Etymological Dictionary of the Norn Language in Shetland*. London etc.

Laurenson, A., 1860: 'Om sproget paa Shetlandsöerne': *Annaler for Nordisk Oldkyndighed og Historie*.

Low, G., 1879: *A Tour through the Islands of Orkney and Shetland in 1774*. Kirkwall

Mackenzie, J., 1836: *The General Grievances and Oppression of the Isles of Orkney and Shetland*. Edinburgh.

Rendboe, L., 1984: 'How "worn out" or "corrupted" was Shetland Norn in its final stage?' NOWELE 3

Rendboe, L., 1985a: *The Shetland Literary Tradition: an introduction*. Odense.

Rendboe, L., 1985b: *The Shetland Literary Tradition: an anthology of modern Shetland poetry*. Odense.

Sibbald, R., 1845: *The Description of the Isles of Orkney and Zetland*. Edinburgh.

Smith, B., 1987: 'The tarry kirk', *Shetland Times*, 24 December.

Smith, B., 1990: 'Shetland, Scandinavia, Scotland 1400-1700: the changing nature of contact'. In: G. Simpson (ed.), *Scotland and Scandinavia*. Edinburgh.

Stewart, J., 1948: 'Norse remains in Shetland', *New Shetlander*, 9.

Terry, C. S. (ed.), 1909: *De Unione Regnorum Britanniae Tractatus*. Edinburgh.

Weber, E., 1979: *Peasants into Frenchmen*. London.

Worthen, J., 1991: *D.H. Lawrence: the early years 1885-1912*. Cambridge.

'WE'RE AA DA SAME HERE - BUT DIFFERENT, TOO' SOME NOTES ON REGIONAL LINGUISTIC VARIATION IN SHETLAND

Gunnel Melchers

Introduction

The utterance quoted in the title of this paper was taken down by Anthony Cohen, a social anthropologist who was a 'participant observer' in the close-knit community of Whalsay, one of the islands in the Shetland archipelago, for a number of years (cf. Cohen 1987: 60f). Admittedly, the utterance originally referred to what Cohen calls 'the allocation of identity' within Whalsay, 'a dialectic of collective and individual identity', but as I hope to show it could equally well apply to the language situation, and to Shetland as a whole.

The linguistic significance of the utterance might then be interpreted in the following way:

'We're aa da same here' — there is a concept such as 'Shetland dialect', a discrete form of language to be distinguished from any other variety of English through certain indexicals. A specification of these would include a sizeable Scandinavian-based vocabulary, uniquely retained in Shetland, containing 'emotive' adjectives such as *haandless, döless, vyndless*; words relating to typical Shetland activities such as *hent, makkin*; names of birds and plants such as *scarf, bonxie, ekkelgirse*; a formal/informal distinction realized in second person pronominal usage (*du/you*). Further indexicals, which may in part be ascribed to the Scandinavian substratum, include the use of BE as a perfective auxiliary, as in 'Da bull lat oot da most gödless gölbröl I'm ever heard' (Graham 1984:31); the character and occurrence of the /ö/ vowel as just exemplified; the structure of the syllable, e.g. the existence of long, possibly geminate consonants; so-called 'TH-stopping', i.e. plosives instead of fricatives in words such as *they, there, think* (represented as *dey, dere, tink* in Shetland dialect writing).

Although the realization of the /ö/ vowel may vary somewhat and the names of flowers as well, the above features are generally shared by all Shetlanders, at least when they speak 'Shetland', i.e. the traditional dialect, and do not adapt to outsiders (*'knappin'*).

'But different, too' — there is considerable dialectal variation within Shetland. When, more than ten years ago, I first set up a research project on Shetland dialect, with special emphasis on its Scandinavian element, I found, for one thing, that a major problem would be 'to unravel the strands of Shetland speech and distinguish those leading back to Norn from those leading back to Scots' (cf. Catford 1957:76). This is not to be wondered at, considering a type of language contact situation where closely related language varieties interweave beyond distinction. Yet the most complicating factor of all turned out to be the regional diversity, which has made it necessary to aim for a dense network of localities investigated. This regional linguistic variation is the main topic of my presentation, which is mainly of a descriptive character. In my attempt to give an account of it, I will refer to Jakobsen and some later scholars, in particular the compilers of the Linguistic Atlas of Scotland and my own research group. In addition, it goes without saying that the perception of linguistic variation conveyed by the speakers themselves should never be neglected.

To what extent it is possible to *explain* the variation is, however, another matter; obviously, our knowledge of settlement patterns will clarify a great deal of linguistic diversity and diffusion, but it also fails to account for many phenomena. Why is it, for example, that — in contrast with the smallish Shetland Islands — there are hardly any regional dialects in Iceland or Australia, despite the fact that there are major geographical barriers in both these countries? Conversely, neighbouring villages in Dalarna, Sweden, may have clearly distinctive dialects, to the point of unintelligibility. It is also worth pointing out that totally unrelated, or at least only remotely related language varieties may show striking similarities, not only in the odd word, but in phonological systems and syntactic constructions. A characteristic of Shetland dialect, as mentioned earlier, is the use of BE as a perfective auxiliary rather than HAVE, not only with verbs of motion and change as sometimes found in other varieties of English, but with all verbs (cf. the example quoted above). The only other variety of English that features a similar construction is African American Vernacular English!

Although any 'genetic' explanation of such similarities is bound to be extremely far-fetched or downright absurd, it seems part of human nature to look for such explanations; this produces folk-linguistic myths, such as the idea that the English language originated in the Swedish province of Dalarna, since a few words such as *swine* and *folk* sound English-like. Similarly, in the Shetland context, there is something of a folk-linguistic myth in the wish to ascribe anything that deviates from Standard English to the Norse substratum.

However, whereas parallel developments such as those described in the preceding paragraph can probably only be 'explained' as independent innovations, many other characteristics and changes are the obvious results of social rather than purely geographical phenomena: the strong sense of togetherness in certain communities (this probably accounts for the 'deviating' accents on Whalsay and Out Skerries); the possibility and frequency of contacts with other groups of people; social mobility and accommodation; urbanization (this will account for the increasing use of glottal stops in Lerwick).

45

Regional differences as perceived by the speakers themselves

As indicated above, I wish to emphasize that I have the highest regard for the perception of differences expressed by the speakers themselves; after all, who can be better judges? Yet it can be difficult for a dialectologist to specify the elicitation and to determine the quality of information of this intuitive kind. In Whalsay, for example, a lady told me that the pronunciation of the word *salt* varies within the island: where she came from, people said /sa:t/, but in the south they said /sa:t/. I have rendered these examples in identical transcriptions, because I was unable to hear the difference. Since I recorded the words on tape, I also analysed them instrumentally (with the help of a spectrograph) and the analysis proved them to be identical. It is, of course, possible that there exist differences as regards the quality of the vowel but my informant may have been unable to imitate other speakers. On the other hand, it is well known to linguistic fieldworkers that informants may exaggerate or invent distinctions, at least when they are of a semantic kind (cf. Chambers 1994:1). I would tend to believe that — at least as to the smaller islands — most claimed differences should be classified as idiolectal, or possibly 'kin-lectal'. This is corroborated by observations made by Anthony Cohen (1987:62f), who writes about 'Glybie talk' (the Glybies are a Whalsay family), and on the uniqueness of the Skaw people (Skaw is a settlement at the extreme north of Whalsay). Similarly, there is a family on Skerries where three members have back R's (so-called 'corbies'); this alone will not justify the inclusion of R variation on a dialect map.

Describing Whalsay as an entity in the context of Shetland as a whole, Cohen claims that there is something atypical about this island community. He even provides a linguistic example not found in other sources, viz. the habit of emphasizing the descriptive content of any word by adding -Y. A boat which fishes well is 'fishy', for example.

Indeed, Whalsay is generally singled out — sometimes together with Out Skerries — by Shetlanders as a 'deviant' community, especially as far as language is concerned, but also, for example, when it comes to knitting where distinctive, favoured patterns and colours can be observed.

A few years ago, I carried out a language attitude study among some 350 pupils of the Anderson High School, Lerwick, who were asked to complete a questionnaire, which contained at least two questions clearly relating to regional variation. They ran as follows:

'Do you think Lerwick people speak differently from other people in Shetland?' (95% answered 'yes') and 'From the way he or she talks, I can tell whether a person comes from ...', listing Whalsay, Fair Isle, Unst, Lerwick, Cunningsburgh, the West Side (Walls), ending with the open suggestion 'somewhere else in Shetland'. 84% claimed to recognize a Whalsay speaker, which is very much in line with data from our interviews, where Whalsay is *always* mentioned as the most deviant accent ('their words are not different,

46

but it's the way they say them'). 58% state that they can tell whether a person comes from Lerwick, which is interestingly low and seemingly incompatible with the 95% positive responses to the previous question. Only 9% indicated Fair Isle, which does have a very distinct accent. However, the low figure can be explained by the fact that only about 80 people live on Fair Isle, and schoolchildren in Lerwick thus rarely meet them. The West Side scored 40%, Cunningsburgh 32% and Unst 31 %.

As to more specified, native-speaker (folk-linguistic) comments, here follow two characterisations that have intrigued us:

1) 'Unst people speak *clippet*', i.e. 'not pronouncing all the letters'. In part, this can be dismissed as a general lack of comprehension of what spoken language is like, but the observation is borne out, to some extent, by recordings of extreme vowel reduction produced by speakers from the north of the island, whereas in the south we have observed the opposite tendency of putting in additional, so-called 'epenthetic' vowels between consonants.

2) Before going to Fair Isle we were told by some people that the delivery of speech on the island is extremely slow; conversely, by others that Fair Islanders speak as well as move quickly (like penguins!). The report on slowness was explained to me by Jim Mather, co-editor of the Linguistic Atlas of Scotland, who held that this referred to certain extended diphthongs, such as /dra:ijøf/ for *drive*. However, carrying out instrumental analysis (spectrograms) of tokens of Fair Isle speech, I found no evidence of extreme quantity either way. It is my belief that the perception of quickness has to do with the gemination of consonants (a Scandinavian feature) and the unvoicing in final position as exemplified in *drive* (ending in /f/ rather than /v/), whereas the unusual, 'widened' quality of certain diphthongs may be related to quantity rather than quality.

A higher level of native-speaker intuition, hardly to be labelled 'folk-linguistic', was demonstrated to us when visiting a Whalsay school, where a teacher gave special instructions in 'writing Whalsa'. She told the children that there are four ways of spelling some words: the English way, the Scots way, the Shetland way and the Whalsay way. It was an interesting effort, though not very consistent: *cake*, for example, was said to be 'tyAEik' in Whalsay but 'cake' in all the other variants, whereas *game* was given as 'gem' in Scots, 'geym' in Shetland and 'dyemm' in Whalsay. Although Whalsay palatalisation/fricativisation was correctly observed, the vowel quality suggested for *cake* is puzzling. On the whole, the rules provided were, if not incorrect, certainly incomplete, i.e. strongly reminiscent of the representation of nonstandard dialect in fiction.

Graham's observations on regional variation

The very highest level of native-speaker knowledge and proficiency is to be found in the works of John Graham — a trained linguist, teacher, writer of fiction and bidialectal speaker rolled into one. His writings include a dictionary, a book on grammar and usage, dialect in fictional dialogue, textbooks for schools and articles for Shetland journals. From personal experience I know that Graham's knowledge of the regional distribution of phonological features and lexical items is encyclopedic. It is to be hoped, then, that his comments on regional variation presented in the introduction to the dictionary will be extended and more detailed in a future edition.

One observation made by Graham has to do with the quality of /a:/, which is said to be what is known as back and slightly rounded, i.e. not too different from Received Pronunciation, in the North Isles (Yell and Unst) and Fair Isle. This is corroborated by a close inspection of the fieldworkers' notebooks from the Linguistic Survey of Scotland; similar vowel qualities were, however, also found on Papa Stour and in Dunrossness.

Another characteristic, shared by Fair Isle and Whalsay, also pointed out by Graham, has to do with the diphthongs in words such as *main* and *fair*, which could be represented in a broad, if not crude, transcription as /moin/, /foir/. This is also borne out by the Fair Isle Notebook from the Survey. Finally, Graham draws attention to the Westside realisation of orthographic WH- as /kw/, in contrast with /hw/ in most areas. This feature is even mentioned in the standard handbook on English accents worldwide (cf. Wells 1982: 399). It may be a regional innovation, but there are clear parallels in Norwegian dialects. On the whole, Graham's claim is borne out by the findings of the Linguistic Survey; however, this feature is variable in certain areas, particularly Cunningsburgh, where a switch often occurs, in that *whisky* may be pronounced as /kwiski/ but *queen* as /hwi:n/. This would appear to be a case of hypercorrection — a well-known phenomenon in language contact situations. A close look at the Survey recordings will reveal scattered examples of the same phenomenon in other districts as well.

Regional variation according to Jakobsen

In his introduction to the *Etymological Dictionary of the Norn Language in Shetland*, Jakobsen (1928: Introduction) claims that there are many distinctive dialects; in fact, he states explicitly that each island in the Shetland archipelago shows dialect variation, postulating nine main dialect areas, which, in turn, consist of several sub-areas. There are, he writes, for example several 'Fetlar dialects' (Fetlar has an area of 15 square miles), such as East and West Herra, Funzie (names of farmsteads). However, the classification is not accounted for. In talking about dialect variation, Jakobsen refers to a 'language map', but this is nothing but an ordinary map, giving no linguistic information whatsoever.

From Jakobsen's notebooks and papers, which I have studied closely in the Tórshavn Library (Landsbókasavn), it appears that he visited and investigated most Mainland districts and most of the islands, yet excluding

Fair Isle and Out Skerries. He paid a very short visit to Whalsay. On the other hand, he managed to interview quite a few 'immigrants' from these areas in Lerwick, relying on self-reported data rather than actual language usage. Yell and Fetlar can be said to be over-represented in his material; this probably results from his contacts with Laurence Williamson, a man with scholarly ambitions but extremely rigid notions.

Jakobsen's magnum opus, the etymological dictionary, is a goldmine of information — above all, of course, for vocabulary, but it is also rich in examples of morphological and syntactic variation, phonetic distinctions and even facts on material culture. The facts are, however, not easily retrievable: important phonological information may, for example, be 'concealed' under a particular lexical entry only. A close comparison with the original notebooks will show that nearly everything collected was incorporated in the dictionary in a somewhat unsystematic way. Clearly, a neat description of regional variation must be based on extremely systematic investigations of semantic fields, 'Wörter und Sachen', phonological inventories, and syntactic structures. For this purpose, I am in the process of setting up a database, classifying each entry in Jakobsen's dictionary and listing it under various headings, including regional distribution.

The only place where Jakobsen spells out generalisations about dialect differences (yet restricted to pronunciation) is found in his 1897 dissertation *Det norröne sprog på Shetland* (The Norn language in Shetland), where he devotes a page and a half to the following issues:

1) establishing the different qualities and distributions of /a:/ — /a:/, as mentioned above;

2) pointing out the deviating West Side vowel quality in words such as *she*: Western /y:/ v. Eastern /ö:/; further examples include *tryni* rather than *tröni* ('pig's snout'). Here the West Side (including Foula) shows more affinity to Norwegian than other dialects;

3) describing the /hw/)(/kw/ distinction. Interestingly, Jakobsen seems to suggest a more consistent pattern for Cunningsburgh than outlined above, i.e. the use of /hw/ exclusively;

4) singling out Dunrossness as the only area where /ð/ has been retained (as in Orkney) and not subjected to 'TH-stopping', i.e. changed to /d/. This is generally corroborated by the findings of the Linguistic Survey, but only occasionally by our project.

A present-day application and elaboration of Jakobsen's data

A first step towards putting together and using a database based on Jakobsen's dictionary (cf. above) was taken by my student Greger Nässén in a study called *Norn weather words. A comparison between dictionary and actual usage* (Nässén 1989). The following questions, of which c) obviously is of immediate relevance for the topic of this paper, were discussed:

49

a) How reliable is Jakobsen's information about individual words, their meaning and distribution?

b) To what extent are weather terms of Norn origin still known in Shetland?

c) Are Norn words used in other areas than those attested by Jakobsen? Nässén collected 700 entries devoted to weather words and selected 646 items for a questionnaire, which was distributed to informants all over Shetland in the summer of 1984. He decided to work with four semantic categories, viz. precipitation, winds, the sky, type of weather, and four 'dialect' areas, viz. The North Isles, North Mainland and adjacent islands, South Mainland and adjacent islands, and finally a general category, where Jakobsen either claims that the terms are used in several districts or does not specify the area.

It is impossible to do justice to Nässén's original and penetrating study here. However, some of his most important findings are:

1) The number of identified words turned out to be quite high. Well over 83% of the words of Norn origin were familiar to the informants.

2) As regards the current geographical distribution of Norn weather words, it was shown that a large majority of the words were also recognised by informants in other areas than those attested by Jakobsen. Only 21% of the words were found exclusively in the same areas as given in the dictionary. This finding should not be ascribed to great changes in the distribution pattern; a plausible explanation is that this result simply reflects the fact that Jakobsen was not able to test his huge body of information on all his informants. Viewed from another angle, however, the results appear to prove that the informants tended to recognise words attested by Jakobsen for their own area only, certainly more often than they recognised words alleged to be representative of other areas.

Regional variation according to the Linguistic Atlas

An extremely important source of information concerning present-day regional variation anywhere in Scotland is, of course, bound to be the Linguistic Survey of Scotland, whose crowning glory — the atlases — have been available for some time. As regards vocabulary, however, regional variation within Shetland is far from striking and offers little of general interest.

Looking at the pioneering phonological atlas, then, the first of its kind in its use of 'phonological systems' and 'frames', we find that recordings (face-to-face, mostly not taped) were made in ten Shetland localities. Curiously, if not shockingly, neither Whalsay/Skerries nor Cunningsburgh — generally acknowledged as somewhat atypical (cf. above) is included. This is especially puzzling, since I know that Whalsay, at least, has indeed been *visited* by a fieldworker, and both Whalsay and Skerries are mentioned in the pilot study by Catford quoted above.

Unfortunately, very little is learnt about consonants from the atlas. Vowels are presented in a very condensed and abstract way; the only significant regional marker to emerge is the fact that Fair Isle has a smaller inventory of phonemes. I agree with Glauser (1994), who, in discussing dialect maps, concludes that the actual, basic material, presented in *tabular form*, is the really fascinating data presented in the atlas, not the maps.

For fine, phonetic detail it is even more rewarding to turn to the original notations as produced by the fieldworkers. This is what I am working on at the moment, collating the findings with our own recordings, using a dense network. When this work is completed, I hope to be able to provide a clearer, if not the final, picture of regional linguistic variation in Shetland.

References

Catford, J.C., 1957: 'Shetland Dialect'. In: *Shetland Folk Book* 3, Lerwick, 71-76.

Chambers, J.K., 1994: 'The Demise of the Canadianism *Chesterfield*'. In: Gunnel Melchers and Nils-Lennart Johannesson (eds.), *Nonstandard Varieties of Language*, Stockholm, 1-10.

Cohen, A.P., 1987: *Whalsay*. Manchester.

Glauser, B., 1994: 'Dialect Maps: Depicting, Constructing or Distorting Linguistic Reality'. In: Gunnel Melchers and Nils-Lennart Johannesson (eds.), *Nonstandard Varieties of Language*, Stockholm, 35-52.

Graham, J.J., 1984: *The Shetland Dictionary*. Stornoway.

Jakobsen, J., 1928-32: *An Etymological Dictionary of the Norn Language in Shetland*. Copenhagen.

Mather, J.Y. and H. Speitel (eds.), 1975-86: *The Linguistic Atlas of Scotland*, Vols. I-III. London.

Nässén, G., 1989: *Norn Weather Words*. Stockholm.

Wells, J.C., 1982: *Accents of English*, Vols.1-3. Cambridge.

SHETLAND LITERATURE AND THE IDEA OF COMMUNITY

Laurence Graham

Does Shetland have what can be called 'a literature'? Is literature, in fact, not too grandiose a word for the few odds and ends of verse and prose that make up Shetland writing? And if there is, how good is it, and what does it have to say to us to-day, what light does it throw on our past and present? These are some of the questions this essay will try to address.

What about the quality of the writing? Can Shetland compare for instance with Orkney which has produced such famous authors as Eric Linklater, Edwin Muir and latterly George Mackay Brown? It could be argued of course that these three Orcadian writers all chose to write in English — giving them ready access to a national, indeed international public, whereas most Shetland writers have opted for their native dialect, and consequently a more restricted, local readership. But that has not prevented the perceptive outsider from appreciating the true worth of our dialect writing. For example, Neil Gunn, the distinguished Scottish novelist, said of Vagaland's poems: 'When the ends of the earth and their savagery worry too much I can take up his poems — They have the Northland in them, the space and the spareness, and they take me back to my beginnings. I find the dialect attractive and not too difficult . . . and always the rocks and the seas, the maas and the divers, the strength and the austerity' (Robertson 1975:xx). In fact it could be argued that Shetland has produced a wider range of writers than Orkney and that the best work of at least a dozen of our local writers should be rightfully included in any representative anthology of Scottish literature over the last hundred years.

Modern Shetland literature began only a little over a century ago. From the period before this little has survived, though Hibbert in 1822 records that a rich native literature had once existed. In fact he says, 'Shetland was from time immemorial celebrated for its native poets.' After 1469 when Shetland was transferred from Norwegian rule to Scotland, the old Norn language gradually became Scotticised, and later anglicised, till we have the dialect that exists today. All that remains of the old Norn traditional literature is the 'Hildina Ballad', a long poem recorded in Foula in 1774 by George Low, the 'Unst Boat Song' recorded more recently in Unst, and various Norn fragments collected by Jakob Jakobson who rescued thousands of old Shetland Norn words from oblivion in the eighteen-nineties.

Three writers laid the foundations of Shetland literature. First we have Basil Anderson, a poet from Unst who died tragically young at the age of twenty-seven, leaving behind his masterpiece, 'Mansie's Crö', a superb description of Shetland life last century. Next we have James Stout Angus who hailed from Nesting and wrote some of the finest examples of the old speech we have. The third writer was Haldane Burgess, poet, novelist and linguist whose popular book of poems *Rasmie's Büddie* broadened the scope of dialect verse to include satire, political comment and philosophical speculation. All three wrote their best work in the dialect and the lasting popularity of their poetry confirms the rightness of their choice of language.

Basil Anderson's long poem 'Mansie's Crö' has been called by local poet and critic, William J. Tait, 'the finest poem ever written in the Shetlandic tongue' (Tait 1949:16). It is about an old Unst crofter and his 'crö' (or 'plantiecrub' as it would be called in other parts of Shetland), how he built it, and how as well as providing food for him and his livestock it became a noted landmark, a 'meid' at sea, even a time-piece for the folk round about and a shelter for sheep, cattle and ponies on the hill.

But it comes to mean far more than an old planticrub on a hillside — as old Rasmie's evening prayer suggests:

Da shapter read, he booed him doon
An prayed at He wha rules abön
His hand roond dem an dirs wid keep
For he wid wauk tho dey sood sleep   .
An gaerd dir herts laek stocks a kale
Fae dat black kyunnen caaed da Deil.   *rabbit*
An staund a waa aroond dem tö
Far surer dan Auld Mansie's Crö.

Later when the poet shows Mansie growing old and feeble and his crö begins to crumble as well, the same resonance comes through:

At last despite baith sheep an kale
Maunsie and his crö began to fail.
Time booed his rigg and shöre his tap   *backbone*
An laid his crö in mony a slap.   *broken down part of dyke*
Snug shoarded by his ain hert-sten   *supported*
He lost his senses een by een
Till lyin helpless laek a paet
Nor kale nor mutton could he aet:
Sae deed, as what we aa man dö
Hae we, or hae we no, a crö.

As Tait has also pointed out, the whole development of the poem is beautifully shaped. It unfolds in ever-widening circles around the centre-point of the crö, like ripples on a pond. It describes in turn the cycle of a typical crofting day from dawn to dark, then the cycle of the seasons, next with Auld Mansie's death — a human life come full circle. And finally the cycle not only of the years, but of the generations:

Bit years gaed by as aye dir geen -
Da winter white, da summer green,
Da voars aye sawn, da hairsts aye shoarn   *seed-time*
Aye some-een dead, aye some-een boarn.

53

Words simple and unpretentious, just right for the context, without a trace of moralising or false sentiment.

His short poem 'Coming Fae da Hill' records a dialogue between an old woman laden under a burden of peats and a young neighbour who offers to help. Here Anderson evokes beautifully the neighbourliness, the quiet dignity and resignation of old Betty and the natural grace of the old tongue he remembered from his early days in Unst:

Lamb, A'll juist cerry what I can
Bit blissins be in every bane
An mak dee, jewel, a stately man
Fir dy sweet kindness. So, du's geen.
Da Loard len me His heevenly staff,
Till Christ sall lift my kishie aff.   *straw peat basket*

James Stout Angus, our next poet in what has been called 'the Golden Age of Shetland Poetry', was born in 1830 and lived to the ripe old age of 93. His rich resources of dialect speech can be seen in his collection *Echoes from Klingrahool* and also in his *Glossary of the Shetland Dialect* which he published when he was 84 years of age. The richness of dialect used can be seen in his poem 'Eels' first published in 1877 as a verse contribution to a local controversy in *The Shetland Times* on, of all things, 'the theory of spontaneous generation of eels from the hairs of pigs and horses'. From this unlikely source sprang a remarkable poem — probably the first truly original poem written in what we know as Shetland dialect. This is how Angus describes the heavy Lammas rainfalls in August in the poem:

Da Lammas spates lek fljuget aets	*heavy showers, winnowed*
Abön a flakki laavin	*straw mat*
Fell frae da lift wi a heavy drift	*sky*
Da sam as hit'd been kaavin	*snowing heavily*
Da burns aa rase abön da braes	
For stanks an stripes were tömed in	*streamlets, poured*
Till every ljoag whar an eel could oag	*hollow, crawl*
A neesik micht a swömed in.	*porpoise*
Da hedderkows upo da knowes	*bunch of heather*
Lay drooket and disjasket.	*exhausted*
Da taatie-shaas an bulwand taas	*mugwort roots*
Were wuppled lek a gasket.	*entangled, rope*

Angus's joy in the rippling flow, sound and vigour of the dialect is very evident in these lines.

Later in the poem he describes a Shetland scene at daybreak:

An noo up ower da aestern sky	
Da daybrak spreads a glöd,	*dawn, glow*
Da leedfoo leverik rives da dim	*diligent, twilight*
Wi a sweet angelic löd,	*tune*
An baess and birds an fock come oot	
Ta seek dir mornin föd.	

A flekket strik be-oot da dek	*stirk*
Rises oot o her böl,	*resting place*
Shakkin da dew fae her sholmet shoks	*white jaws*
Shu njoags an sets a kröl	*moans, humps her back*
An waanders awa ta da burn ta tak	
Her slokkin at a pöl.	*quenching drink*
Da muckle skerry be-oot da teng	*rock, flat point of land*
Is covered ower in raas,	
Wi flachterin scarfs an plootshin looms	*shags, paddling guillemots*
Dunters an swabbi maas,	*eider ducks, black-backs*
An da lang banks girse waves fitfully	
Ta every pirr at blaas.	*very light breeze*

Seldom do we find such a beautifully articulated picture of man and Nature, 'baess an birds an fock', all part of a harmonious whole — a seamless garment of living things, a true community.

But communities are fragile things too, subject to pressures from within and without. Another of Angus's poems 'Da Lad at wis taen in Voar' shows the violent intrusion of the Press Gang on the Shetland scene and the feelings of a young lass who has seen her lad taken away in early spring, and who still waits loyally for his return long after. It is a ballad of love, longing and loyalty told with all Angus's apparent artless ease and clarity of vision.

Haldane Burgess, the third of the group, is probably the best known of the three. He was an amazing personality, immensely gifted, and possessing an irrepressible sense of humour. He was a scholar, a brilliant linguist, a prolific writer and a socialist in later life — and all this despite the fact that he was struck with blindness in his twenties when at Edinburgh University. His long narrative poem 'Scranna' which tells of an old crofter's battle with the devil can be read and enjoyed on more than one level: as a superbly comic poem in the vein of Burns' 'Tam o Shanter' or as an allegory of the poet's own rejection of the dogmas of the established church of his time. Burgess himself had intended to enter the ministry, but began to question some points of Church doctrine and cut short his divinity course rather than compromise his beliefs. It can be seen as another fine portrait of a Shetland crofter like Anderson's Mansie — a man secure and self-sufficient within the hill-dykes of his convictions, philosophical, untouched by the lure of ambition, shrewd and outspoken in his perception of hypocrisy, greed and pride. This is a theme which recurs again and again in Shetland writing. It is another aspect of that strong sense of community already alluded to. And here we see the significance of Burgess' choice of the dialect for his poetry. The dialect was the language of the ordinary working folk, the community whose voice was seldom to be heard in public places. He wanted that voice, the voice of the oppressed, to be heard and recorded. Unconsciously he was following Brecht's words written many years later: 'The most important teaching of

Socialism is that a future for mankind can be seen only from underneath, from the standpoint of the oppressed and exploited.'

I have emphasised up to now the positive side of the old community, its virtues, its strengths. But it must always be remembered there was a darker side too, the endless toil, the poverty, the hunger, the fear, the lives shadowed by superstition, disease, ignorance, threat of eviction and above all the iron rule of uncontrolled Market Forces. That is the background of Burgess' 'Jubilee Ode'. Here Rasmie the old crofter sits down to write an ode to Queen Victoria on her fifty 'glorious' years as monarch. Tennyson, the Poet Laureate, and others had all joined in the general chorus of applause for Victorian values and prosperity, so Rasmie thinks he'll have to have *his* say on the great divide between Royalty with its 'roogs and roogs a siller' and the 'poor wi his aald rivlin girnin at da tae' *(moccasin open mouthed at the toe).*

JUBILEE ODE

Fifty voars I'm dell'd an set da taaties,
Noo my aald rig complains ipo da wark;
Fifty simmers ower da Muckle Watter
I'm sailed, an rouwed, an striven, an set on;
Fifty hairsts I'm gaddered in da coarn, —
An hirdit my sma crop;   *harvested*
An fifty winters peyd my rent, and grudged it,
For it was dooble what it sood-a-been;
Fifty years I'm heard da wolf o hardship
Jöst snuffin wi his nose alow da door;
Fifty times I'm clampit my aald troosers   *patched*
Till no anidder clamp dey'll had ava;
An du sat on dy tronn awa in Lundin,
An never sae muckle as said, 'Rasmus. yun's you.'
Or raekit oot dy haand ava ta help me,   *reached*
For aa 'at du hed roogs an roogs o siller,   *heaps*
An laand oot in Ameriky, dey tell me, an idder pairts.
O du, du, Wheen Victorey! I raelly widna-a-tocht it o dee;
I hae a picter o dee, whin du wis a lass —
It's hingin ben abön da shimley-piece —   *mantelpiece*
A boanie face, göd feth, as e'er I'm seen,
An fu o kindness; bit dat wis dan
Whin du wis onnly laernin ta be Wheen;
An weel I mind da hoops I hed o dee,
O aa da grit an nobble things du'd dö,
Whin du cam up ta be a wife; hoo du'd no bear
Ta view da poor wi his aald rivlin girnin at da tae:
O less-a-less! What is du döne trou aa da lang half-centiry o time
At du's been Wheen? I kno no what
An dan, —
Ach! dis be blow'd
For a Jubilee Ode!

56

A young friend of Burgess, sharing his interest in poetry and politics was Jack Peterson (b. 1895, d. 1972). He first came into prominence as a First World War poet writing under the pen-name of Private Pat. His first book (in English) *Roads and Ditches* reflected his experiences in the war where he was wounded in action. They are, for the most part, bitter, angry poems showing intense disillusionment at the horrors and waste of war. *Streets and Starlight* published in 1923 is a mellower book which contains some poems in the dialect. But 'Seine-netters' written in the 1960s shows best his skill in the old tongue and his love for the sea and a community bred to that sea. It conveys vividly the harsh rigours of the fishermen's lives, the awareness of a sea-going tradition spanning the centuries from Norse times to the present day, and the urgent need to cope with the uncertainties not only of wind and weather, but of market forces in the highly competitive world of to-day:

Black aa roond, an da steep seas makkin;	*building up*
Gunwale to gunwale, til da decks rin white;	
Mast-head licht in a swirlin moorie	*blizzard*
Loopin aboot laek a thing geen gyte	*leaping, mad*

Hullo! — Hullo! — Hullo! —
'Daybreak' callin 'Venture' —
'Venture' — 'Venture' — Venture' —
'Daybreak' calling 'Venture' ....

Fag-end glint i da wheel-hoose window;	
Tide-lumps brakkin laek ghosts on da baem;	*massive tidal waves*
Lost aa sicht o da laand fir an oor noo —	
Dis is da rodd da Norsemen cam haem.	

Swein, an Hal, an da Bare-legged Magni,	
Brusi da Black, an Kol Brokkenbanes,	
Day an nicht, wi der een ta da wastard,	
Strampin da seas laek der ain briggiestanes.	*striding*

Hullo! — Hullo! — Hullo! —
Twa drags — forty boxes —
Twa drags — forty -
Twa drags — forty boxes ....

Androo John an Grace Ann's Robbi,	
Willi by Nort an Hugh frae da Hadd,	
Day eftir day, i da hert-hol a winter,	*depth*
Shuttin, draggin an guttin laek mad.	

Oot an awa afore you an me's waakin,	
Niver dune till lang eftir dark;	
Trivvlin der wye by baa an by Voder,	*groping, underwater reef*
Fishermen, makkin fur haem frae der wark.	

'Venture' calling 'Daybreak' —
'Daybreak' — 'Daybreak' — 'Daybreak' —
What's da price a haddocks
In Aberdeen da day? ....

57

Da price! Da price! An da Nort Baas brakkin!
What's da price, braks a winter's gale?
Senses tuned ta a world obstropolus   *obstreperous*
Ready ta act sood onything fail.

What's da price, an da squall comes dirrlin; *hurrying*
Black aa roond, nor iver a glaem -
Compass, wheel, an a ee ta windward,
Haddin da rodd da Norsemen cam haem.   *holding*

Shetland poetry since the last war owes a tremendous debt to Peter Jamieson,
another socialist writer and poet, who launched in 1947 *The New Shetlander,*
a quarterly magazine which had as its chief aim the encouragement of local
writers. In its pages first appeared the poems of T.A. Robertson or 'Vagaland'
as he called himself. Though a quiet gentle poet, Vagaland was fiercely
passionate about the virtues of the old tongue and the old traditions — the
heritage which had shaped and formed so much of his own attitude to life. 'A
Skyinbow a Tammie's' is a fine tribute to that language — its beauty, strength
and significance for to-day. Here are the concluding verses:

Trowe wir minds wir ain aald language
    still keeps rinning laek a tön;
Laek da laverik ida hömin,   *twilight*
    sheerlin whin da day is döne;   *singing*
Laek da seich o wind trowe coarn   *sough*
    at da risin o da mön,

Hit's da skriechin o da swaabie,   *screeching*
    an da kurrip o da craa,   *croak*
An da bulder o da water   *bubbling noise*
    in aboot da brakkin baa;
Hit's da dunder o da Nort wind   *thunder*
    whin he brings da moorin snaa.   *drifting heavily*

Hit's da soond da sheep maks nyaarmin   *bleating*
    whin you caa dem on afore,
An da noise o hens, aa claagin,   *cackling*
    layin Paece-eggs ida Voar;
And da galder at da dug gies,   *loud barking*
    whin a pik comes ta da door.   *knock*

Wirds laek Freddie Stickle's music
    whin he played 'Da Trowie Burn',
Wirds wi fire an frost ita dem,
    wirds at nearly maks you murn.
Some we hae, baid coorse an haemly,
    nane can better dö da turn.

Things at maks dis life wirt livin,
  dey're jöst laek da strainin-post;
Whin he's brokken, hit's no aesy
  gettin new eens — an da cost,
Hit'll shön owergeng da honour
  if da aald true wyes is lost.

Just as the straining-post, firmly imbedded in the ground, helps to hold together the crofter's fence which surrounds his livelihood, so the culture, the music, the old speech and the web of associations these invoke — the 'things at maks dis life wirt livin', strengthens the whole community.

Another of *The New Shetlander* group of poets is Stella Sutherland. She writes highly accomplished verse on often complex and delicate themes and is equally at home in both English and dialect. Her two books of poetry *Aa my Selves* and *A Celebration* (which won the Shetland Literary Prize for 1992) contain poems which could take pride of place in any collection of modern verse. Outstanding among them is 'At da Croft Museum'. It is a beautifully written poem, vivid in its detailed particulars of bygone crofting life, its joys and sorrows — especially the 'winters a hert's bittersie', that came with the evictions. Yet, through it all, survival is the keynote, a quiet determination — 'dybin on an on becaase dey most', towards the promise of a better future. A celebration of endurance:

Dey büre an strave; gret sair, or keepit in —   *wept*
better ae hert ta brak as aa da world ta winder!
Boady an breath dey gae wis, an da foond   *foundation*
o aa at's wirs eenoo, an da regaird   *just now*
we feel for aa at's right ta inward sense.
Dey yearned forever upward, laek da flooers
bund i da seed under black tons o time —   *bound*
draemin o light, strivin towards da light,
an dybin on an on becaase dey most —   *toiling*

till dis caald eart sood tak a warmer cant,
an da frost melt an lat da simmer trow,
an burst dir laef, dir blossom an dir sang!

'A Celebration' is one of her finest poems in English. It celebrates the life of her father even though that life was crippled by the social and economic circumstances of his time: the lack of opportunity, the war and the years of the Depression — circumstances which created 'a web in wait, a snare, a net', the 'cage' he had to wear.

A CELEBRATION

The cage my father wore was made,
that crippled all his day,
before his parents ever met
and close together lay:

A web in wait, a snare, a net
of intricate design
a tender fret that closed and cut
of filigree too fine.

He was caught and set at naught,
confined without reprieve,
without avail, to toil and fail,
and little to achieve.

But in one poignant surge of bliss
he let me here begin:
my world, as I uncurled, to his
converse, and yet akin.

For me, the cruel filigree
sprang jewels at the tips;
the gift he gave that's mine to have,
they shine without eclipse
And now, too late, I celebrate
him and his cripple day:
He never had a gift so glad
as that he gave away.

That poem could stand as epitaph for many who went through those troubled, constricting times.

Rhoda Bulter (1929-94) is one of our most popular poets to-day. She published four volumes of verse all in the dialect: *Shaela, A Nev Foo o Corn, Link-stanes* and *Snyivveries.* Humorous, satirical, meditative and always vividly descriptive her poetry is a triumphant assertion of the vitality of the Shetland dialect to-day. Her poems reflect an intense love of the local scene, the land and the sea, the flowers, the birds, the animals and the crofting communities she knew when young. Her pictures of the old traditional life could have been simply nostalgic, but she is saved from this by the vivid realism and intimacy of detail which vitalises these scenes. She is conscious too of the darker side of life and is moved to bitterness and anger by the destructive side of man, his greed, his abuse of the land, his cruelty to wild life, industrial exploitation and the ultimate crime of nuclear war. She would have agreed with the writer who said, 'We abuse land because we regard it as a *commodity belonging to us.* When we see land as a *community to which we belong,* we may begin to use it with love and respect' (Aldo Leopold). Rhoda Bulter never regarded land as a commodity. She saw herself as belonging to that land — a land to care for and to love, as she shows at the end of her poem 'Wir Inheritance' describing the impact of oil on small communities.

60

Dan a caald braeth blew across me face,
An I lookit aroond at a different place,
Back ta da hertless giddy race
O life da day.
Ley crofts wi juist a yowe or twa,
Wi nane ta work an nane ta maa.
Whaat wis it at gluffed da fok awa,   *frightened*
An left caald clay?

Could it be dem wi da might an means,
At cam here wi dir muckle machines
An ruined da place as we kent it eence -
Baith mine, an dine?
Nae towt for da hame at anidder med,
Nae towt for da life at anidder led,
Nae towt for da laand in beauty cled,
No lang sin syne.

Juist bore an dreel an gurm an shap,   *engage in dirty work*
Roog in da siller athin dir lap,
Dan birze da aert for da hidmost drap   *squeeze*
Dey tink is tane.
An sae up anchor an pit ta sea,
Rubbin dir oily haands wi glee,
Laevin da brucks ta da twa or da tree   *remnants*
At widna geng.

Dir aye da twartree at hae da care
Ta bide an bigg up whaat lies wasted an bare,   *build*
Ta lave somethin livin for idders ta share,
Laek dey hed wance.
Tho da gaet might be herd an da night be lowng,   *path*
Lat it be lightened wi wird an sowng,
Aye uttered idda midder towng —
Wir inheritance.

Among recent Shetland poets, W.J. Tait has been the most ambitious, in choice of theme, technical skill and use of language. His translations of Villon, Ronsard, and other foreign poets are amazing achievements and show how the dialect can be extended in surprising contexts. His masterpiece is 'A Day Atween Wadders'. It is a love poem celebrating a memorable day in early spring when sunlight and shadow, love and death, Past and Present are all caught up, blended and transformed by the poet's heightened awareness into something new and beautiful.

'A day at we'll hae but eence — wha cares? Gie tanks fur da day.'

His long poem 'Hogmanay Sermon 1964' was sparked off by an article in *The New Shetlander* — 'Muness Sixareens' — which vividly described the storms the haaf fishermen had to battle against last century. He contrasts this vivid piece of writing with the tired, sugary sentiments on trivial themes local writers too often indulged in, and chastises them for failing to tackle the realities of life to-day:

Dir aald men, young men, weemen, lasses — or dey wir.
Dey canna be aa gien blude spring ta boutiques!   *with great speed*
Dey tüilye ower hooses; plan mills, naachtify   *quarrel, belittle*
Dem at plan mills; dey fish an sometimes droon;
Dey drink an dunna drink; dey even lie
Drunk up a closs; dey spin lang yarns — or fine   *lane*
Lace wirsit, still; write letters ta da papers;
Bigg boats an paet-stacks; elt wi motor-bikes;   *work*
Dance, feycht, mak love — toh dat as laek as no,
We canna mention i da *New Shetlander*
'Open da box', I said. I say: Open your een
Dunna glinder i da aze. Hit maitters little   *peer, blaze*
What wye you look, as lang as you look hard.
Look atween your taes, look back, look up,
Look foarward even. Lang sycht comes wi age -
Or so dey say: I doot it. If your een's gien fae you
Get glasses; but no rose-tinted eens. An write.
Write wis up; write wis doon; write wis aff;
bit fur Goad's sake write
As if you meant it. Mean it. An göed luck!

As we have seen Shetland poets have achieved much over the past hundred years. What of the prose writers? A look at three novels portraying different periods in our island history reveals creditable achievement in this field too: *Tang* by Haldane Burgess, *Thin Wealth* (a novel from an oil decade) by Robert Alan Jamieson and *Shadowed Valley* (a novel based on the Weisdale evictions) by John Graham.

Tang was written in the closing years of the last century. It tells the story of a young girl, Inga, and her divided love for two men: one, her devoted admirer, a steady, hard working fisherman, and the other, a newly arrived minister, young, idealistic, unsure of himself and very susceptible to feminine charm and persuasion. It also presents a picture of a small community of crofter-fishermen, their women-folk, the merchant, the teacher, the minister and the laird. Burgess brings out the darker side of this community, the hypocrisy and occasional dishonesty, the servility of some crofters towards the gentry, the malicious gossip, the petty jealousies and spitefulness within the congregation and the damage done by itinerant hot-gospellers and 'their infernal, illegitimate-producing revival meetings' as Hakki, the agnostic schoolmaster, calls them. The novel certainly gives an unflattering picture of what passed for religious life at this period. Here is old Magnus, the shoe-maker, who no longer goes to church, giving his views on public worship and the congregation to the new minister:

Public worship! Yea, it's public anoff, but I don't know aboot da worship. Hoo mony o da fok, tink ye, goes dere ta worship? Da most o da lasses goes to shaa aff dir bits a claes, da most o da lads ta sit an glower at dem agen, an da most o da aald fok becaase it's da custom ta go an dey're frightened fur what dir neebors wid say if dey didna. Tink ye at da laek o Hansi Bolt wid budder wi da kirk if it wisna fur his shop? Not he, feth, sir.

The arguments between Hakki, the outspoken agnostic, and the minister and laird are among the highlights of the book and it is obvious where the author's sympathies lie. It is certainly an unusual novel for its time when the Scottish Kailyard school of writing was still at its height.

Our second novel *Thin Wealth* depicts the sudden impact of North Sea Oil on the life of an island community. It is a swiftly moving story, sensitively told, with a wide range of characters all reacting in their various ways to the new and rapidly changing environment: the young vulnerable, the old stoical, some taking what they can get out of it, some confused, angry, alienated and lost. As a local critic has said, 'The central character, Linda, can in many ways be regarded as symbolic of Shetland itself. She carries with her the buried memories of a troubled past, is caught up and loses her way in the turmoil of the oil-boom, strikes back and eventually through a series of traumas finds her true self through a new insight into her traditional past.' The turbulence of the times leaves many characters bruised and scarred but some at least emerge with a new understanding of the other side of affluence and a reappraisal of their old loyalties and roots.

Our last novel *Shadowed Valley* has the clearances for its theme. It is a story of the life and death of a crofting community in Weisdale. But it is more than that. It is a commemoration of these half-forgotten folk, giving them a voice hitherto unrecorded. As a critic has said, 'it is the community itself which is the central character'. We see it in all its variety, enjoying itself at the Beltane and Lammas Foys and in story-telling sessions round the fire; joining in the excitement of caain the whales, bidding farewell to the whaling-men bound for a six-month voyage to Greenland and the hectic activity at the fishing station, and finally the sad exodus of the families from 'all the emptied homes of Weisdale'. The book has a wealth of characters: Johnie Hunter, the outspoken Radical, Seemon, the young hero's father crippled with frost-bite from the whaling, the imperturbable Rasmie, a Trafalgar veteran, Da Sodger, the laird's 'watchdog', Baabie, the hard pressed anxious mother, Aald Maalie, the midwife and Hakki himself, the young boy through whose eyes the story unfolds. And worlds apart from these folk, we have the ministers, the lairds and the lawyers debating the priorities between people or profit, crofter or sheep-farmer, compassion or progress. Only the Rev. Turnbull of Tingwall and Duncan, the Lerwick lawyer, emerge with any credit from these discussions. Turnbull in fact pays a fine tribute to an almost invisible section of the community, the women folk:

I find the Shetland women have a simple quality of enduring which is remarkable. The Shetland men are fearless at sea but irresolute ashore. It is the women who are at the heart of the community, shaping it in their own quiet way.

Shadowed Valley tells a tragic story but it is one which still has lessons for us to-day.

What kind of common theme or attitude emerges from the works we have been discussing? I would say that a strong sense of community and its survival against the odds permeates most of these poems and novels. Endurance is the keynote throughout as the last quoted extract suggests.

A recent Prime Minister said not so long ago that there is no such thing as community or society, only individuals. A study of Shetland literature shows how utterly wrong she was.

Bibliography

Anderson, Basil J., 1889: *Broken Lights*. Lerwick.
Angus, J.S., n.d.: *Echoes from Klingrahoul*. Lerwick.
Burgess, J.J. Haldane, 1891: *Rasmie's Büddie*. Lerwick.
Burgess, J.J. Haldane, 1898: *Tang*. Lerwick and London.
Bulter, Rhoda, 1976: *Shaela*. Sandwick.
Bulter, Rhoda, 1977: *A Nev Foo o Coarn*. Sandwick.
Bulter, Rhoda, 1980: *Link-Stanes*. Lerwick.
Bulter, Rhoda, 1986: *Snyivveries*. Lerwick.
Graham, John J., 1987: *Shadowed Valley*. Lerwick.
Hibbert, S., 1822: *A Description of the Shetland Isles*. Edinburgh.
Jamieson, R.A., 1986: *Thin Wealth*. Edinburgh.
Peterson, John, 1920: *Roads and Ditches*. Lerwick.
Peterson, John, 1923: *Streets and Starlight*. London.
Robertson, T.A., 1975: *Collected Poems of Vagaland*. Edinburgh.
Sutherland, Stella, 1980: *Aa My Selves*. Lerwick.
Sutherland, Stella, 1991: *Celebration*. Bressay.
Tait, W.J., 1949: 'London Letter', *New Shetlander*, xix, 15ff.
Tait, W.J., 1980: *A Day Between Weathers*. Edinburgh.

SHETLAND: THE LAND, SEA AND HUMAN
ENVIRONMENTS

James R. Coull

I doubt whether anyone has ever questioned that there is a distinctive quality about Shetland; nor that this distinctive quality applies both to the islands and to their inhabitants. There too will be considerable consensus on just what constitutes the distinctive quality, but it will also to some extent be a matter of individual (or subjective) appraisal. The aim of this paper is to show how this distinctive character has appeared to an outsider who has been acquainted with the islands over a period of well over thirty years.

No doubt the Oil Age has brought Shetland within the ken of people in other parts of Britain more than ever before — not least, unfortunately, because of the *Braer* disaster. However, the popular image of the islands has, I fancy, changed little. The old perception of islands which are 'bare, bleak and windswept, with a summer without night and a winter without light' can only have been fortified by TV camera catching the great storm waves breaking up the Braer as she lay on the rocks at Garths Ness; and this despite the fact that there was obviously enough light in January for the TV camera to function without difficulty.

None the less one look at the map does emphasise the character of the location of Shetland, the old 'Ultima Thule' position. In the rare occasions on the map of Britain when Shetland is not relegated to an inconvenient map inset, it is clear that it is over 100 miles north of the nearest part of the Scottish mainland, or about 200 kilometres in metric distance. It is also over 1,000 kilometres from Brussels in the day when more and more of our lives depend on decisions taken in the E.C. From any normal British, and still more any European, perspective, the location of Shetland is marginal and isolated.

However there are other perspectives. What might be called the conventional view of Shetland is what might be called the landsman's view. It is otherwise from the maritime perspective, as numerous traders, fishermen and navymen have realised for centuries; and to these may be added the modern oilmen. When it comes to movement by sea, or the exploitation of marine resources, the position of Shetland is essentially nodal (or central) and not marginal.

Another matter which has gained increasing significance in the modern age is simply the limited size of the Shetland community. One of the great dangers in our modern world village is that of the loss of identity, as more and more wants are catered for in the mass; and the politicians based in distant cities, backed by the cost accountants, make decisions that affect even the detail of life for millions of people. One of the great developments of the Oil Age has been the return of confidence in their own future on the part of Shetlanders, and the reassertion of Shetland identity. Perhaps this is in no way better shown than in the present debate on the returning of local government in Scotland to single-tier all-purpose authorities: surely the manner in which an all-purpose local authority in Shetland has been able to cope with, and turn to account, the pressures and demands of the Oil Age is something of a guiding light or model here. Shetland has become something of a living test case or proof of E. F. Schumacher's principle that 'small is beautiful'.

The physical environment

The characteristics of the physical environment of Shetland are well enough known, and are set out in a number of works, at least in broad outline. However, it is due partly to the remoteness of Shetland that modern work by environmental scientists has been selective and in some ways limited. Ornithologists have been attracted in strength to study the rich bird life, and more recently palaeo-botanists have worked out the vegetation history. However the contribution of geomorphologists has been limited. The Oil Age has of course brought a high intensity of work in petroleum geology under the sea bed for a wide area around Shetland, although much of the detail of the findings is still in confidential files in the offices of the oil companies.

Essentially Shetland consists of an archipelago towards the north-west margin of the European continental shelf, and the continental edge (in Shetland the 'brow of the deep water') lies only about 30 miles (50 km) to the north-west of the islands. In direct distance the islands are as near to western Norway as they are to the mainland ferry terminal of Aberdeen.

Geologically the bedrock of the 'Auld Rock' consists of a mixture of Dalradian and Old Red Sandstone rocks. The former are Precambrian: geologically they are very old, and are comparable in age with much of the Scottish Highlands. It is rocks of this series which underlie most of the islands. They are mainly metamorphic schists, but also include limestone bands in Tingwall and Weisdale, and serpentine outcrops in Fetlar and Unst. The Old Red Sandstone consists of a discontinuous strip in the south-east part of the Mainland between Bressay and Sumburgh, along with a bigger area in the West Mainland and in part of Northmavine. Also on the west side are a variety of igneous intrusions, like the granite of Muckle Roe and Roeness Hill, and the volcanic rocks of Papa Stour and Esha Ness.

Like land areas generally, Shetland has seen various phases of uplift, and also various phases of erosion, although much of the detail of the geological and geomorphological history is still obscure; and there is the essential problem of relating the sequence of events in Shetland to the better known sequence on bigger land masses, like that of Mainland Britain. It is the processes of erosion, acting over many millions of years of geological time on the rock assemblage already outlined, that has produced the present form of the islands. The essential characteristics of the relief of Shetland is that it is hilly, and it is only in a small area on Roeness Hill that the altitude exceeds 1,000 feet. The general implication is that the main lines of the relief are due to long periods of water erosion, but that much of the surface detail is due to the geologically recent Pleistocene glaciation.

At some stages of the Pleistocene Shetland was under a local ice cap, and there are also some signs that at one stage the much bigger ice sheet from Scandinavia reached across the North Sea and left its mark on the islands. An effect of glaciation has been to roughen part of the land surface, as can be seen, for example, around Mavis Grind; but the ice has also coated a large part of the land surface with a thin deposit of glacial drift. The generally smooth outline of the great part of the Shetland landscape is due partly to this, but also to the large scale post-glacial growth of peat. Also important for an archipelago like Shetland were the complicated changes in sea-level related to the glaciation: these were due to the land being depressed by ice loading, but also to the general fall in world-wide sea-level through part of the earth's water being locked up in the ice sheets. The net effect in Shetland was that the sea rose relative to the land: the Shetland coast is one of submergence, and it lacks the raised beaches characteristic of the Scottish mainland.

The coast of Shetland is in general the most scenic and spectacular part of the landscape of the isles, and owes its forms to this fact of submergence, allied to the effects of powerful wave erosion. Over 120 years ago the pioneer harbour engineer Thomas Stevenson was amazed by the power of storm waves in Shetland to move blocks of rock weighing five to ten tons and more at heights as much as 70 feet above normal sea level (Stevenson 1874: 38-45). Shetland voes are drowned inlets, and submergence has also promoted one of the most prominent landscape characteristics of the isles, the development of the cliff coast, which includes numerous cases of near-vertical cliffs hundreds of feet high, as at Noss and Esha Ness; there is also a series of other features due to wave attack at the margins of the land, including the caves, natural arches, and stacks like the Drongs and the Vee Skerries. It is also characteristic of a submerged coast that where deposition of eroded material has taken place it is in the form of such beach features as the tombolas at St. Ninian's Isle and Fora Ness (Delting), and the bay bars at Spiggie and Tresta in Fetlar, as well as the numerous bay beaches of shingle or sand.

The climate of Shetland reflects both the northern location and the pervading influence of the sea: it is classed as extremely oceanic, and though cool compared to the remainder of Britain, this is really a feature of the warmer half of the year: average winter temperatures are little different from London, and it has been pointed out that because of the great northwards transfer of warmth by the circulation systems of both atmosphere and ocean in winter, the January temperature in the isles is over 20°C. above the average for the latitude. Statistically there is little remarkable about Shetland rainfall figures with a recorded average of 45 in. (or 1140 mm). The isles are well

68

known for being prone to gales, although popular misconception does tend to exaggerate wind strength and frequency: recorded windspeed has an annual average of 16.9 m.p.h., and in Britain only the Butt of Lewis has average wind strengths on a par with those recorded at the Lerwick Observatory.

The world has never been as conscious and concerned about ecological issues as it now is, and Shetland has its own characteristics here too. Isolation inevitably limited the extent to which the isles were colonised by plants and animals after the retreat of the ice, although of course it has done little to restrict the rich bird life. The land came to be dominated by peat moorland, especially after the climatic deterioration which followed the early Bronze Age. This is essentially because of cool conditions and a water balance which entailed that most organic decay would take place in saturated conditions. The peat cover at one time would have been general: the main exceptions to this are the steepest slopes, along with the best drained areas, such as sandy areas at the coast. Many generations of peat cutting have removed the peat cover from extensive areas, and this has been one of the biggest man-made impacts on the isles.

For long there have been reports of parts of trees being dug up in the peat, and recent work by palaeobotanists has now established that the islands at the post-glacial climatic optimum had a considerable tree cover despite the effects of isolation, and of wind and salt spray.

Naturally a part of the environment that has always been important in Shetland is the sea itself. As well as the effects of waves, tides and strong tidal streams around the islands, the sea also provides a very important part of the resource base. This in the past has included seaweed as a fertiliser and a winter stock feed, but more important are the fish stocks, with herring, haddock, cod and many others having part or the whole of their life cycles in the waters around Shetland. It is hardly necessary now to add the oil and gas under the sea bed in the East Shetland Basin, and also in known locations to the west of the islands.

The development of Shetland society in its environmental context

Shetland has had a long history of human occupation, and for generations the abundance of its Prehistoric remains have been noted. The Ancient Monuments Inventory lists over 600 sites in the isles (R.C.A.H.M.S. 1946); and since these data were collected in the inter-war period, it has become clear that the number of sites is around double this figure, illustrating its attraction over thousands of years for pre-literate peoples, whose life was dominated by the needs of subsistence rather than commerce. In early times part of the attraction of Shetland was that forest was less well established and easier to clear; and in addition the resources of the land could be easily supplemented from those of the sea. Also movement over longer distances was frequently by sea, and right into modern times goods of any weight or bulk were more easily moved on water: thus in addition to the advantages of its resource base, Shetland was not inaccessible. Early farming too had often an emphasis on livestock rather than cropping, and even at the post-glacial climatic optimum there are likely to have been considerable open areas both on the higher hills and on the more exposed parts of the isles. This would have rendered Shetland preferable for stock farming to lower ground on the Scottish Mainland, which was generally well covered in forest.

Early immigration to Shetland would have been from the south, via Orkney, and must have been aided by the intervisiblity of high ground between the archipelagos; and there is sufficient in the archaeological record to show that such contacts were repeated. While such contacts made Shetland to an extent part of considerably bigger cultural provinces, notably at the time of the megalith builders, Shetland also developed its own individuality, as (for example) the heel-shaped tombs show. Shetland is also clearly shown to be part of larger cultural provinces at the times of the Iron Age and the Dark Age Celtic Church.

Among the wide range of prehistoric remains, especially important are the prehistoric houses and the brochs. The known number of early house sites is difficult to parallel anywhere of similar size in Britain. In addition to pointing to the attraction of the wide resource base of Shetland to early man, this is also probably related to the more favourable conditions for grain ripening during the Sub-Boreal phase, and the pollen record shows that wheat was cultivated. Also there was the probable early emergence of the practice of building in stone in islands with relatively few substantial trees at a time when on the Scottish Mainland buildings were mainly of timber.

Brochs are one of the several types of fortifications which were constructed in Western Europe during the unsettled period of the Iron Age, which was characterised by deteriorating climate and considerable migration and warfare. In Shetland, brochs are found all around the islands, and there is also a range of other less prominent Iron Age structures and remains, many of them around the brochs (Fojut 1984: 47-84). These Iron Age complexes probably represent the earliest identifiable pattern of community foci.

Of course, of basic importance in Shetland history was the Norse settlement, and to this day both the place-name map and the dialect emphasises this. How far the earlier inhabitants were replaced or swamped by this new seaborne invasion from the east is indeed a problem. That there was a considerable Iron Age population can not be doubted, and on the peripheries of Britain cultural elements from the Iron Age frequently survived well into the Dark Age. Modern ideas on social evolution hardly favour the notion of the elimination of the earlier peoples, followed by resettlement on a blank map. It would appear more likely that the culturally and militarily dominant Norse absorbed the earlier groups, as (for example) the Anglo-Saxons absorbed the Celts in Eastern England.

The traditional life in Shetland has been discussed in very full detail by Prof. A. Fenton in his major modern work on Orkney and Shetland (Fenton 1978). This details the various activities and implements by which the land and resources were effectively utilised to provide for the needs of the people: it covers such matters as techniques of husbandry, types of building, the securing of peat fuel and fishing methods.

One of the most important environmental adjustments which becomes clearer with the adaptation of the Scandinavian odel system to the island situation is the pattern of land holding under Shetland udal law. The principle of holding land 'fra den effste stein i fjelde till den neste i fjoren' (from the highest stone in the hill to the lowest on the beach) in fact incorporates the right to an ensemble of resources which were all needed in a subsistence economy (Fig.1). As well as land for cultivation and grazing, it included provision for peat as the essential fuel; and unlike feudal law, in giving foreshore rights it gave in this environment valuable extra rights which included driftwood, as well as seaweed and sand which could be put on the land; in addition it gave access to the sea for fishing.

In the evolution of settlement, it has also been shown that the scattald is also of basic significance. The word itself is an interesting one, and Brian Smith has shown how its meaning developed over time (Smith, B. 1984: 99-125). It features an essential link between settlement and cultivated land on the one hand, and rights to various other privileges, of which the most important was grazing rights on the hill, on the other hand; and 'scatt' dues

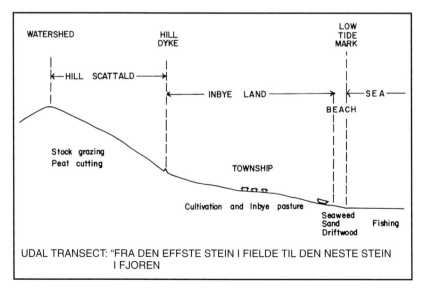

UDAL TRANSECT: "FRA DEN EFFSTE STEIN I FIELDE TIL DEN NESTE STEIN I FJOREN

were paid by the older settlements, whereas later settlements were unscatted and were excluded from the privileges. Over the centuries settlement and population expanded by a process of growth at the edges of the already cultivated area by means of new reclamation, or 'outsets'.

In the working of the land, ploughs and delling spades were used through all recorded history. Which was used depended on a combination of circumstances. Ploughs had more scope on bigger holdings and for wealthier people, while delling was used more on smaller holdings, and on small pockets of land. When we come forward to the 18th century, and the 'haaf' fishing and associated population growth, it has long been claimed that the sub-division of holdings resulted in a greater emphasis on delling; and as late as 1883 Tudor records it as the only method in general use (Tudor 1883:149). The traditional main crops were the grain staples of oats and bere, and these were ground in the traditional click-mills, or sometimes by the hand quern. As in most of Northern Europe, the potato was added in the 18th century as a crop well suited to cool and wet conditions. The isles had their own distinctive stock breeds, and cattle, sheep and ponies (or shelties) all had something of a diminutive characteristic.

In Scotland the Improving Movement, which greatly raised productivity in Lowland farming, had a different and lesser impact in the Highlands and Islands. Here the main single change was the stimulation of commercial sheep farming and the creation of sporting estates. In the absence of deer and grouse the latter hardly affected Shetland, and the remoteness of the islands delayed the main impact of the laying down of land to sheep till the second half of the 19th century, after the establishment of regular service transport to the mainland. At the same time, improved varieties of crops and stock, as well as modern methods and implements of husbandry have become parts of Shetland life.

Shetland fishing

While fishing was engaged in as part of the subsistence economy from earliest times, it is clear for many centuries that the main resources used in the islands were those of the land rather than the sea. This was characteristic of Faroe and Iceland too, although agricultural conditions in these islands were still more marginal than in Shetland.

In such island groups it took the rise of commercial fisheries for the sea to be seen as the more important part of the resource base. As so often happens in outlying areas, the main initiative in stimulating this came from the outside, with the German merchants from places like Hamburg and Bremen coming to Shetland and providing the market links from the 15th century (Smith, H. D. 1984: 10). This was to lead to ambitions for Shetland landlords and merchants to replace the outsiders, and from the late 17th century this in turn was to lead to the development of the well known 'haaf' fishing for cod and ling. It was to be the essential basis of the commercial economy for the best part of two centuries. In these centuries, Shetland became more fishing dependent than any other part of Britain. Production was very much export-oriented to the Mediterranean as well as to nearer parts of Europe, and Shetland in most of the 19th century accounted for over 80% of the British exports of cod and ling.

The 'haaf' was characteristically a fishery which was prosecuted for about two months in the summer in the open sixareens. The bases were mainly outlying points in the islands which gave access to greater areas of sea, and where members of the crews lived in lodges, or bothies. In some cases operation reached forty miles offshore, and one or two trips to the haaf in a week were the norm.

It is trite to say that the organisation of the 'haaf' fishery was enmeshed in controversy. 'The Shetland method' has been much debated: it essentially involved the monopoly position of the lairds (or their agents) in dealing with the fishermen, and participation in fishing for the laird being a condition of tenure of house and land. It took a long historical period before trade acquired the degree of freedom that it now has, and such freedom was long constrained, especially in outlying areas; and Shetland, like other comparable areas with fishing-based economies like Newfoundland and North Norway, was long involved in a truck system, whereby one merchant bought the fish and provided stores and equipment on his own monopoly terms. This is just the situation that in many instances and parts of the world has been, and is, open to abuse. As Dr. Wilfred Grenfell recognised in Labrador, alternative systems are not simple to develop in sparsely scattered populations where the total volume of trade is restricted. The lairds and merchants regularly argued that this type of system was inevitable in the Shetland situation, and it did persist as a dominant system longer in Shetland than anywhere else in Britain: there was a national Truck Commission in 1872 devoted entirely to the Shetland situation — a clear illustration that it had become an anachronism.

It was inevitable that the fishermen should chafe at their bonds of truck, and numbers of them sought opportunities in other activities, although these very generally also involved sea-faring. In the late 18th and much of the 19th centuries, a main alternative opportunity was going as crew members on Scottish boats going to the whaling at Greenland or the Davis Straits.

The great 19th century expansion of maritime trade also gave employment in the merchant marine: and from especially the middle of the century, and continuing to well into the 20th century, Shetlanders here participated in big numbers. Service in the navy, which had generally involved recruitment by the Press Gang, also in time passed to less drastic methods of engaging manpower.

Another new activity in the 19th century was the offshore cod fishery from decked smacks, which developed with the encouragement of government bounties. This was taken up at various places in Britain, but

Shetland was one of the main locations, and as well as resulting in the fishing of offshore banks around the islands, this also led to cod fishing at Faroe.

In the new opportunities which appeared in the 19th century there was of course also the herring fishery, although here the path of development in Shetland is anomalous in the Scottish context. In the light of Shetland having been the main base of the Dutch in the centuries when they dominated the North Sea herring fisheries, the isles were remarkably late in attaining their potential when the British herring fishery was the world's leading fishery in the 19th and early 20th centuries. Earlier British attempts to develop this main resource in Shetland waters had essentially tried to copy the proved Dutch method of fishing from decked busses, and curing the catch aboard. By contrast the method that was to give outstanding success in Scotland relied on shore-based curing. This easier expedient proved feasible as the herring were generally caught within 15 miles of the coast; they could be caught at night and cured onshore when the boats returned next morning.

This fishery saw an upsurge on the Scottish coasts from the second decade of the 19th century, and it was also taken up a little later in Shetland; and until the late 1830s it appeared to be on a parallel upward trajectory to that on the Scottish mainland. However it failed badly in a complex situation from 1840. Part of the problem was that the haaf fishery had pride of place in July and August, which was also the main herring season. None the less it did expand, and appeared to promise to give the fishermen a new degree of freedom as on the Scottish mainland, and it also drew in Scottish curers from established centres. It showed a growth phase until severe damage to boats and gear in a big gale in 1840 was followed by the great failure of the major Shetland merchant house of Hay and Ogilvy in 1842. This was the firm that had by far the greatest involvement in the herring fishery, and in addition to its own failure it also brought down the Shetland Bank, in which the firm had a major share, and which had been much involved in financing the fishermen (Coull 1983: 123-140). A background issue was that with the many scattered catching points in Shetland it was more difficult to supervise an adequate quality of cure, and quality gained a higher premium in the second half of the 19th century as the Scottish cure came to dominate the main continental market: and until late in the century that market could be satisfied from centres on the Scottish East Coast.

Thereafter Shetland effort was concentrated in other activities until the end of the 1870s. By this time a bigger Scottish fishery was dominating the main herring markets which were on the continent, and curers and fishermen were looking for new opportunities to extend their operations, especially in the early summer before the Scottish East Coast fishing began in July. This led to a major boom (Fig.2), and within five years Shetland had advanced from being a district of no real significance for the herring fishery to being its leading single district (Coull 1988: 25-38). Although the fishery was dominated by Scottish boats and curers, it stimulated great developments in

74

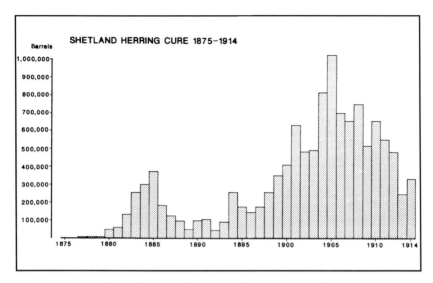

SHETLAND HERRING CURE 1875-1914
Barrels

the isles, and a fleet of over 400 herring boats was rapidly built up in the 1880s. Balta Sound, as the main centre of the early summer fishing, rose to special prominence, although curing stations were established all around the isles. The fishermen too enjoyed a new degree of freedom, as they could engage to incoming curers rather than their old masters. There was a serious recession in the herring fishery for about eight years from 1885, which did cause great problems in what had rapidly become the dominant economic activity, although with a fresh surge of growth from 1893, the fishery reached a spectacular new peak with well over a thousand boats engaging in the fishery each year, and Lerwick came quickly to the fore as the main landing point. At this point the earlier engagement system of seasonal contracts began to be replaced by the auction system of disposing of the herring, and Lerwick was the only place in Shetland where it proved feasible to establish auctions; and when the more mobile steam drifter rapidly replaced the sailboat after 1900 as the main catching vessel, the size of the Lerwick market and the competition on it by the many buyers concentrated the bulk of landings at the port.

Shetland itself never had more than a few steam drifters, although by installation of motors in their sailboats, Shetland men were able to persist in the herring fishery in the difficult inter-war period. The main fishery outside the herring in the 20th century became the line fishery for haddocks, for the fresh market or for smoking. There had been a major change in the structure of the market for demersal species in Britain: it was now dominated by fresh trawl-caught fish, and trawlers operated on the fishing banks around Shetland, but landed their catches at mainland markets. However during World War II Shetland men started to copy the men on the Moray Firth who

75

had taken up the ground seine for demersal fish, and in modern times this has become a major fishery, although there has been considerable diversification in more recent times with the adoption of different types of trawl. Shetland too has developed its own fleet of very efficient purse-net boats in the modern pelagic fisheries for herring and mackerel.

Outside contacts

Despite its apparently isolated location, developments in Shetland in all of history have been influenced by repeated external contacts. In many cases insular situations which were relatively stable in the circumstances of earlier economies dominated by subsistence have been put under strain with the growth of the highly specialised modern commercial economy. During the modern age, Shetland, like many peripheral communities, became poorer relative to the main centres of national life, and it has lost people.

The modern period has seen the growth of regular transport services with the mainland, first by sailing packet and then steamer; and since the inter-war period air services have been added. However transport services to small populations on islands can never be as good as those between main population centres, and the commercial economy necessarily involves the carriage of a great assortment of goods in small amounts to the islands. Freight rates have become a permanent modern problem, and it is generally recognised by governments of all parties that acceptable modern living standards can only now be attained with subsidised transport. The modern combination of ro-ro services to the mainland and between the islands, with air services is essential for the islands to participate in modern life.

Population

The modern population trend can be followed through the Census, but any attempt to estimate historical population can only be approximate. To judge by what is known of population trends elsewhere, and by the capacity of local resources to support a population mainly at subsistence level, the estimate of the population at between 10,000 and 12,000 around 1600 is likely to be of the right order of size (Donaldson 1958: 136).

There is also evidence to suggest that there had been significant population growth by the late 18th century with the sub-division of holdings that accompanied the development of the haaf fishing; and this point is specifically made in the Old Statistical Account in the leading haaf parish of Northmavine (O.S.A. XII: 355-356).

During the Industrial Age Shetland has seen a rise and fall of population, followed by a stabilisation that is now seen as a norm for rural areas. Increasing concentration of people and employment in cities inevitably generated increasing stress in peripheral islands like Shetland, and although the population rose to its 1861 peak, there was an increasing exodus as it was realised that for many opportunities were better on the British mainland and in Commonwealth countries than in the isles. This led to the persistent fall in numbers for a full century from 1861 to 1961, and the isles were left with a shortage of the younger age groups and with a problem of morale. At the same time there has been significant redistribution of population within the isles, as Lerwick has grown and there has been retreat especially from isolated islands and crofts.

It is not always realised that the population tide had actually turned in advance of the Oil Age, thanks to new developments in fishing and knitwear, and to the general improvement in living conditions with improvements in housing and the general extension of basic modern amenities like electricity. The hectic development of oil of course brought numbers of Shetlanders back to employment in their native isles, as well as bringing in many incomers, especially at the construction stage. At the same time the major developments of the Oil Terminal and oil servicing have been achieved with remarkably little disruption to Shetland life.

Conclusion

The goal in the medium and long term must now of course be to look beyond the Oil Age. There is now a real political challenge to establish a sustainable economy in the wake of the oil; but that will have to be met by a new generation of Shetlanders.

References

Coull, J.R., 1988: 'The boom in the herring fishery in the Shetland Islands, 1880-1914', *Northern Scotland* 8, 25-38.

Coull, J.R., 1983: 'The herring fishery in Shetland in the first half of the nineteenth century', *Northern Scotland* 5:2, 123-140.

Donaldson, G., 1958: *Shetland life under Earl Patrick*. Edinburgh

Fenton, A., 1978: *The Northern Isles: Orkney and Shetland*. Edinburgh.

Fojut, N., 1985: 'Thoughts on the Iron Age'. In: Smith, B. (ed.), *Shetland Archaeology*, Lerwick, 47-84.

Old Statistical Account (O.S.A.), XII. Northmaven, 346-368.

R.C.A.H.M.S. (Royal Commission on Ancient and Historical Monuments in Scotland) (1946): *Orkney and Shetland*. Edinburgh.

Smith, B., 1984: 'What is a Scattald? Rural Communities in Shetland 1400-1900'. In: Crawford, B.E.. (ed.), *Essays in Shetland History*. Heiðursrit to T.M.Y. Manson, Lerwick, 99-124.

Smith, H.D., 1984: *Shetland Life and Trade 1550-1914*. Edinburgh.

Stevenson, T., 1874: *The Design and Construction of Harbours*, (2nd edn.). Edinburgh.

Tudor, J.R., 1883: *The Orkneys and Shetland: their Past and Present State*. London.

THE AULD ROCK: THE PHYSICAL ENVIRONMENT AS AN ELEMENT IN THE INTERPLAY OF CONTINUITY AND CHANGE IN SHETLAND'S HISTORY

Ian A. Morrison

One of the paradoxes and pleasures of the study of history is that the past is not immutable. Our perceptions of it are always changing. New information comes to light, whether through archive work or archaeology, and seemingly established data are re-evaluated. These re-assessments may reflect either the application of new practical techniques, or changing fashions in philosophy. Often it seems to be a two-way interaction: either may enable or indeed demand the other, and lead to data being approached differently and re-assembled on frameworks which may vary radically from those used by previous scholars. Because of their small scale, and physical though not cultural isolation, the North Atlantic islands offer a particularly interesting theatre to observe the interplay of different schools of thought on basic themes such as the relationship between continuity and change within societies, and between people and their environments.

The nature of the relationship between continuity and change has emerged as a major theme in recent publications on the Northern Isles as well as other areas of Scotland (e.g. Bigelow 1987, 1992; Crawford 1984; Fenton 1984; Fenton and Pálsson [eds.] 1984; Irvine & Morrison 1987; Morris and Rackham 1992; Lynch, Spearman & Stell 1988; Stoklund 1984; Thomson 1987; Whyte 1987). It figured at the 1993 Conference of our Society. The theme had indeed been a leitmotif of the preceding Settlement Conference in Lerwick in 1988, not least in the contributions by William Thomson and John Baldwin, who both gave us particularly vivid views of the evolution of agricultural patterns in Shetland and in the Faroes. They highlighted the way that a propensity for dynamic change has been woven through elements of long-term continuity in the landscape. This pattern is not dissimilar to that found by the present writer in exploring the relationship between traditionalism and innovation in the maritime technology of Shetland and other North Atlantic communities (Morrison 1992).

Professor Bjarne Stoklund (1984), focusing on vernacular building traditions, concluded that most of the earlier studies on the cultural history of the Northern World have been preoccupied by the phenomenon of 'continuity', while 'change' was mostly considered in connection with the process of modernisation beginning in the 19th century and accelerating during the 20th. Because of the apparent 'primitiveness' of the older houses to be found in the Northern Atlantic isles, they were regarded in light of an evolutionistic model of explanation as 'survivals' i.e. representatives of earlier stages in an unbroken continuity from the Viking age, or even earlier. The Black-House of the Hebrides, for instance, was once widely believed to go back to the Iron Age, but it has now been shown that some of its characteristic features may well be relatively recent (Fenton, 1978). Stoklund talks (1984: 96) of 'evolutionistic thinking in grooves... which has played a dominating role and is very hard to escape'. He emphasises that more recent investigations of vernacular buildings in the North Atlantic isles show that 'primitiveness' is not necessarily a question of age, and that change is not always a more recent phenomenon than continuity. He doubts the value of a mechanistic idea of culture embodying this type of concept of 'survival'.

Stoklund suggests, however, that another meaning of the word 'survival' has real relevance to Northern studies: that of culture as a means of adapting to environment, and surviving harsh conditions. He goes as far as to say that 'it is an aspect that is more distinct here than in any other part of Europe, because these marginal settlements have been most vulnerable in the face of climate as well as economic changes' (1984: 96). One suspects that, *pace* Stoklund, cases could be made that certain southern European areas also display environmental problems which have rendered them equally marginal and vulnerable: for example, those rugged limestone regions which have suffered loss of vegetation and soil erosion through centuries of overgrazing. Uniqueness is not however what is at stake here, and his basic point is surely a valid one, that those concerned with the history of the Northern Atlantic islands can not afford to omit the physical environment from their considerations.

To say this is not however to advocate a return to simplistic environmental determinism. This would be manifestly unprofitable, not to say unattractive. Much of the fascination of the study of these island communities lies in the way that they are small enough for the historian to get to know them sufficiently well to test out hypotheses at a very direct human level. If one is interested in the interplay between, say, social structures and economic systems on the one hand, as against the role of individuals in shaping the development of the community on the other, in island polities of such small scale there is a fair chance of making one's assessment in very specific terms. Sweeping generalisations regarding, say, 'the Effect of Environment on Man' would add little to such debates.

As R. G. Collingwood put it in 'The Idea of History':

> ... when people speak (as Montesquieu, for example, did) of the influence of geography or climate on history, they are mistaking the effect of a certain person's or people's conception of nature on their actions for an effect of nature itself. The fact that certain people live, for example, on an island has in itself no effect on their history; what has an effect is the way they conceive that insular position; whether for example they regard the sea as a barrier or as a highway to traffic. Had it been otherwise, their insular position, being a constant fact, would have produced a constant effect on their historical life;

whereas it will produce one effect if they have not mastered the art of navigation, a different effect if they have mastered it better than their neighbours, a third if they have mastered it worse than their neighbours, and a fourth if everyone uses aeroplanes... In itself, it is merely a raw material for historical activity, and the character of historical life depends on how this raw material is used (Collingwood 1946: 200).

The views of Stocklund and Collingwood accord well with the findings of James J.A. Irvine and the present writer, regarding historical and geographical aspects of the fishing activities of the Shetland community (Irvine and Morrison 1987). We concluded that popular stereotypes of 'traditional folk life' are often more hide-bound and less flexible than those ways of life themselves ever were in actuality. As in the case of vernacular architecture, so too with fishing technology: the stereotypes tend to assume to be 'continuity from an immemorial past' what is frequently no more than an eclectic recollection of elements from the experience of relatively recent generations. Thus, rather than perpetuating the practices of Viking times, the Far Haaf fishery and the particular form of sixareen used to pursue it appear to have been essentially 18th century developments. It would seem that in much of the past as at the present day, the story of fishing in Shetland has essentially been one of change. What is more, these changes have arisen as much through responses to conditions created elsewhere as to local environmental factors within the islands. They have involved a complex multi-way interplay of social, economic, technological and indeed psychological elements. We concluded that things as tangible as not only boat types but the geographical location of fishing stations might be viewed as the varying resultants of these interacting forces. Through time, their patterns have altered markedly, and sometimes very rapidly. The potentials and problems of the physical environment have been re-evaluated periodically as perceptions and aims have changed.

Nonetheless, just as one must reject simplistic environmental determinism, so too is untrammelled 'possibilism' an unrealistic framework for research. Subconscious acceptance of this is however, perhaps a more subtle and insidious danger than that of embracing discredited determinism. Few people in these allegedly ecologically-conscious days would overtly deny that economic, social and political acts have their environmental constraints and consequences. But in practice it seems all too easy to disregard or under-rate the importance of the physical environment in historical studies, for three reasons.

Firstly, there is the seductive convenience of interpreting history as if the stage upon which it is played out were some featureless isotropic plane, which refrained from adding geographical complications to socially or economically based conceptual models. Secondly, attempts to take account of the physical environment can run up against the problem of divergences in interests and training: specialists in the natural sciences and in historical studies do not necessarily have either the background or the inclination to work together. Thirdly, it takes a determined historian of the particular turn of mind of an Emmanuel Le Roy Ladurie (e.g. 1972) to identify and extract information on the physical environment from historical documents. In terms of environmental data, little short of a catastrophe tends to 'hit the headlines' in the types of records with which historians normally deal. Conditions which are constant, or which are changing so slowly that trends are imperceptible to those living through them, are unlikely to be forced on the historian's consciousness by contemporary comments, however important those continuities or changes may be in the long term.

This is an extreme case of what Fernand Braudel (1972: 16) identifies as:

> . . . the basic problem confronting every historical undertaking. Is it possible somehow to convey simultaneously both that conspicuous history which holds our attention by its continual and dramatic changes [conjuncture, denoting short-term realities] - and that other, submerged, history [structure, denoting long-term realities] almost silent and always discreet, virtually unsuspected either by its observers or by its participants, which is little touched by the obstinate erosion of time?

Braudel's own solution for his classic and immense analysis of Mediterranean history was to adopt as his starting point an in-depth consideration of 'the role of the environment':

> The resulting picture is one in which all the evidence combines across time and space, to give us a history in slow motion from which permanent values can be detected. Geography in this context is no longer an end in itself but a means to an end. It helps us to rediscover the slow unfolding of structural realities, to see things in the perspective of the very long term. Geography, like history, can answer many questions (Braudel 1972: 23; also 1958).

In adopting this approach, Braudel specifically rejects 'the doubtful pursuit of a determinist explanation' (loc.cit.). His interest is focused on distinguishing between long-term and more changeable factors in the lives of those who lived in his area of interest. It is in this spirit that the present writer offers the remainder of this paper. The nature of the interplay between factors inducing continuity and change is likely to be subtly different in every period, so the objective here is not to provide 'the solution'. Instead, the aim is to offer those interested in particular periods an overview of the physical environment of Shetland, indicating some of the problems of the information available. The Conference made it clear that we are at an interesting phase in the development of settlement studies in the North Atlantic isles. With new concepts being applied and primary archive work and fieldwork going forward afresh, it would seem a shame if the excitement of these developments distracted us from giving due weight to those basic realities of life in the islands arising from their location and configuration. The aim here is therefore to review characteristic elements of the physical environment of

Shetland, to encourage us to keep these factors in mind while carrying on our main-line historical studies in whatever period we may specialise.

In embarking on this, it is necessary to reiterate that we must beware of too simple an approach in which we equate long-term continuity with 'constant' factors from the world of nature, and change with 'recent human activity'. This can certainly sometimes be the case. However as we saw, for example, in our study of fishing (Irvine & Morrison 1987), human factors (political, economic, social, psychological) can sometimes conspire to delay change. When such a situation occurs, the appearance of long-term continuity may create an erroneous impression, in which undue importance may be attributed to the constraints set by the physical environment as the context within which the society is operating. But then quite suddenly the nature of the multi-dimensional interaction between people and their habitat can alter, weaving a new pattern across those warp threads of continuity which do come running through from the islands' past and off into its future.

We have to keep in mind also that some of the elements in the environmental equation have themselves changed through time due to natural processes. Furthermore, in as fragile an environment as Shetland, aspects of the habitat will inevitably have been modified (directly and indirectly, intentionally and inadvertently) by people and their animals.

Environmental implications of Shetland's location and configuration

One inescapable fact of Shetland's physical geography is the high latitude of the archipelago. While London lies at 51 degrees North, Shetland is mostly between 60 and 61. The Arctic Circle is as near to Shetland as Shetland is to Newcastle or Belfast. The islands thus lie north of Stockholm, and share the same latitude not only with Bergen and Oslo but Helsinki, Leningrad and much of Siberia. Moscow is far to the south. Indeed Shetland is well north of such snow-bound places as Churchill on Hudson's Bay, Juneau in Alaska, the Aleutians and most of the Bering Sea. It is indeed on the same latitude as Cape Farewell at the tip of Greenland.

Because of the obliquity of the sun's rays in these latitudes and the amount of cloud cover sweeping in off the Atlantic, the total insolation received at the surface in Shetland each year averages less than 80 g.cal. per square cm, i.e. less than half that characteristic of much of the Mediterranean (data from I. Budyko, in Fisher 1978). This is less disadvantageous for agriculture than it perhaps sounds however, because of the marked seasonality which the high latitude also brings. Certainly, at mid-winter, the sun is below the horizon for eighteen of the twenty-four hours. In compensation, however, during the latter part of the growing season leading up to Hairst, the land is virtually without night. Though not quite far enough north to qualify for the Midnight Sun, instead of any real darkness Shetland enjoys the bright twilight of 'da Simmer Dim', giving crops a better chance to ripen than farmers used to the less extreme daylight regimes farther south tend to assume. Nonetheless, with this low basic level of solar input, conditions for reliable cropping have always been marginal, and the possibility of crop failures due to both short and long-term climatic variations can never be left out of the reckoning in considering the history of Shetland.

Because of their clearer skies, inland parts of southern Greenland in fact receive more insolation than cloudier Shetland. Their great contrast in climatic harshness, despite this, emphasises the fact that climatic zones are not simply latitudinal. The effects of continental masses and oceanic circulation have to be taken into account. Most of the other northerly places noted in the latitude comparison above are subject either to continental effects or to cold ocean currents, and have severe winters. Shetland lies however in the track of moderating westerly winds coming in across the ocean, which is warmed here by the North Atlantic Drift, the continuation of the Gulf Stream. The result is an equable climate, with winter temperatures almost the same as those of London, ten degrees of latitude farther south but more susceptible to the winter cooling of the landmass of continental Europe. Indeed, winters in New York (twenty degrees farther south but subject to harsh continental effects) are often much more bitter than in Shetland.

In Shetland, the average number of mornings with snow cover tends to be 15 or less (Chandler and Gregory 1976), whereas for substantial inland areas of mainland Scotland, both in the Highlands and Southern Uplands, it is often over 50. The average dates of the first air frost of the year tend to be as late as November in Shetland, compared to September in much of Highland Scotland, and October in many of the mainland Scottish lowland areas. The last frosts of the spring are more important for agriculture, and again the beneficial effect of the North Atlantic Drift is apparent, with Shetland tending to have had its last air frosts before April is out, whereas much of mainland Scotland has to wait until June is in (Burnett [ed.] 1964).

These figures for snow cover and incidence of frost are based on runs of statistics gathered in the earlier part of the present century, yet their relevance to our immediate future is in dispute. The present preoccupation with the possibility of anthropogenic 'Global Warming' emphasises the difficulty of evaluating trends even in this heavily instrumented age. Some historians may accordingly feel that it is injudicious to involve themselves with the possibility of climatic variations in periods before scientific meteorological records were kept. There are however many indirect lines of evidence which suggest, for example, that the efficacy of the ocean currents for warming the North Atlantic has varied significantly through the centuries. These include the positions where pack-ice was logged by the 17th and 18th century whaling ships, and a wide range of other indirect documentary and natural science data from Iceland, the Faroes and Norway as well as the British Isles (e.g. inter al.: Grove 1988; Lamb 1982; Gissel & Jutikkala 1981; Parry 1978).

The importance of climatic change to a community set at so high a latitude as Shetland is such that the probability of significant variations ought not to be discounted, despite the need for much further research. Happily, the prospects for this going forward seem positive. Not least because of the topical interest in using historical data to evaluate the current concern over 'Global Warming', it seems likely that there will continue to be inputs of funds for researching the climatic changes of recent centuries. Results from this may offer routes by which some of the basic problems of the history of Shetland may be approached. For example, Dr Hance Smith has drawn attention to the dearth of reliable direct data on the varying population levels of Shetland, right up until the 18th century. He casts doubt on estimates for the Viking era and notes that 'there is practically no information for the intervening period' (Smith 1984: 6). An assessment of the changes in the subsistence base available in the islands in earlier centuries would at least help to provide a framework for conjecture on demography, and the climatic research now proceeding offers one route towards this. While data on the sequence of climatic changes derived from Shetland itself remain scanty, recent reviews of results from Iceland and Norway suggest that a sufficiently consistent picture is emerging to justify some interpolation to our intervening islands (e.g. Teitsson 1981; Grove 1988; Ogilvie 1984). Since the area of ground in Shetland with any potential for arable land-use is of such limited extent (see Fenton 1978, and below), it is practicable to consider surveying its viability under specific conditions, and apportioning confidence limits for its possible productivity under different climatic regimes (cf Parry 1978).

The North Atlantic Drift has clearly been crucial in saving Shetland from the frigid winters commonly characteristic even of latitudes much farther to the south. In summer however, while the temperature curve can rise quite steeply in continental areas protected from the influence of a major ocean, the great mass of sea water works as a heat-sink and inhibits the rise of summer temperatures in the islands. At 12 degrees Celsius, Shetland in July is about three degrees cooler than Edinburgh and six degrees cooler than London. This may not seem much, but this flattening of the curve relative to more continentally-influenced areas means that relatively few day-degrees of energy are available above the threshold temperatures for plant growth and ripening. The relative mildness of Shetland's winters certainly makes the islands a more convenient place to live than Greenland or Labrador, but this is of scant advantage for arable farming, since little crop growth occurs in the gloom of winter. The importance of this factor of 'oceanicity' relative to 'continentality' in the summer growth season is brought out by the fact that in a European perspective, all Scotland has been mapped (Parry 1978: 85) as having a more marginal climate for cereal cropping than part of Finland, despite the marked contrast in the severity of their winters.

The oceanic inhibition of the rise of summer temperatures makes everything more marginal: not only is there less scope for evaporating excess soil moisture, but the cooling effect of increasing height above sea level becomes critical at a much lower altitude than in regimes where summer

84

temperatures show a higher peak. Crops ripen reliably in the Alps and other inland continental locations (including parts of eastern Scandinavia) at considerably greater heights than the practical limits of arable farming in Shetland. Thus, just as we have to qualify our interpretation of Shetland's latitude in terms of the 'oceanicity/continentality' axis, this in turn leads us to take on board the concept of 'vertical norths'. This term was coined by Strzgowski (and adopted by Braudel 1972: 27) as shorthand to indicate the way in which vertical movement up a hillside at a single locality can lead through a succession of ecological zones, equivalent to those which would be encountered in a considerable horizontal traverse northwards. The oceanicity of the climate in the Northern Isles has compressed these zones dramatically, so that despite the low amplitude of relief in the islands, viable agricultural land is soon supplanted by habitats that are technically sub-Arctic, as one ventures up hill.

Thus, Shetland's growing-season at sea level is no more than that at Dalwhinnie at 1150ft (350m) in Scotland's central Highlands, while by the time that 1000ft (305m) above sea level is reached in Shetland, the mean summer temperature is the same as at 2500ft (762m) in the central Highlands (Spence 1979). Because of exposure, one does not have far to climb to encounter 'patterned ground' features. These are stripes and other shapes sorted in loose stones by frost-heaving on bare, wind blasted ground. They are characteristic of periglacial conditions, and though found down to sea level in the Arctic and Antarctic, they tend to develop only at relatively high altitudes elsewhere. On the Keen of Hamar on Unst, however, they may be seen on slopes of serpentine gravel at only 200ft (60m) above sea level: the lowest post-glacial, frost-patterned ground recorded anywhere in Britain. Ronas Hill, though the highest point in Shetland at 1486ft (453m), is hardly a notable peak in European terms. Yet a whole range of periglacial phenomena are to be seen 'more clearly here than on any other British site' (Ball & Goodier 1974), and because of this and its Arctic-Alpine flora it has been designated a Site of Special Scientific Interest. It is a measure of the marginality of conditions in all the Northern Isles that despite the advantages of lowland Orkney for agriculture (see below), Ward Hill on Hoy, which at 1565ft (477m) just tops Ronas Hill, also has widespread examples of patterned ground.

Although the patterned ground emphasises how closely the isles come to the Arctic in terms of their 'vertical norths', as noted earlier the buffering effect of the surrounding ocean both limits the time in which snow lies and in which killing frosts may affect agriculture, at least at sea level. However, exposure to the wind is a factor which has to be taken into account throughout the year in the isles. There is no shelter as far as Greenland or Newfoundland to the west, or the Pole to the north. Scotland as a whole ranks as:

. . . one of the most exposed countries in the world, with wind forces and frequencies greater than elsewhere in Western Europe and comparable only to the coasts of NW America, Tierra del Fuego, the Falkland Islands, and other high latitude islands (Tivy 1983: 79). Shetland is among the windiest parts of Scotland. There are no records for Ronas Hill, but Sandness Hill at just 817ft (249m) registers 80% of the mean annual windspeed of the summit of Ben Nevis itself (4406ft; 1343m). For eight months of the year, the average windspeed in much of Shetland does not drop below 15mph, and through December, January and February it stays over 20mph. There are between 200 and 250 hours of full gales per year, and some of the highest windspeeds known anywhere in Britain have been recorded in Shetland. A gust registered 177 knots at RAF Saxa Vord, Unst, but as it took the head of the anemometer off downwind with it, nobody is quite sure what speed it actually reached! (Morrison 1974).

Besides causing direct mechanical damage to crops, high wind forces tend to curtail productivity by increasing evapo-transpiration and lowering temperatures by wind-chill. Furthermore, since none of Shetland is more than three miles (under 5km) from the sea, the turbulent air off the ocean is often heavily salt laden, and can damage plants throughout the year. Taking these features into account, Dr David Spence (1979) has classified the upland part of Shetland as subarctic oceanic, in terms of climate and vegetation. He puts the lower limits today of this inhospitable environment at around 200m in sheltered valleys, but at no more than 100m (c330ft) on summit ridges, since exposure depends on relief as well as altitude. This is the situation in the relatively bland climate of the late 20th century. We must assume that in many of the phases of the Little Ice Age which are now being identified (as reviewed for example by Grove 1988), the constraints on subsistence agriculture in Shetland and the other Atlantic Islands were even more severe. Indeed, recent work in Norway suggests that some phases characterised by milder winters, which favoured inland parts of that country, were marked by increased storminess which actually restricted vegetation growth on the exposed western Norwegian seaboard (Teitsson 1981). Complications such as these may well have to be taken into account in our Isles, because of their degree of exposure.

Most of the terrain with which the climate interacts in Shetland has never favoured agriculture. Although absolute heights are not great, the narrowness of the islands and the degree of coastal indentation is such that steep slopes from ridge to shore are common. Glaciation has worked over the very ancient and often highly contorted bedrock to produce landscapes of erosion, with many bare rock outcrops and characteristically shallow soils. In some areas, as we shall see, the soils appear to have been further attenuated by the activities of people and their animals. Where recent deposits of any depth have formed, these are generally of blanket peat, capable only of supporting low-intensity grazing. The extensive peats (covering, for example, two thirds of Yell) reflect the combination of the cool wet climate with bedrock which is often acidic, rather than base rich.

86

There are relatively few areas where geology has favoured agricultural activity. The Old Red Sandstones of Dunrossness resemble those of Orkney in their gentler topography and sweeter soils, and give some of the best farming land in Shetland. Narrow bands of limestone, outcropping from Scalloway to Nesting, make part of the Tingwall area more productive than the acidic soils on the surrounding schist and gneiss. In Unst and Fetlar, basic gabbro and serpentine offset the acidity, so that Fetlar has sometimes been called 'the Garden of Shetland' (Whittow 1977).

These exceptions however emphasise the limited agricultural potential of the greater part of the archipelago. When considering this in terms of traditional economies, it is perhaps more realistic to avoid figures from the current EC and Oil era, and join Fenton (1978) in looking to those from the pre-war period. Thus, even in 1931 just 3.4% of Shetland's total land area was classified as Arable: less than a tenth of the corresponding figure for Orkney (37.3%). As we have seen, climatic variations must certainly have reduced the amount and productivity of Shetland's limited stock of arable land, particularly in phases of lower summer temperatures, and greater storminess. As Goodlad (1971: 2) puts it:

> . . . with Shetland close to the limits of tolerance of many crops... a small annual fluctuation in the amount of sunshine, or strength of wind or occurrence of frost... on occasions in history caused famine, and even today they can severely strain the resources of a small farmer.

Just as human factors may sustain long-term continuity as well as precipitate change, so too can quite evanescent short-term physical events like some of the great storms which Shetland has experienced change the fortunes of communities, through losses of crops on land, and crews at sea.

Although the present climatic phase is relatively bland compared with many in previous centuries, it can not be assumed that this 3.4% figure represents the maximum, from which subtractions for negative climatic phases should be made. The reservoir of land of arable potential may have been slightly greater in the past. It is not merely the prospect of some periods of better climate which needs to be taken into account. As suggested above, allowance must be made for the deleterious impact of people and their animals, in over five millennia of occupation of this fragile habitat.

The limitations of Shetland for cropping have led to a traditional emphasis on livestock, with the hill land being used to feed cattle, ponies, swine and particularly sheep (Fenton 1978). Even in recent years Shetland has carried more sheep than the much larger county of Caithness and as Spence has pointed out, these have degraded the upland vegetation and soil significantly by trampling, as well as reducing its nutrient status with the removal of their wool and carcasses for consumption elsewhere (Spence 1979). The burning-over of the pastures has contributed to erosion. The hill land has also served at least since the Iron Age as a source of peat for fuel. According to Spence, failure in the past to follow the practice of replacing the top sod on the bare peat surface may account for the stoney areas so common in areas of cut-over blanket bog, as at Staneydale in West Mainland. Turf scalping may account for the bareness of upland Papa Stour, and for the thin soil cover on the areas around many townships, as at Muness in Unst. Overall, the extent to which potentially productive land has been lost is difficult to assess, and it may be that the impact has been more on the uplands and rough grazings than on patches of better arable land, cherished because of their very rarity. Certainly, until the last century peat used to be brought off the hill to be mixed with manure to supplement the topsoil of infields.

Whatever detailed variations there may have been in the area of ground capable of supporting cultivation in Shetland, it has certainly been one of the factors of long-term continuity in the human geography of the islands that this area has only been of the order of one twenty-fifth of the total extent of the archipelago. This underlies the stereotyping of the Shetlander as 'a fisherman with a croft', i.e. one who turned for subsistence from the limited potential of the land to relative fertility of the surrounding seas, despite the difficulties and dangers of working these far northerly waters.

Since Orkney and Shetland both lie in the same broad climatic regime, the contrasting stereotype of the Orcadian as 'a farmer with a boat' requires consideration. We have already noted that the proportion of arable land in Orkney is ten times that in Shetland. Underlying the rich complexity of the history (e.g. Thomson 1987), there is a bold geological contrast between the island groups (Whittow 1992). Except for areas such as Dunrossness mentioned above and part of western Mainland, most of Shetland is essentially a geological stepping stone between the Grampian Highlands and the equally ancient rocks of the western Norwegian mountains. It is akin to them in structural complexity, with many contorted and metamorphosed beds set on edge, their differences in hardness picked out by glacial erosion. Orkney, however, is primarily an extension of the sandstones characteristic of Caithness. Their almost horizontal strata give broader islands, with more extensive plains in the crucial climatic zone close to sea level. The sandier soils tend to be less acid, to drain better and to warm earlier in the spring. At the same time as it has fostered agriculture, this geology has given Orkney a coastline which is very different from the point of view of traditional small-boat fishing. Though there are great roadsteads such as Scapa Flow, and fine sandy beaches, the erosion of the sandstone strata has often created wide shallow rock shelves which make approach difficult in heavy weather (Goodlad 1971). These shelves are frequently backed by unbroken clifflines. Shetland on the other hand, though certainly beset by complex stretches of skerries and iron-bound coastlines, is penetrated by many narrow arms of the sea which offer sheltered havens.

Shetland's physical geography can also be set in perspective by comparison with the Faroes (Jackson 1991). Lying around two hundred miles to the northwest, conditions there tend to be more extreme versions of those encountered in Shetland. There is less insolation, due not only to the even higher latitude, but to more persistent cloud cover and fogginess. The terrain is yet more dissected. Agriculture is thus even more difficult. The surrounding fishing grounds are at least as fecund as those around Shetland, so it is hardly surprising that in the Faroes, fishing has traditionally been of far greater importance than farming. However, as Goodlad notes (1971: 8) 'this is not entirely due to the attractiveness of the marine environment.' Factors such as the nature of the historical relationship to Denmark and changing access to European markets can not be left out of account.

Conclusion

As suggested above, Shetland and the other North Atlantic isles have an especial attractiveness as a theatre for re-assessing one's ideas on the processes of history. They have advantages for evaluating the extent to which the interplay between elements sustaining continuity and those promoting change has varied from period to period, and for investigating the ways in which human and environmental factors each have the potential to influence the development of a community and its landscape in both long-term and short-term ways. Thus, all these island communities are sufficiently small and relatively well documented for their internal dynamics to be accessible, and there is a rich legacy of previous scholarly study to provide starting points. The very fact that they are islands also tends to make the evolution of their relationships (for good or for ill) with other societies elsewhere more explicit and visible than is necessarily the case for inland communities set amidst the artificial political boundaries of a continent. The northerly and oceanic habitats which they offer are also sufficiently exacting to make the nature of relationships between the environment and the social or economic organisation of the communities rather more direct and clearer than in many parts of the world which are climatically blander.

In this paper, both the obsolescence of traditional determinism and problems involved in evaluating aspects of the physical environment have been stressed. It is nonetheless difficult to escape the conclusion that this high-latitude North Atlantic oceanic realm provides an environment of sufficiently pronounced characteristics to deserve serious attention by historians concerned with most aspects of life in these islands.

Bibliography

Ball, D. & Goodier,R., 1974: 'Ronas Hill, Shetland: a preliminary account of its ground pattern features resulting from the action of frost and wind'. In: Goodier, R. [ed.], 1974, 89-106.

Bigelow, G., 1987: 'Domestic Architecture in Medieval Shetland'. *Review of Scottish Culture No3.*, Edinburgh, 23-38.

Bigelow, G., 1992: 'Issues and prospects in Shetland Norse archaeology'. In: Morris and Rackham [eds.], 9-32.

Braudel, F., 1958: 'Histoire et sciences sociales, la longue durée'. *Annales E.S.C.* Oct-Dec, 725-753.

Braudel, F., 1972: *The Mediterranean and the Mediterranean World in the Age of Philip II,* Volume I. London.

Burnett, J. [ed.], 1964: *The Vegetation of Scotland.* Edinburgh.

Chandler, T. & Gregory, S., 1976: *The Climate of the British Isles.* London.

Clapperton, C. [ed.], 1983: *Scotland: a New Study.* Newton Abbot.

Collingwood, R., 1946: *The Idea of History.* Oxford UP.

Crawford, B., 1984: 'Papa Stour: Survival, Continuity and Change in one Shetland Island'. In: Fenton & Pálsson, 40-58.

Crawford, B., 1987: *Scandinavian Scotland.* Leicester UP.

Fenton, A., 1978: *The Island Blackhouse.* Edinburgh.

Fenton, A., 1984: 'Northern Links: Continuity and Change'. In: Fenton & Pálsson, 129-145.

Fenton, A. & Pálsson, H. [eds.], 1984: *The Northern and Western Isles in the Viking World: Survival, Continuity and Change.* Edinburgh

Fisher, W., 1978: *The Middle East.* London.

Gissel, S. & Jutikkala, E., et.al., 1981: *Desertion and Land Colonisation in the Nordic Countries, c1300-1600.* Stockholm.

Goodier, R. [ed.], 1974: *The Natural Environment of Shetland.* Lerwick.

Grove, J., 1988: *The Little Ice Age.* London.

Irvine, J. & Morrison, I., 1987: 'Shetlanders and Fishing: Historical and Geographical aspects of an evolving relationship'. *Northern Studies* 24, 43-56.

Jackson, A., 1991: *The Faroes.* London.

Le Roy Ladurie, E., 1972: *Times of Feast, Times of Famine.* London.

Lynch, M., Spearman, M. & Stell, G. [eds.], 1988: *The Scottish Medieval Town.* Edinburgh.

Morris, C. and Rackham, J. [eds.], 1992: *Norse and later settlement and subsistence in the North Atlantic.* University of Glasgow.

Morrison, I., 1973: *The North Sea Earls.* London.

Morrison, I., 1992: 'Traditionalism and innovation in the maritime technology of Shetland and other North Atlantic communities'. In: Smout, C. [ed.], 114-136.

Parry, M., 1978: *Climatic Change, Agriculture and Settlement.* Folkestone.

Smith, Hance, 1984: *Shetland Life and Trade 1550-1914.* Edinburgh.

Smout, C. [ed.],1992: *Scotland and the Sea.* Edinburgh.

Spence, D., 1979: *Shetland's Living Landscape: a study in island plant ecology,* Sandwick, Shetland.

Stoklund, B., 1984: 'Building Traditions in the Northern World'. In: Fenton & Pálsson, 96-115.

Thomson, W., 1987: *History of Orkney.* Edinburgh.

Tivy, J., 1983: 'The Bio-Climate'. In: Clapperton,C. [ed.], 64-93.

Whittow, J., 1977: *Geology and Scenery in Scotland.* London.

Whittow, J., 1992: *Geology and Scenery in Britain.* London.

Whyte, I., 1987: 'Agriculture in Aberdeenshire in the 17th and 18th centuries: continuity and change'. *Review of Scottish Culture No3*, Edinburgh, 39-52.

TREES IN SHETLAND? A PALYNOLOGICAL EXPLORATION

Graeme Whittington

Introduction

In 1774, the Reverend George Low undertook a perambulation through the 'Islands of Orkney and Schetland'. He kept a journal of his tour but it had to wait a century before being published. He approached Mainland from the south and made the following observation:

> . . . a clear view of the whole south part of the country, which indeed affords no very prepossessing appearance, the whole vista of ranges of dreary wilds, black and dismal mountains, whose tops are covered with almost perpetual fogs, their sides swampy bogs, without either good heath or shrub; the rocks in most places being the only support the eye has under the general dusk, which sticking thro' the sides of the hills is a sort of variety in this wretched prospect (Low 1879: 65).

He certainly pre-dated the romantic view of mountains purveyed by Walter Scott. He was not as caustic, however, about the appearance of trees as Johnson, who commented :

> A tree might be a show in Scotland, as a horse in Venice. At St Andrews Mr Boswell found only one, and recommended it to my notice; I told him, that it was rough and low, or looked, as I thought, so. This said he 'is nothing to another a few miles off' (Johnson 1775: 6).

Low left arboreal comment with:

> Busta, a large house with a good garden, planted with different sorts of wood but all stunted as soon as it comes above the garden wall. I observed Common Elder, Rowan and Plane Trees, grow highest, but even these could not stand the climate (Low 1879: 129).

Low was making his visit during the Little Ice Age when European temperatures were greatly depressed, so much so that glaciers re-advanced in The Alps and Scandinavia. It can be asked, therefore, if Low's views on the vegetational appearance of Shetland were aberrant due to the timing of his visit. Are things different today and were they different in the distant past? This paper will examine these questions with the main emphasis being on woodland.

Present-day Shetland

Today, Shetland's vegetation differs to no great extent from the descriptions presented by Low in his journal. Blanket bog provides a peat cover over most of the islands and is almost continuous over Yell, the western part of Unst and central and western Mainland. In general, it is about 1.5m deep but can be 6-

7m in some places. An area which nourishes such deposits is unlikely to be propitious for tree growth and Spence has pointed out that 'there are no native trees, only planted ones in Shetland' (Spence 1960: 73). He does correct that statement by pointing out that there is one, a solitary *Populus tremula* (aspen), growing at sea level and reaching 4m in height (Spence 1969: 91).

The Shetland Crofting, Farming and Wildlife Advisory group does, however, encourage the planting of trees and yet all the evidence advanced so far suggests that it would be a forlorn task. Can these views be reconciled and what are the grounds for suggesting any investment in silviculture?

The peat cover of Shetland has already been referred to and it preserves evidence of former woodland in the islands which, according to legend, was destroyed by men from Lewis and by the Vikings. Near the kirk of 'Scalsta'[1], Low records the remains of an extensive woodland under 3m of peat, apparently of *Corylus avellana* (hazel) and other species which he called 'Aquatick woods' (Low 1879: 146). A further example comes from Foula where peat cutting was yielding trunks and branches (Low 1879: 103).

It would appear, therefore, that at some time in the past Low would have been greeted by a rather different landscape from the one which actually confronted him. The possibility of looking at the nature and timing of any vegetation changes which have occurred on Shetland is made feasible by the application of pollen analysis (Moore *et al.* 1991). The existence of peat deposits is especially important for the exploitation of this technique so Shetland's vegetational history ought to be readily explored. Figure 1 shows the location of sites which have been subjected to pollen analysis (for site names and analysts see Appendix 1).

The earliest evidence

Two sites, Fugla Ness in North Roe (Hall *et al.* 1993) and Sel Ayre (Hall *et al.* 1993) in the Walls peninsula provide the earliest information on vegetational history. The latter site revealed three vegetational regimes; the first and last had Poaceae (grass) as their dominant constituent while the central period was characterised by Ericaceae (heaths). Trees and shrubs were rarities; some *Betula* (birch), *Pinus* (pine), *Alnus* (alder) and *Quercus* (oak) pollen was recovered but it is quite feasible that this was windborne to Shetland from a non-local source.

Fugla Ness presents a different picture. The vegetation was dominated by Ericaceae but the peat contains cones, needles and wood fragments of *Pinus*, providing unequivocal evidence for tree growth on Shetland at that

---

1. The printed version of Low's writings has mistranscribed the name of the place to which he is referring; it should be Scatsta. Since the time of Low's journey there has been considerable erosion of the coast at Scatsta and the deposits to which he referred are no longer preserved.

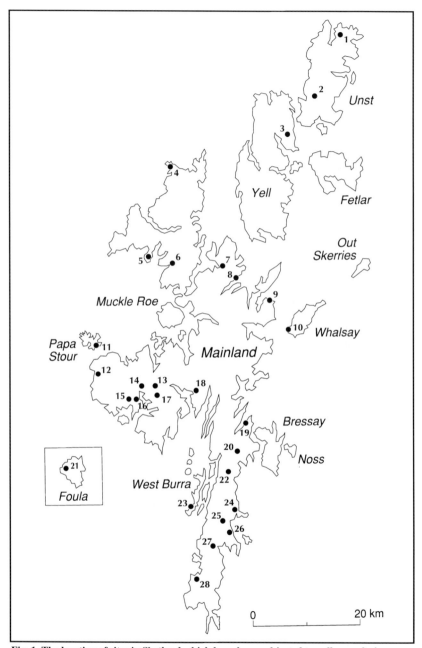

Fig. 1. The location of sites in Shetland which have been subjected to pollen analysis.

93

time. The period to which Sel Ayre and Fugla Ness belong is uncertain. Claims for an interglacial age, which would mean at least 100 Kyr BP (thousand years before present), have been made and Fugla Ness, at least, does seem to warrant such an attribution. With woodland existing at Fugla Ness, it would seem probable that it also occurred elsewhere in Shetland.

The Devensian Ice Age

From c.100 000 to c.10 000 BP Scotland witnessed the waxing and waning of the Devensian glaciation. As yet, virtually no evidence has been forthcoming as to the nature of vegetation on Shetland during possible ice free periods which are known to have existed elsewhere in Scotland during this period. Only one site, at Tresta, west Mainland (Hall & Whittington 1993) has allowed a glimpse of conditions around 11 000 BP. Shetland, as might be expected during a period of extremely low temperatures, supported a very restricted flora; only dwarf willow provided variety in a landscape which was dominated by sedges and grasses. This may not be a complete representation of Shetland's vegetation at this time but, until more sites offering organic deposits belonging to this period are found, nothing more can be established.

The Holocene period

With the removal of permanent ice from Shetland came climatic amelioration and with it a marked change in the flora. The pollen of *Juniperus communis* (juniper), *Salix* spp. (willows), *Empetrum* (crowberry), *Armeria maritima* (thrift) and *Thalictrum* (meadow-rue), among others, is found in the deposits at Murraster (Jóhansen 1975) and Lang Lochs (Hulme & Durno 1980).

a) *The establishment of woodland*

In the Holocene, by about 10 000 BP, recent research has shown that temperatures rose rapidly and had reached a level higher than those of today (Birks 1990). On the Scottish mainland, the vegetational response was one of colonisation by arboreal species. *Betula* was established in the eastern and central areas by 10 000 BP and in the north and west by 9500 BP. *Corylus avellana* was present in western Scotland at 9500 BP, *Ulmus* (elm) had appeared over virtually the whole country by 8500 BP and *Quercus* was north of the Forth-Clyde lowlands by the same date.

   The evidence of tree trunks and root systems in the peat on Shetland (Lewis 1907; 1911) suggests that this colonisation also affected the islands, although the view is still held (Lowe 1993) that both the Outer Hebrides and Shetland remained treeless. The first substantial pollen-based evidence to refute this idea came from the work of Jóhansen at Murraster on the Walls peninsula. (In 1924 Erdtman examined 20 sites in Shetland and showed that tree pollen existed but his analyses were rudimentary by today's standards.) Jóhansen showed that, at its peak, tree and shrub pollen provided 40-50% of

94

the total pollen and, in keeping with the evidence from the peat, this was mainly derived from *Betula* and *Corylus*. Three other important investigations have not only confirmed this finding but have taken it further. Keith-Lucas (1986), working at Scord of Brouster, has shown the local importance of birch and hazel, and at even higher levels than at Murraster. Bennett *et al.* (1992) examined lake muds from Dallican Water at Catta Ness. Their results revealed that from 9350 BP until about the beginning of the fifth millennium BP, tree and shrub pollen was consistently about 40%. More recently, pollen analysis from Loch of Brunatwatt (Edwards and Moss unpubl.), on the Walls peninsula, has shown that tree pollen alone reached 70% [Fig. 2]. The investigations at Dallican Water and Loch of Brunatwatt have, however, gone further than merely putting the existence of extensive woodland on Shetland on a firm footing. At both sites, the pollen of *Pinus*, *Ulmus*, *Quercus* and *Alnus* has been recovered, perhaps indicating that a wide range of woodland species was present.

In the face of this evidence, why has there been reluctance to accept that Shetland was once wooded? Part of the answer lies in the difficulty of avoiding present day perceptions of Shetland when trying to evaluate its past because of its stormy, salt-laden climate and bog-ridden surface. There is, however, a more deep-seated problem, one that faces all palynological investigation. The fact that much pollen relies on wind for its dispersal always raises the question of the provenance of any that is recovered at a site; this is especially the case where *Pinus* is involved, because it is specially adapted for aerial dispersal. As no fossil root or wood evidence of *Pinus*, apart from the very old deposits at Fugla Ness, has been found on Shetland, it is reasonable to deduce that the pine pollen found at Dallican and Brunatwatt has resulted from long distance wind transport. Studies have been undertaken (Tyldelsley 1973) of the modern windborne introduction of tree pollen into Shetland. It is calculated to be somewhere of the order of 15% (Birnie 1981; cf. Hawksworth 1970). The high levels of *Betula* and *Corylus* pollen and their remains in peat deposits, however, put their presence in Shetland beyond doubt. *Quercus* pollen reaches nearly 10% at Brunatwatt and 14% at Dallican, making its presence on Shetland a strong possibility. The status of *Alnus* and *Ulmus* has to be less certain as their values do not exceed about 5%, although in the case of *Alnus*, macroscopic remains have been recovered from Foula (Hawksworth 1970) and Mainland (Lewis 1911). There is every indication, therefore, that for a very long period following the recovery from the depressed temperatures of the Devensian Ice Age that Shetland not only supported an extensive woodland cover but that it was varied, perhaps even containing *Ulmus* and *Fraxinus excelsior* (ash).

b) *The demise of the woodland*

The contrast between the vegetational conditions revealed by the palynological investigations discussed above and the situation today, or even

95

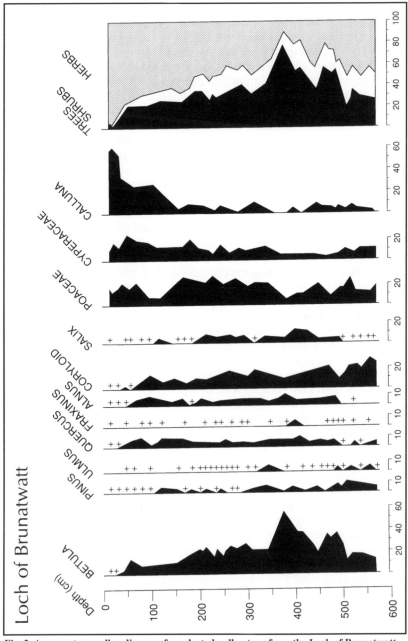

Fig. 2. A percentage pollen diagram for selected pollen taxa from the Loch of Brunatwatt.

96

that described by Low for 1774, is very striking. The hand of humans is seen in the demise of the woodland according to the myths concerning the activities of Lewis men and Vikings. The pollen analyses show that the disappearance of woodland pre-dates such activity, if it occurred, by several thousand years. It is noticeable in the pollen diagrams, particularly those from Murraster and Dallican that the change in the woodland status came very suddenly. This has been linked to the arrival in Shetland of Neolithic farmers who cleared the woodland to pasture animals and cultivate crops. Such a suggestion has been given weight by the start of a continuous pollen curve for *Plantago lanceolata* (ribwort plantain) at 4680 BP (Jóhansen 1978), a plant which is associated with soil disturbance. The remains of enclosure walls, as on Shurton Hill, near Lerwick, is also dated to this same period (Whittington 1980). The palynological investigations undertaken at Scord of Brouster and those currently occurring at Brunatwatt and Troni Shun in the Walls peninsula are also in areas where considerable Neolithic activity occurred. The Scord of Brouster pollen record (Keith-Lucas 1986) shows that *Betula-Corylus* woodland was cleared by Neolithic people.

Such woodland clearance took place generally over north west Europe, but in most areas, including mainland Scotland, regeneration of woodland followed, to be succeeded by further clearance and regeneration episodes (see e.g.Whittington *et al.* 1991). This did not happen on Shetland although it is now becoming clear that clearance and regeneration had occurred before the Neolithic settlement. *Betula* and *Corylus* pollen percentages had already fallen at Murraster before the Neolithic period. The woodland pollen frequencies also show a fall and then a rise prior to the Neolithic at Brunatwatt and Scord of Brouster. This phenomenon has been explored more fully at Dallican. Vegetational and erosional changes occurred there at about 7500 BP which has led the investigators (Bennett *et al.* 1992) to suggest that there was a Mesolithic hunter-gatherer presence, for which there is as yet no archaeological evidence, on Shetland. The vegetational changes, which seem to be equivocal (Hirons & Edwards 1990), or to go unrecorded (see e.g. Whittington *et al.* 1991) in other areas where Mesolithic peoples are known to have lived, are, at Dallican Water, laid at the door of red deer which could have been brought in by the settlers. By about 5400 BP, woodland regenerated at Dallican and remained intact until the Neolithic clearance, a fact attributed to the extinction of the deer by over-hunting or natural population crash (Bennett *et al.* 1992: 267).

Whether the Mesolithic-deer suggestion is true or not, there is proof at Dallican Water that woodland could regenerate on Shetland. This leads to the question as to why it did not occur at any time in the post-Neolithic period. It is possible to put forward several reasons which may have operated singly or in unison.

First, it should be pointed out that the Mesolithic period clearance and that of the Neolithic took place under very different circumstances. The

Mesolithic clearance was, if red deer were involved, an unintentional act; it would have been consequent upon animal rather than human population pressure. Furthermore, the land area of Shetland had become increasingly circumscribed by the Neolithic period due to a rising sea level (Flinn 1974). That factor, together with the increasing population pressure which might be expected in the transition from hunter-gathering to farming economies, would have strained the land resources of Shetland even further, preventing woodland regeneration. There would, however, have been woodland areas that were unsuitable for arable agriculture and so might be expected to have escaped clearance. The browsing activities of animals would have conspired against that. In his investigation of present-day remnant scrub in Shetland, Spence found native *Betula* bushes on an island in a lochan near Sandy Water, North Roe. He noted that in August 1953 they were readily apparent, due to the bright green of their leaves, but could not be seen the following summer; close examination showed them to have been cropped and sheep's wool tangled in the branches (Spence 1960: 77). Such predations had been noted over a century earlier. Bryden, writing on the parishes of Sandsting and Aithsting, had noted that 'mountain ash, hazel, honeysuckle, the hip-brier and willow are native in many islets in freshwater lochs'. He concluded that it was only their insular position that saved them, 'for horses, cows and sheep browse upon and destroy everything that comes in their path when hard pressed for food' (Bryden 1845).

To these factors must be added a consideration of climatic change. It is generally held that northwest Europe has undergone a series of climatic shifts (Lamb 1977), two of which, the so-called Atlantic and sub-Atlantic periods, were believed to have witnessed great increases in wetness and storminess. The consequent development of peat and the possibility of increased exposure to strong westerly, salt-laden winds would provide conditions which were not conducive to tree growth. The current status of research on climatic change suggests that no such widespread alterations have taken place since 10 000 BP (Birks 1990). That, however, does not preclude local or regional changes brought about by such features as latitude, oceanicity or altitude. Where areas are at the margin of tree growth even a slight shift in temperature would have repercussions, unmarked in the vegetation of more favoured areas. This combined with the continued assault by humans and animals would ensure that woodland regeneration would be a most unlikely event. Whether the human or the climatic factor is the more important, it is difficult to judge. An assessment of the present scrub and tall-herb vegetation on Shetland shows it to be related to communities which have an altitudinal range from sea-level in south west Greenland to 640 m in the Cairngorms of mainland Scotland (Spence, 1974: 86). On the other hand, tree growth is possible on Shetland, as is demonstrated by the frequent occurrence of *Acer pseudoplatanus* (sycamore) and the now rather neglected *Picea sichensis* (sitka spruce) plantation at Kergord in Weisdale.

Conclusion

The existence of extensive and in some cases spectacular prehistoric settlements in Shetland, especially with regard to their associated field systems, can clash with our perceptions of the conditions and resources of the areas in which they are found. To ignore the fact that environmental changes of considerable magnitude may occur, but are concealed from us, can lead to misapprehensions about life in earlier times. The employing of pollen analysis has shown that the vegetational landscape of Shetland was once very different. On arrival any Neolithic immigrants would have found a verdant and wooded prospect which would have gladdened the heart of the Reverend George Low, but it was one which they most probably unwittingly destroyed.

Acknowledgements

Thanks are due to Dr K. J. Edwards for permission to use unpublished data from his investigations at Loch of Brunatwatt and to Graeme Sandeman who drew the figures.

Bibliography

Bennett, K.D., Boreham, S., Sharp, M.J., & Switsur, V.R., 1992: 'Holocene history of environment, vegetation and human settlement', *Journal of Ecology* 80, 241-273.

Birks, H.J.B. & Ransom, M.E., 1969: 'An interglacial peat at Fugla Ness, Shetland', *New Phytologist* 68, 777-796.

Birks, H.J.B. & Peglar, S.M., 1979: 'Interglacial pollen spectra from Sel Ayre, Shetland', *New Phytologist* 83, 559-575.

Birks, H.J.B., 1990: 'Changes in vegetation and climate during the Holocene of Europe'. In: M.M. Boer & R.S. de Groot (eds.), *Landscape-Ecological Impact of Climatic Change*. Amsterdam, 125-138.

Birnie, J. F., 1981: *Environmental changes in Shetland since the end of the last glaciation*. Unpublished Ph D thesis, Department of Geography, University of Aberdeen.

Butler, S.B., 1992: *Archaeopalynology of ancient settlement at Kebister, Shetland Islands*. Unpublished Ph. D. thesis, University of Sheffield.

Bryden, J., 1845: 'Sandsting and Aithsting', *New Statistical Account of Scotland* 5, 97.

Edwards, K.J., 1972: *A pollen diagram from Saxa Vord, Unst*. Unpublished M.A. project, Department of Geography, University of St Andrews.

Edwards, K.J. & Leese, S.: *Palynological investigations at Sandwater Hill, Yell*. (unpubl.).

Edwards, K.J. & Moss, A.: *Palynological investigations at Troni Shun, Walls peninsula, Shetland*. (unpubl.)

Edwards , K.J. & Moss, A., 1993: 'Pollen data from the Loch of Brunatwatt, West Mainland'. In: J.F. Birnie, J.E. Gordon, K.D. Bennett, & A.M. Hall, (eds.), *The Quaternary of Shetland; Field Guide*, Cambridge, 126-129.

Erdtman, G., 1924: 'Studies in the micropalaeontology of postglacial deposits in northern Scotland and the Scotch Isles, with special reference to the history of woodlands,' *Journal of the Linnean Society: Botany* 47, 449-504.

Flinn, D., 1974: 'The coastline of Shetland'. In: R Goodier (ed.), *The Natural Environment of Shetland*, Edinburgh, 13-23.

Hall, A.M. & Whittington, G., 1993: 'Tresta'. In: J.F. Birnie, J.E. Gordon, K.D. Bennett & A.M. Hall (eds.), *The Quaternary of Shetland : Field Guide*, Cambridge, 121-122

Hall, A.M., Whittington, G. & Gordon, J.E. 1993: 'Interglacial Peat at Fugla Ness, Shetland'. In: J.F. Birnie, J.E. Gordon, K.D. Bennett, & A.M. Hall (eds.), *The Quaternary of Shetland : Field Guide*, Cambridge, 62-76.

Hall, A.M., Gordon, J.E. & Whittington, G, 1993: 'Early Devensian Interstadial Peat at Sel Ayre'. In: J.F. Birnie, J.E. Gordon, K.D. Bennett, & A.M. Hall (eds.), *The Quaternary of Shetland: Field Guide*, Cambridge, 104-118.

Hall, A.M. & Whittington, G.: *Late glacial deposits at Clettnadal, West Burra, Shetland*. (unpubl.)

Hall, A.M. & Whittington, G.: *Palynological and lithological investigations at Channerwick, Mainland, Shetland*. (unpubl).

Hawksworth, D.L, 1970: 'Studies on the peat deposits of the island of Foula', *Transactions and Proceedings of the Botanical Society of Edinburgh* 40, 576-591.

Hill, K, 1990: *Holocene vegetational history of north Mainland, Shetland*. Unpublished M.Phil. thesis, Queen's College, Cambridge.

Hulme, P. & Durno, S.E., 1980: 'A contribution to the phytogeography of Shetland', *New Phytologist* 84, 165-169.

Hoppe, G., 1965: 'Submarine peat in the Shetland islands', *Geografiska Annaler* 47A, 195-203.

Jóhansen, J., 1975: 'Pollen diagrams from the Shetland and Faroe Islands', *New Phytologist* 75, 369-387.

Jóhansen, J., 1978: 'The age of the introduction of *Plantago lanceolata* to the Shetland Islands', *Danmarks Geologiske Undersøgelse Årbog* 1976, 45-48.

Johnson, S., 1775: *A Journey to the Western Islands of Scotland.* J.D. Fleeman (ed.), 1985. Oxford.

Keith-Lucas, M., 1986: 'Neolithic impact on vegetation and subsequent vegetational development at Scord of Brouster'. In: A. Whittle, M. Keith-Lucas, A. Milles, B. Noddle, S. Rees, & J.C.C. Romans, *Scord of Brouster. An early agricultural settlement on Shetland,* Oxford University Committee for Archaeology, Monograph No. 9, Oxford, 92-118.

Lamb, H.H., 1977: *Climate, past, present and future.* Vol. 2. *Climatic history and the future.* London.

Lewis, F.J., 1907: 'The plant remains in the Scottish peat mosses. III. The Scottish Highlands and the Shetland Islands', *Transactions of the Royal Society of Edinburgh* 46, 33-70.

Lewis, F.J., 1911: 'The plant remains in the Scottish peat mosses. Part IV. The Scottish Highlands and Shetland, with an appendix on the Icelandic peat deposits', *Transactions of the Royal Society of Edinburgh* 47, 793-833.

Low, G, 1879: *A Tour through the Islands of Orkney and Schetland in 1774.* Kirkwall.

Lowe, J.J., 1993: 'Isolating the climatic factors in early- and mid-Holocene palaeobotanical records from Scotland'. In: F.M. Chambers (ed.), *Climate Change and Human Impact on the Landscape,* London.

Moore, P.D., Webb, J.A. & Collinson, M.E, 1991: *An Illustrated Guide to Pollen Analysis.* 2nd edition. Oxford.

Mitchell, D.A., 1972: *A pollen diagram from Watlee, Unst.* Unpublished M.A. project, Department of Geography, University of St Andrews.

Spence, D.H.N., 1960: 'Studies on the vegetation of Shetland. III. Scrub in Shetland and in South Uist', *Journal of Ecology* 48, 73-95.

Spence, D.H.N., 1974: 'Subarctic debris and scrub vegetation of Shetland'. In: R. Goodier (ed.), *The Natural Environment of Shetland,* Edinburgh, 73-88.

Tyldesley, J.B., 1973: 'Long range transmission of tree pollen to Shetland. I. Sampling and trajectories. II. Calculation of pollen deposition. III. Frequencies over the past hundred years', *New Phytologist* 72, 175-190 & 691-697.

Wakefield, G., 1976: *A palynological study of an infilled lake in Shetland.* Unpublished undergraduate thesis, Department of Geography, University of Hull.

Whittington, G., 1980: 'A sub-peat dyke on Shurton Hill, Mainland, Shetland', *Proceedings of the Society of Antiquaries of Scotland* 109, 30-35.

Whittington, G. & Edwards, K.J., 1993: 'Vegetation change on Papa Stour, Shetland, Scotland: a response to coastal evolution and human interference?', *The Holocene* 3, 54-62.

Whittington, G., Edwards, K.J. & Cundill, P.R., 1991: 'Late- and post-glacial vegetational change at Black Loch, Fife, eastern Scotland - a multiple core approach', *New Phytologist* 118, 147-166.

101

Appendix 1

The location of sites in Shetland used for pollen analysis and the names of the investigator(s). The numbers refer to the sites shown on Figure 1. Sites investigated by Erdtman are not listed.

	Site	National Grid Reference	Investigator(s)
1.	Saxa Vord	HP 631165	Edwards
2.	Watlee	HP 590054	Mitchell
3.	Sandwater Hill	HU 535984	Edwards & Leese
4.	Fugla Ness	HU 311912	Birks & Ransom
			Hall *et al.*
5.	Hillswick	HU 279756	Birnie
6.	Gunnister Water	HU 325746	Hill
7.	Garths Voe	HU 409733	Birnie
8.	The Houb	HU 449723	Birnie
9.	Dallican Water	HU 498674	Bennett *et al.*
10.	Symbister	HU 538632	Hoppe
11.	Papa Stour	HU 188602	Whittington & Edwards
12.	Sel Ayre	HU 177541	Birks & Peglar
			Hall *et al.*
13.	Unnamed	HU 275540	Wakefield
14.	Scord of Brouster	HU 256517	Keith-Lucas
15.	Loch of Brunatwatt	HU 252512	Edwards & Moss
16.	Troni Shun	HU 251506	Edwards & Moss
17.	Murraster	HU 275518	Jóhansen
18.	Tresta	HU 363510	Hall & Whittington
19.	Kebister	HU 455445	Butler
20.	Shurton Hill	HU 442402	Whittington
21.	Foula	HT 949401	Hawksworth
22.	Lang Lochs	HU 430378	Hulme & Durno
23.	Clettnadal	HU 359301	Hall & Whittington
24.	Aith Voe	HU 440290	Birnie
25.	Ward of Veester	HU 413268	Birnie
26.	Leebotten	HU 430248	Birnie
27.	Channerwick	HU 404230	Hall & Whittington
28.	Spiggie	HU 370170	Birnie

NOT SEEING THE WOOD : AN ARMCHAIR ARCHAEOLOGY OF SHETLAND

Noel Fojut

Introduction

Twenty years ago, as one of his geography students at Aberdeen University, the author followed Dr Coull around Shetland, a first visit which was to lead to a fascination with the islands, and in particular their rich archaeological heritage, and indirectly to a career as an archaeologist, albeit increasingly from the office chair.

One of the usual problems in preparing an account of the archaeological background for a gathering of non-specialists is that it requires the summarising and codification of large quantities of excavation reporting and specialist analyses. For Shetland the situation is somewhat different. Although there have been a good number of recent excavations, very little of this material is published in other than interim summary form. So it is necessary to present an account based on what little has been published, supplemented with personal knowledge and communications from unpublished sites and their excavators, plus the observations of some 20 years fieldwork, first as a research student and nowadays with Historic Scotland.

In research into Shetland's past, in particular the Iron Age brochs and the economic requirements of their inhabitants, it rapidly became clear that the question of land, its availability, ownership and control, were factors which stretched back into the Neolithic and forward to the present. So matters such as the history of the islands' vegetation, and its inter-relationship with climatic changes, or the pattern of coastal change since the Ice Age, are almost as important to the archaeologist as is the human evidence. Environmental determinism may be outmoded as an academic fashion, but that does not necessarily imply that its basic principles do not apply, especially in a landscape and climate such as Shetland's, where one can be environmentally determined on a regular basis.

In many ways, the ideal popular archaeology of Shetland might take the form of a prospectus, the work of an estate agent trying to sell to Shetland settlers through the ages: what had the islands to offer, how could they be developed, what particular building plots were available, what desirable properties could be sympathetically converted, what skills and trades were in demand locally, and what business opportunities were to be opened up. Unfortunately, we are still far from this goal, and it has to be said that the archaeological part of the necessary inter-disciplinary approach seems to be further away than the geomorphological or the palaeoenvironmental.

103

What follows is a brief summary of the archaeological story of Shetland, with a number of asides pointing out where favoured assumptions are based on less than stable ground. As will be seen, such an exercise requires almost as many asides as summary, so sketchy is most of received archaeological 'knowledge'. (For a more expansive summary, see Fojut 1994).

Cairns and crops: the Neolithic

Archaeologically, dead Shetlanders come first, by a long way. The first dated site in Shetland was the multiple burial at Sumburgh radiocarbon dated to around 3100 BC (Hedges and Parry 1980). Conventional wisdom would put the chambered tombs also early in the sequence of sites, although in Shetland there is only the evidence of field survey to rely upon, for not a single chambered tomb has provided reliable dates, the earliest cairn dated being at Brouster, where a Late Bronze Age kerbed cairn stands (interestingly enough) within a settlement which may have been abandoned by the time of the cairn (Whittle 1986).

Shetland has its own type of chambered tomb, the 'heel-shaped' cairn, and most chambered cairns with discernible plans belong to this group. There are exceptions, round and square chambered cairns without the elaborate facade. These seem to be direct fore-runners of later cairns, ascribed to the Bronze Age, where the burial is in cists or pits below a usually round, usually kerbed, cairn. Shetland has no proven surviving examples of the long cairns so common in Orkney (Henshall 1963), although two unconvincing contenders exist.

Of course, dead Shetlanders had to be Shetlanders first, and dead second. Somewhere they must have had settlements. So far we have failed to date any of the settlements as early as the Sumburgh cist. But there are plenty of opportunities left. About 160 individual house sites of the typical oval plan, often incorporating very large boulders as dividers and roof supports, have been dated to the Neolithic and Bronze Age periods by the simple fact that they lie on old soil horizons below the blanket peat. Around these house sites are irregular fields and scatters of cairns of field-gathered stones (Calder 1958, Calder 1965, Winham 1980). This is, with the possible exception of parts of the West Coast of Ireland, the richest upstanding prehistoric landscape in Britain. Not rich in the sense of the individual set-piece monuments (although one or two are superb in their own right) but rich in the assemblages and inter-relationships of sites. However, interpreting this evidence is fraught with problems.

The first problem is when people first reached Shetland. By about 3300BC we must assume there was agricultural settlement, on the basis of Sumburgh and Scord of Brouster. In the absence of dated sites we cannot push the date back earlier.

Is there any inherent reason why visits, perhaps seasonal encampments, could not have been taking place for many centuries previously? What did Shetland have to offer nomadic hunter-gatherers of the pre-agricultural mesolithic period? Rich coastal fishing, extensive seabird colonies, seals, perhaps small whales, wildfowl, shellfish: but all of these were available on the Scottish mainland coast at this early date. Shetland apparently lacked the larger mammals, particularly the herds of red deer which seem to have been central to at least some mesolithic economies. These were forest animals, and Shetland had no forest, or at best one which, except for a few sheltered groves, a well-nourished red deer might have looked down upon. If there were mesolithic visitors to, or residents in, Shetland they would have come not because of any special attractiveness in Shetland but because of pressure from behind, on the mainland, where their seasonal round was capable of being sustained only at low population densities. To date there is no archaeological evidence for a pre-agricultural human presence.

[Since this paper was given, Niall Sharples has drawn my attention to a recent study of the vegetation record showing a decrease in herbage during the period 5500-3500 BC which might be consistent with grazing, and it has been tentatively suggested that red deer were, indeed, introduced and that there was mesolithic settlement for well over a millennium, with the deer finally being wiped out by disease, over-exploitation or inbreeding not long before the arrival of agricultural settlers (Bennett et al, 1992).]

When agriculturally-skilled groups began to explore, and settle, northern Scotland, perhaps sharing their skills with the inhabitants in return for local knowledge and partnership, the balance in favour of Shetland swung decisively into the positive. What these early agricultural groups seem to have practised was something akin to slash-and-burn, although perhaps slash-and-rot was more likely, even given a marginally better climate. Without dense forest cover, Shetland would have been very attractive. The likely absence, at that date, of vermin and larger predatory animals would have been a bonus.

There is a possibility, based on the way in which the land appears to have been divided early on with large dykes and earthen banks, that this Neolithic settlement was in numbers and with some degree of organisation. This should not be a surprise: a society which could build boats capable, reliably, of reaching and returning from Shetland could probably cope with allocation of land, especially with no pre-existing settlement pattern or land-holders.

Crops were cereals, especially barley, with domestic animals. What was the balance: was it cereal farming with stock, stock farming with cereals, a mixed regime or something half-Mesolithic: fishing or seal-hunting with a crofting sideline? There is no hard evidence. While the evidence certainly demonstrates that these settlers were farmers, we would be wrong to assume they were only farmers. They were skilled quarrymen, they worked in polished stone, flint and quartz. By analogy (if it is permitted), they probably had just as varied a lifestyle as recent crofter-fishermen. One of their more high-value products, stone axes, appeared on the 'international', or at least 'furth of Shetland' market. One of the best-preserved artefact-working areas in Britain lies on the barren rocky slopes of Beorgs of Uyea, north of Ronas Hill.

Surviving evidence for the agricultural and domestic centres of these people's lives, in the form of ruined stone buildings, clearance cairns and walls, is spread unevenly throughout Shetland, being particularly rich in the West and North Mainland and in Whalsay. It appears mainly in areas which have been cut over for peat (not surprisingly, since it was burial below peat which preserved most of these sites), and is particularly rich in areas where extensive cutting has been relatively recent. Most of the surviving sites are on marginal land, used only for sheep grazing.

However, we should assume that the earliest settlers took the best land first, and that would have been the coastal land: low-lying, probably more fertile, and without a dense forest cover to remove. The relative absence of archaeological remains in these areas is a result of partial survival, because this same coastal land has continued to be the focus of settlement ever since. That said, the surviving pre-peat settlement sites are not necessarily atypical, because there are a few examples near to the shore where peat was never cleared, and these seem to be much the same, in terms of house size and field patterns, as the more upland sites. But a distribution map of recognised sites might suggest that early settlers preferred to live in the uplands, and this was not the case.

A slow fade: The Neolithic-Bronze Age transition

Looking at points on a map, it is easy to fall into the error of assuming that each is equivalent. It cannot be the case that the entire Neolithic and Bronze Ages were homogeneous. There must have been changes over time, in farming methods, in architectural styles, almost certainly in burial rites. But the number of dated, well-excavated, sites is so small that only the most generalised of statements are possible: houses seem to have become more circular in plan over time, and perhaps began to be grouped into small villages; the higher hillslopes were gradually abandoned as peat grew, so settlement would have become more concentrated onto the coast. The climatic and environmental processes which brought this about are described elsewhere in this volume.

By the end of the Bronze Age, at the depth of the climatic gloom (helped on, recent research suggests, by spectacular volcanic eruptions in Iceland creating or assisting climatic deterioration), life was certainly harder than at the time of the first settlement. The factors persuading people to remain were the inertia of established settlement and, doubtless, that nowhere else within reach was any more attractive.

Only the burnt mounds survive as a numerous monument class ascribed to the Bronze Age, and although how these worked as water-boiling points is well-known, just what they were — kitchen, bake-house, sauna — is not proven. Nor, as Brian Smith has recently observed, are we secure in the assumption that they are communal: they appear to be about as numerous as ruined 'Norse' mills, they were built over no longer a span of time, and the mills were not in general communal, although they were frequently the focus of social intercourse in the winter months. Might a similar ancillary social function be adduced for burnt mounds?

Whatever the inner meanings of burnt mounds (and the ubiquitous suburban barbecue of recent years springs to mind as analogy), it seems on the basis of present evidence that by the start of the Iron Age, around 600 BC, the broad pattern of use of the land that we know today was established. Indeed, the picture of prosperous-looking coastal farmland with rough grazings spreading onto the hill, often incorporating the ruins of earlier settlements and traces of their fields, was remarkably like the recent scene in many areas, but for the different shapes of the houses and byres.

Celtic cowboys: Iron Age preconceptions

Archaeologists have for many years been confident that Iron Age Shetland was primarily cattle-raising country, with small arable acreages and a fair bit of fishing and wild-fowling on the side. The evidence for this, especially in quantitative terms, is scanty. True, excavations at Jarlshof (Hamilton 1956) and more recently at Upper Scalloway broch (Sharples, pers comm) detected many bird-bone fragments: great auk, puffin, cormorant, and so on. They also indicated the use of cattle and sheep meat. But the total number of actual individual birds or animals recovered would not have fed a large family for much more than a week. There is actually no hard evidence that Iron Age Shetlanders were 'Celtic cowboys' rather than smallholders who kept the odd cow.

We have been misled over the years by circular argument: the archaeologist has a preferred picture, the palaeoenvironmentalist tells him that it can be sustained by the evidence. Then the archaeologist thinks he is being told his preconception is the correct answer, and the palaeoenviron-mentalist, reading archaeological accounts based on these preconceptions, designs his research accordingly. Few archaeologists have put any real effort into searching out patterns of life which challenge preconceptions, and the Iron Age preconceptions by which Shetland is interpreted are from southern Scotland at best, southern England more usually. Is it not remarkable that the understanding of the society which produced some of the most spectacular prehistoric remains in Britain, if not Europe, should be interpreted in the light of Wessex hillforts? It was in the north that exciting things were happening in the Iron Age, and Shetland was in the swim (Hingley 1992).

Polemic aside, how did the brochs, and their lesser cousins the forts, not to mention the unenclosed Iron Age settlement sites which are increasingly being discovered, fit into everyday life? Are they the strongholds of an egalitarian society, united in strength and equipped to ward off those of more militant tendency, or are they the castles of a native aristocracy, the bloated plutocrats of the export tammie-norie cartels? [Non-Shetland speakers note: tammie-norie = puffin.] Are they, in modern jargon, the fashionable residences of the upwardly mobile, or simply desperate bolt-holes against slave-raiders?

Has archaeology helped to answer these questions, which we might characterise as "what people want to know"? In practical terms, no. Almost all it has told us so far is that the inhabitants of brochs had a diet based on agricultural products with some non-farmed contribution: surely any Shet-lander could have told us that.

The nearest we have come to understanding broch society, at least the economics, has come not from digging brochs but from looking around them, at the land, its relationships with the sea, and trying to imagine what the best, most stable, economic base would have been (Fojut 1980, Fojut 1982). And so far as this research has gone, it appears that arable land ranks higher up in the scale of importance and grazing land lower, with the sea very important. But then again, perhaps the arable land was growing hay for the cattle of the Celtic cowboys....

One thing we do know about Shetland brochs, and that is that they were not isolated, a group of structures standing splendidly apart. There were other sorts of forts: small island duns with thin walls, fortified promontories, blockhouses (if these were forts at all) (Lamb 1980, Fojut 1985). And there was plenty of Iron Age settlement in slight oval or round houses similar to those of earlier periods. Because we cannot distinguish it in the field it is found only by accident, when digging sites which on surface indications could equally well be Neolithic or Bronze Age, as at Mavis Grind (Cracknell and Smith 1983) or at Kebister (Owen, pers comm). Taking these, the only two dated sites together, there might be a case for a small sub-circular thick-walled early Iron Age house-type.... but that is a classic example (saving the pun) of circular argument: these two were Iron Age, therefore all unexcavated sites which appear to be almost circular in plan are Iron Age. Two similar sites can so easily equal one generalisation.

One of the interesting aspects of recent Iron Age research has been a tendency for workers in the Western Isles to look past Orkney to Shetland for parallels (Armit 1990). It has, to date, been less common for Shetland researchers to look west, despite the fact that Audrey Henshall remarked, many years ago, that Shetland's Neolithic pottery had more of the Hebridean about it than the Orcadian (pottery report in Calder 1958). There has been a rather blinkered, Shetlandocentric, approach from many workers, the present author not excepted.

Are the Picts hidden in the same place as the Vikings ?

It is perhaps not with great expectations that the archaeological evidence for the Pictish period in Shetland is examined. This is not the place for yet another examination of 'who were the Picts'. The term is used simply as a label for a period between the end of the monumental roundhouses, brochs and wheelhouses, and before the Norse settlement.

At Jarlshof there are the 'passage houses', and at Sandwick in Unst there are two burials (Hamilton 1956, Bigelow 1985). There are unimpressive little hutments around the brochs at Clickhimin and at Upper Scalloway (Hamilton 1968, Niall Sharples pers comm). It appears that both forts (at Scatness) and brochs (at Eastshore) may have been in use, at least in some modified form, as late as the sixth and seventh centuries AD (Steven Carter, pers comm). There were circular houses of pre-Norse date at Jarlshof and Underhoull (Hamilton 1956, Small 1966). There are a few carved stones, mainly of later types (probably mid eighth to early ninth century, although a few fragments may be as early as the late seventh) (RCAHMS 1946). There is placename evidence which is taken to suggest there were pre-Norse Christian establishments, and at some sites (which except for Papil in West Burra do not coincide with the placename evidence) there are physical remains of ecclesiastical structures which are definitely pre-Norse, albeit only marginally so.

Above all, there is the magnificent St Ninian's Isle treasure, which we have recently been encouraged to see as hidden in the church not so much in fear of marauding Norsemen but precisely because Norsemen might have respected the church in their depradations. Thus is proto-history woven out of scraps of archaeology.

We can be sure that the Viking settlers would not have found the islands empty of population, but so far the evidence for a numerous Pictish farming population is slight. This problem has been dismissed as unimportant. Alan Small dealt with the problem of an apparent shortage of Norse houses many years ago, when he pointed out that the specifications for a Viking house plot were much the same as those for a nineteenth century croft: above farmland, overlooking a good landing beach, with access to plenty of rough grazing (Small 1969). Since then there has been a tendency, not least on the part of the present author, to push the argument back in time. The Picts lived a similar lifestyle, so used similar house-sites, therefore the Vikings built over the Pictish houses and later crofters built over those of the Vikings.

It was partly to examine this largely untested theory of the repeatedly-used house site that Olwyn Owen recently excavated the site at Kebister, beside Dales Voe, north of Lerwick. A typical ruined post-medieval settlement site with nearby burnt mounds suggested that the area had been occupied over a long period. Here was an opportunity to test for continuity of Bronze Age > Iron Age > Pictish > Viking > Medieval > Recent. The results? A limited extent of Bronze Age settlement activity, extensive Iron Age unenclosed settlement, a trace of an Early Christian presence followed by no Viking or other remains, but instead a beautiful post-medieval teind barn, complete with the owner's coat of arms, and the most northerly circular-plan corn drying kiln so far identified.

Clearly, the excavation was not a failure, even though neither Viking nor Pictish farms were found. Much important information was gathered about a range of periods, particularly the Iron Age and the later Medieval. The information about prehistoric ploughing was particularly exciting, with broken stone plough-shares embedded in the ground.

However, we cannot argue that Small's theory is invalid, because it was never stated that *every* medieval croft was underlain by a Viking farm. What has been interesting is the considerable effort that has been made by those commenting on the absence of a Viking-period farm in the area excavated. With the benefit of hindsight we can see that the site was not promising: north-facing slope, waterlogged ground..... all ignoring the fact that the hillside supported a flourishing Bronze Age and Iron Age settlement, as well as post-medieval farming settlement.

This defence of the vanishing Viking farm theory is all the more remarkable because there are only three sites where there actually *is* evidence for a predecessor Viking farm: Underhoull (Small 1966), Jarlshof (Hamilton 1956) and da Biggins (Crawford 1985). What is most interesting about these sites is that all three offer glimpses, at da Biggins an almost complete view, of an alternative technology which has been almost ignored in the settlement archaeology of 'treeless' Shetland, although it is so central to the studies of colleagues in marine archaeology: timber construction.

No-one has looked systematically in Shetland for houses of turf or wood: if Iceland had them in the tenth and eleventh centuries, why not Shetland? Small's elegant solution to the absence of Viking farms, while doubtless valid in large degree, has lulled archaeologists into a false sense of understanding, and diverted searches for alternatives. Not only may much, if not most, of the architecture of Pictish Shetland have been in turf and timber (if there was enough timber to equip Iron Age brochs, there was enough to roof turf houses), but in this period and the succeeding Viking period it may well be that the very finest, and highest status, buildings were of wood, not stone. This is perhaps the single greatest unexplored possibility of Shetland archaeology.

One last diversion, before looking to the future: Norse mills. Not until the last few years has anyone succeeded in finding a Norse mill in the northern Isles which actually dates into the Norse period, when Chris Morris excavated one from the tenth or eleventh century at Orphir in Orkney. Unfortunately for the theory of Norse importation of mill technology from the

Mediterranean, a much more sophisticated direct-drive horizontal tide-driven mill has recently been dated, in Ireland, by radiocarbon and tree-rings, to the seventh century. But rather than considering a pre-Norse origin throughout Scotland, including Shetland, for such mills, it seems to be acceptable to assume that they were still brought by the Vikings, only now from Ireland.

A prospectus

What is it, then, that needs to be done to place Shetland's archaeology onto a firmer footing ? The answers are conventional, but no less valid for that: build up survey, environmental and artefactual data-bases, publish excavation and research results, undertake new research targetted on emerging patterns and problems, and repeat this prescription regularly.

First, we need a thorough, detailed, survey of the whole of Shetland to the same standards as Bradford University's work in Fair Isle and South Nesting. This is a programme of work which will take many years, and cannot be left to the efforts of the islands' lone official archaeologist, whose task should be to collect, collate and direct.

Unlike the researchers who used to materialise from 'Sooth' in the thirties, forties and fifties, and as mysteriously disappeared again, the surveyors of the nineties and of the next century need to be seen and known locally, they must talk to the local residents as they survey, and seek to share their results. The return will be an enhanced understanding of what the structures and systems they are recording may have meant in terms of the functioning of communities. On this first objective, progress looks promising.

Second, all those boxes of stray finds in the Shetland museum, and in universities and Scottish (and English) museums, (and in archaeologists' garages and attics) need to be dug out, and people must be encouraged to bring in their own mantelpiece collections, so that corpora of artefacts can be compiled and related to the remains of structures and to more recent parallels. There is material here for any number of PhD theses. A particular effort needs to be made to interest researchers from as far afield as possible, not just Scotland and northern England. Perhaps some researchers might be attracted from Scandinavia or Ireland?

Third, thumbscrews need to be oiled, the oxen and wain-ropes prepared, and the outstanding excavation reports, and conference proceedings, dragged from excavators, contributors and editors. Many excavations since the mid-1970s have been paid for by public funds, and the results should be made available to the public. What excuse is there for excavations, of modest scale, in the late seventies and early eighties still to remain unpublished? And when they are published, could this not be done in some format, and vehicle, accessible and available locally, not in Glasgow or Edinburgh-based journals? Let us have local publication, so that all of the pensioners who visited the sites as schoolchildren will be sure to see the reports. But let us also have national, or international publication, so that researchers elsewhere can have access to, and be attracted by, the fascinating material coming out of studies in Shetland. But let us have publication.

Attracting others is important. Using the ammunition supplied by the three processes above, we need to tempt people. We need to tempt the period and specialist experts on the rest of Scotland who have 'never quite managed to get to Shetland', we need to tempt teachers to include archaeology in developing curricula (and here Val Turner has made a splendid start) and we need to tempt schoolchildren to become archaeologists, amateur or professional, extracting the knowledge stored in their own families as much as in the landscape. We need to tempt tourists to appreciate more than the set-piece monuments. We need to tempt environmentalists to take into account the human dimension. Regrettably, we need to tempt some archaeologists to do the same.

What will be achieved, at the end of the day, will never be perfect. It will be full of biases and individual idiosyncracies, quirks and special pleading. It will have written all over it 'this came from Charles Calder' or 'this was done by Peter Winham'. But it will be a living body of archaeological theory based on a growing framework of real knowledge. It will be accessible to people at all levels of interest and expertise, both as a resource to draw upon and as a repository to deposit within. And it need not cost the earth: indeed there is a good case against undertaking too much large scale digging for years to come, while survey, synthesis and publication catch up.

All of this will take commitment, but I am confident that in Shetland, largely due to the efforts of the Islands' Archaeologist, together with the assistance of the Shetlanders she is increasingly drawing into archaeology and the archaeologists she is drawing into Shetland, this Utopian vision of a truly popular archaeology is perhaps closer to being realised than anywhere else in Scotland.

Appendix

Excavations in Shetland

As a small contribution to the process of encouraging openness, here is a list of those excavations of which the author is aware. Only sites with elements pre-dating AD 1469 are listed. The status of publication is given thus:

F = full report (to standards of the time)
A = full report in archive form, not published
Y = full report at press at end of 1994
*   = full report in active preparation at end of 1994
-   = no full report: interim report or note only

Site	Type	Year	Director	Pub
Benie Hoose	Neo house	1954-5	Calder	F
Da Biggins	Norse farm	1980-90	Crawford	*
Breckon	Norse/medieval	1983	CEU	Y
Byrelands	BA house	1986	Exton	Y
Catpund	steatite/ house	1988	Smith,Carter,Turner	*
Clickhimin	multi-period	from 1850	Hamilton	F
Clugan	IA house	1970-1	Beveridge	-
Clumlie	broch	1888	Goudie	F
Cross Geos	steatite/IA midden	1987	Buttler	-
Eastshore	broch	1983	CEU	Y
Fair Isle	survey	1984-6	Hunter	Y
Fethaland	IA ? house	1904	Abercromby	F
(Gravlaba)	chambered cairn/house	1957	Calder	F
Gruting School	Neo/BA houses	1950	Calder	F
Grutness	medieval burial etc	1982	Smith	A
Hestensgot	BA/IA house	1960-3	Rae	-
Islesburgh	chambered cairn	1959	Calder	F
Islesburgh	Neo/BA house	1959	Calder	F
Jarlshof	multi-period	from 1897	Hamilton	F
Kebister	multi-period	1983-7	Owen	*
Kirkigeo	IA midden	1983	CEU	Y
Levenwick	broch	1869-70	Goudie	F
(Loch of Brindister)	dun	1888	Goudie	F
(Loch of Huxter)	IA fort	1863	Mitchell	F
March cairn	chambered cairn	1949	Calder	F
Mavis Grind	BA houses	1978-9	Cracknell, Smith	F
(Mousa)	broch	1919	Paterson	F
Ness of Burgi	IA fort	1935	Mowbray	F
Ness of Gruting	Neo/BA houses	1950	Calder	F
Ness of Sound	burnt mound	1972	Small	-
Outnabreck	Neo cairn	1990	Hamilton	F
Papa Stour	survey	1980-3	Allen	A
PettigarthsField	chambered cairn	1954-5	Calder	F

Site	Type	Year	Director	Pub
Punds Water	chambered cairn	1959	Calder	F
Quendale Bay	Neo/BA house	1957-8	Rae	-
St Ninian's Isle	Early medieval, etc	1955-7	O'Dell	F
Sae Breck	broch	1949	Calder	F
Sandwick Unst	Norse farm/Pict grave	1978-80	Bigelow	-
Scatness	IA fort	1983	CEU	Y
Scord of Brouster	Neo/BA settlement	1977-9	Whittle	F
Shetland	survey	1930-6	RCAHMS	F
Shetland	Neo/BA survey	1949-59	Calder	F
Shurton Hill	field wall	1977	Whittington	F
South Nesting	survey	1991-	Dockrill	-
Stanydale	Neo/BA hall & house	1949	Calder	F
(Sulma Water)	chambered cairn	1957	Calder	F
Sumburgh	Neo houses	1974	Lamb	-
Sumburgh Airport	Neo burial cist	1977	Hedges, Parry	F
Tougs	BA house, burnt mound	1977	Hedges	F
Trondra	BA/IA house	1965-6	Goodlad	-
Trowie Knowe	chambered cairn	1904	Abercromby	F
Trowie Loch	burnt mound	1991	Dockrill	*
Underhoull	Pictish/Norse houses	1962-5	Small	F
Upper Scalloway	burials, broch	1989	Smith, McCullagh	*
Upper Scalloway	broch, outbuildings	1990	Sharples	*
West Burra	survey	1877	Parry	F
Wiltrow	BA house/ smithy	1935	Curle	F
Yoxie	Neo house	1954-5	Calder	F

( ) indicates a site cleared of stone but not excavated
CEU = Central Excavation Unit, Scottish Development Department, now AOC (Scotland)
RCAHMS = Royal Commission on the Ancient and Historical Monuments of Scotland

Bibliography

Text references plus excavation and survey reports.

Abercromby, J., 1905: 'Excavations at Fethaland and Trowie Knowe'. *Proceedings of the Society of Antiquaries of Scotland* 39, 171-184.

Armit, I. (ed.), 1990: *Beyond the Brochs: Changing Perspectives on the Later Iron Age in Atlantic Scotland*. Edinburgh.

Bennett, K.D., Boreham, S., Sharp, M.J., Switsur, V.R., 1992: 'Holocene history of environment, vegetation and human settlement on Catta Ness, Lunnasting, Shetland'. *Journal of Ecology* 80, 241-73.

Bigelow, G.F., 1985: 'Sandwick, Unst and late Norse Shetland economy'. In: Smith, B. (ed.) 1985 (below), 95-127.

Calder, C.S.T., 1952: 'Report on the excavation of a neolithic temple at Stanydale in the parish of Sandsting, Shetland'. *Proceedings of the Society of Antiquaries of Scotland* 84, 185-205.

Calder, C.S.T., 1953: 'Report on the partial excavation of a broch at Sae Breck, Shetland'. *Proceedings of the Society of Antiquaries of Scotland* 86, 178-186.

Calder, C.S.T., 1958: 'Report on the discovery of numerous Stone Age house-sites in Shetland'. *Proceedings of the Society of Antiquaries of Scotland* 89, 340-397.

Calder, C.S.T., 1963: 'Excavation in Whalsay, Shetland, 1954-5'. *Proceedings of the Society of Antiquaries of Scotland* 94, 28-46.

Calder, C.S.T., 1965: 'Cairns, Neolithic houses and burnt mounds in Shetland. *Proceedings of the Society of Antiquaries of Scotland* 96, 37-86.

Cracknell, S. & Smith, Beverley, 1983: 'Archaeological investigations at Mavis Grind, Shetland'. *Glasgow Archaeological Journal* 10, 13-39.

Crawford, Barbara, 1985: 'The Biggins, Papa Stour - a multi-disciplinary investigation'. In: Smith, B. (ed.), 1985 (below), 128-158.

Curle, A.O., 1936: 'Account of the excavations of an iron-smelting workshop and of an associated dwelling and tumuli at Wiltrow in the Parish of Dunrossness, Shetland'. *Proceedings of the Society of Antiquaries of Scotland* 70, 153-69.

Fojut, N., 1980: *The Archaeology and Geography of Shetland Brochs*. Ph.D. thesis, Glasgow University.

Fojut, N., 1982: 'Towards a geography of Shetland brochs'. *Glasgow Archaeological Journal* 9, 38-59.

Fojut, N., 1985: 'Some thoughts on the Shetland Iron Age'. In: Smith, B. (ed.), 1985 (below), 47-84.

Fojut, N., 1994: *A Guide to Prehistoric and Viking Shetland*. Lerwick (3rd edition).

Goudie, G., 1872: 'Notice of excavations in a broch and adjacent tumuli near Levenwick in the parish of Dunrossness'. *Proceedings of the Society of Antiquaries of Scotland* 9, 212-219.

Goudie, G., 1889: 'Notice of some recent broch excavations in Shetland'. *Proceedings of the Society of Antiquaries of Scotland* 23, 246-253.

Goudie, G., 1904: *The Celtic and Scandinavian Antiquities of Shetland*. London.

Hamilton, J.R.C., 1956: *Excavations at Jarlshof, Shetland*. Edinburgh.

Hamilton, J.R.C., 1968: *Excavations at Clickhimin, Shetland*. Edinburgh.

Hamilton, J., 1991: 'Excavation of a cairn at Wind Hamars, Outnabreck Hill, Scalloway, Shetland'. *Proceedings of the Society of Antiquaries of Scotland* 121, 45-49.

Hedges, J.W., 1984: 'Gordon Parry's West Burra survey'. *Glasgow Archaeological Journal* 11, 41-60.

Hedges, J.W., 1986: 'Bronze Age structures at Tougs, Burra Isle, Shetland'. *Glasgow Archaeological Journal* 13, 1-43.

Hedges, J.W. & Parry, G.W., 1980: 'A Neolithic multiple burial at Sumburgh Airport, Shetland'. *Glasgow Archaeological Journal* 7, 15-26.

Henshall, Audrey S., 1963: *The Chambered Tombs of Scotland*, 1. Edinburgh.

Hingley, R.C., 1992: 'Society in Scotland from 700 BC to AD 200'. *Proceedings of the Society of Antiquaries of Scotland* 122, 7-53.

115

Lamb, R.G., 1980: *Iron Age Promontory Forts in the Northern Isles*. Oxford.

Lamb, R.G., 1985: 'Sumburgh: prehistory under sand'. In: Smith, B (ed.) 1985 (below), 27-46.

Mitchell, A., 1881: 'Notice of Buildings designed for defence on an Island in a loch at Hogsetter, in Whalsay, Shetland'. *Proceedings of the Society of Antiquaries of Scotland* 15, 303-315.

Mowbray, Cecil L., 1936: 'Excavation at the Ness of Burgi, Shetland'. *Proceedings of the Society of Antiquaries of Scotland* 70, 381-386.

Paterson, J.W., 1922: 'The Broch of Mousa: a survey by H M Office of Works'. *Proceedings of the Society of Antiquaries of Scotland* 56, 172-183.

RCAHMS = Royal Commission on the Ancient and Historical Monuments of Scotland, 1946: *Inventory of Monuments in Orkney and Shetland*, vols i and iii. Edinburgh.

Small, A., 1966: 'Excavations at Underhoull, Unst'. *Proceedings of the Society of Antiquaries of Scotland* 98, 225-248.

Small, A., 1969: 'The distribution of settlement in Shetland and Faeroe in Viking times'. *Sagabook of the Viking Society* 17, 145-155.

Smith, B. (ed.), 1985: *Shetland Archaeology*. Lerwick.

Thomas, C. & Wilson, D.M., 1973: *St Ninian's Isle and its Treasure*. (2 vols). London.

Whittington, G., 1980: 'A sub-peat dyke on Shurton Hill, Mainland, Shetland'. *Proceedings of the Society of Antiquaries of Scotland* 109, 30-35.

Whittle, A., 1986: *Scord of Brouster: An Early Agricultural Settlement on Shetland*. Oxford.

Winham, R.P., 1980: *Site Morphology, Location and Distribution: a survey of the settlement archaeology of Shetland, investigating man-environment interaction through time*. M.Phil. thesis, Southampton University.

ASPECTS OF VIKING SOCIETY IN SHETLAND AND THE FAROE ISLANDS

Steffen Stummann Hansen

There seems to be a strong tradition in Norse archaeology of dealing with the Faroes and Shetland as a more or less defined unity. This tradition of combining and comparing the two groups of islands appears in various fields of research, e.g. environmental studies (Jóhansen 1985), place-name studies (MacGregor 1984, 1986) and human geography and archaeology (Small 1969).

Why should we look at the two archipelagos as though they form a whole? As far as environmental conditions are concerned the differences between the Faroes and Shetland are small as compared to the West Norwegian landscape. As pointed out by Alan Small, the differences from Norway are of such magnitude that they must have presented the Norse with many problems in a new and alien environment (Small 1970:179).

On the other hand, the Faroe Islands and Shetland differ from Orkney and the coasts of Caithness in Scotland to the south, for their landscapes are much more hilly and mountainous and have relatively less room for agriculture.

The Faroes and Shetland have another thing in common, as they both seem to play a rather anonymous role in the Viking Age compared to that of, for instance, Orkney. As Small points out, the political dominance of Orkney has tended to overshadow the importance of Shetland as a major Norse colony (Small 1970:182). An attempt to illustrate the strategic position of the two groups of islands in a North Atlantic context and their role in the amalgam of events and processes that characterized the Viking period was made by Alan Small twenty-five years ago [fig. 1].

The present paper will follow this tradition but it will not try to summarize our present knowledge in all fields of research into the Viking Age in the two groups of islands. Neither will it deal with the question of the place-name evidence and the related discussion about the settlement structure (see for instance MagGregor 1984, 1986; Small 1969; Thorsteinsson 1978, 1981). It will, however, on the basis of the archaeological finds, put the focus on some aspects and perspectives concerning trade and communication links in Viking-Age rural society in Shetland and the Faroes.

Although we have chosen to deal with Shetland and the Faroe Islands as one, there are certainly environmental differences between the two groups of islands. For instance, the mountains of the Faroes rise to a height of approximately 850 m, while the highest mountains in Shetland are only about half this height. At the same time, the space available for agriculture is much more limited and determined by the environment in the Faroes, where settlements are restricted to low-lying coastal areas, than it is in Shetland.

The landscape that met the Norse settlers in Shetland and the Faroes respectively differed markedly. In the Faroes the Norsemen found a virtually uninhabited landscape. Although there might have been some early settlement by Irish monks in the 7-8th centuries, there seems to have been no intensive exploitation of the environment. In Shetland, however, the Norse settlers found a landscape that had been populated for about five thousand years, and this means that the vegetation was quite different.

For instance, juniper was abundant in the Faroe Islands, while it had become extinct thousands of years before the Norsemen's arrival in Shetland.

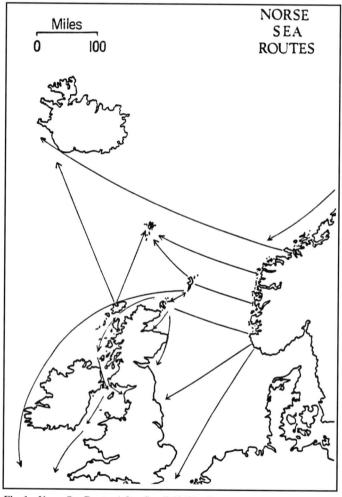

Fig. 1. Norse Sea Routes (after Small 1968A: 2).

118

The exploitation of juniper for different purposes — wicker-work, repair material etc. — was known in Norway, and was practised by the Norse settlers in the Faroes (Hansen 1988: 72; Larsen 1991). Juniper is a good example of how the Norse settlers changed the landscape of the Faroes, as juniper declined rapidly after their arrival (Jóhansen 1985). The character of the human impact and the reason for the decline of juniper has in recent years become a matter of discussion (Hansen 1988: 77; Jóhansen 1971: 151; Jóhansen 1985: 55, Larsen 1991:54ff; Small 1992: 3ff).

The situation that met the Norse settlers in Shetland was a different one, as the islands had been inhabited since the neolithic period. The vegetation was thus different, as the shrubs had been in decline for a long time before the arrival of the Norsemen. At the same time, juniper had disappeared a long time before the Norse settlement. Birch (betula) was present, although only on a small scale, as was hazel (corylus) (Jóhansen 1985: 81).

Although the Faroe Islands and Shetland share some geographical and environmental features, there are nevertheless important differences in geology. While the only types of stone to be found in the Faroes are basalt and tuf, Shetland is much more favoured, as it yields steatite, schist and sandstone, materials that were very important to the Norse settlers, as they were preferred for hones, querns, net- and line-sinkers, spindle-whorls, loom-weights and cooking and drinking vessels. So while Norse settlers in Shetland were well supplied with these materials, their neighbours in the Faroes had to import them from either Norway, Shetland or somewhere further away.

In spite of such differences Small in 1969 found the similarities to be of such basic substance as to allow him to propose a 'geographical model' for the Norse settlement in Shetland and the Faroe Islands, stressing that the environmental conditions in both groups of islands only allowed settlement in a rather limited number of areas (Small 1969: figs. 1-2). The model was based on the following preconditions for a primary Norse farmstead: 1. access to the sea, with a reasonable site for pulling up a boat; 2. a patch of fairly flat, reasonably well-drained land suitable for the construction of a farmstead and with the potential for some grain cultivation; 3. extensive grazing areas, since the number of animals which the poor vegetation of the islands could support would be rather low (Small 1969:149). Viking-Age sites in the Faroes fit well into this model (Hansen 1988: 78).

The environment provided the framework for the Norse settlement, and it is still very important to investigate the environmental conditions for these Viking-Age communities and the economy that they established. Although environmental studies are important, archaeological finds can actually provide evidence on issues where the value of environmental studies and place-name studies will normally be more limited. One of these issues is that of trade and communication.

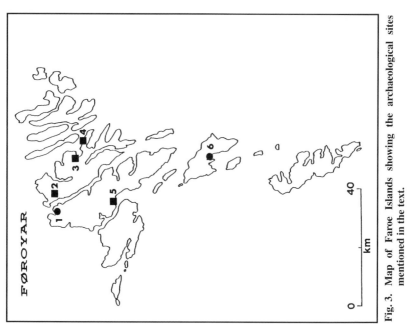

Fig. 3. Map of Faroe Islands showing the archaeological sites mentioned in the text.

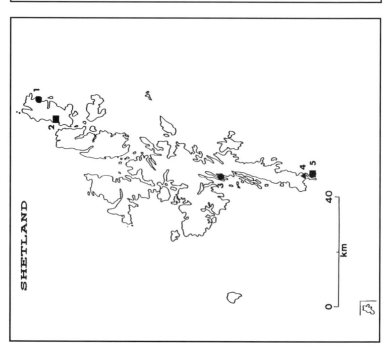

Fig. 2. Map of Shetland showing the archaeological sites mentioned in the text.

120

Norse archaeology in Shetland and Faroe

Archaeological research into the Norse period has a rather short history in both Shetland and the Faroes, which means that any new information will normally contribute essentially to our present knowledge. As new archaeological research has been going on both in Shetland and in the Faroes since Small's paper appeared in 1969, it may therefore be appropriate to give a short presentation of the most important Viking-Age sites in Shetland and Faroe [figs. 2-3].

In Shetland, one of the most famous and well-documented excavations of a Norse settlement in the North Atlantic took place at the site known as Jarlshof on the southern tip of Mainland in the 1930-1950s. The excavator described the settlement as a primary farmstead that was later joined by secondary farmsteads during the Norse period (Hamilton 1956: 5) [fig. 4]. A lot of objects from the Viking Age turned up in stratified layers at the site. J.R.C. Hamilton's publication from 1956 is still the most important publication of any settlement site in the Faroes and Shetland.

Only one other presumed Viking-Age site has been excavated in Shetland and this not on the same scale as Jarlshof. At Underhoull on the west coast of Unst, Small excavated a single Norse building in the 1960s and dated it to the Viking Age (Small 1967, 1968B). Small's dating of Underhoull to the 10th century has been questioned by other archaeologists (Bigelow 1992: 10). The author of the present paper has recently had the opportunity to study the archaeological finds from the site and would on the basis of that preliminarily

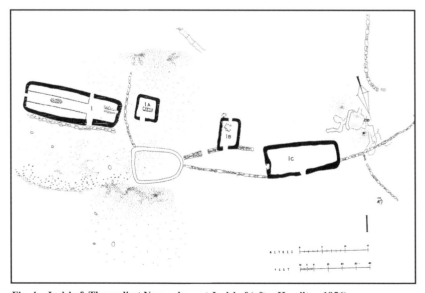

Fig. 4. Jarlshof. The earliest Norse phase at Jarlshof (after Hamilton 1956).

121

suggest a date within the late 10th to 12th century. While there is no doubt about some of the material being Late Norse, it is more difficult to determine at what time exactly this farmstead was established.[1]

Excavations of Norse settlement sites in the Faroe Islands began in the 1940s, when the late State Antiquary of the Faroe Islands, Sverri Dahl, commenced his pioneer work. Excavations were carried out on a number of sites uncovering parts of ancient settlements (Dahl 1971A, 1971B). The dating of the settlements has caused many problems, as it is difficult to give more than just a rough dating of the excavated structures. However, these investigations gradually began to yield the archaeological evidence for the Norse settlement in the Faroe Islands in the Viking Age, thus supporting in general the information of written sources such as the so-called 'Saga of the Faroe Islanders'.

Dahl excavated settlement structures at the important Viking-Age sites 'niðri á Toft' in Kvívík and 'við Gjógvará' in Fuglafjørður (1971A, 1971B) and at a number of other sites which he dated to the Viking Age. With our present knowledge it is obvious that some of the sites dated by Dahl to the Viking Age or Early Norse period have to be dated to the Medieval or Late Norse period. However, Dahl's excavations demonstrated convincingly that Viking-Age farmsteads could be located and investigated in the Faroes and that they tended to occur close to present-day farms.

In the 1980s some large-scale excavations took place in the Faroes. For the first time since Dahl's investigations Føroya Fornminnissavn got the opportunity to excavate a Viking-Age settlement at the site called 'Toftanes' in the village of Leirvík (Hansen 1988, 1989, 1991, 1993). The excavation uncovered four contemporary buildings, all forming part of the same farmstead. The topographical location fits very well into Small's model for 'primary farmsteads' [fig. 5]. A corroboration of the archaeological dating has been provided by three C-14 datings from floor-layers in Building I, which provide dates ranging from ca. 890-975 AD (Hansen 1988: 75).

Another important site to be excavated in the 1980s was that of 'Argisbrekka' near the northern tip of Eysturoy (Mahler 1991). This site, which comprised some fourteen buildings, was interpreted by the excavator as a shieling or 'sæter' and was dated to the Viking Age and Late Norse period (Mahler 1991). This excavation formed the starting-point for a renewed interest in the whole concept of shielings as a part of Norse economy and settlement structure in Viking-Age Faroe Islands (Mahler 1991).

The three farmsteads in Kvívík, Fuglafjørður and Leirvík all contained rather comprehensive archaeological assemblages which can be compared with that at Jarlshof. Similarly Toftanes in Leirvík can in many respects

---

1. The author has recently studied the extensive material of steatite from Underhoull stored in the Shetland Museum. The assemblage contains circular rounded as well as oval and square-sided types of vessels. I am grateful to Alan Small for his help and permission to look at the material.

Fig. 5. Aerial view of the excavation of a Viking-Age farmstead at Toftanes, Faroe Islands. The building just above the Viking site is the present day farm at Toftanes. Photo: Steffen Stummann Hansen/Føroya Fornminnissavn.

regarding both artifact assemblage and house structures be compared with the earliest phase at Jarlshof.

Only a few Viking-Age graves are so far known from Shetland and in all cases they were excavated in the last or early in this century by non-professional local people. In 1861 a grave was excavated on Unst. The grave contained a bronze tortoise brooch and a small circular bronze box. The character of the items suggests that it was a female grave but there is no information about the grave itself (Grieg 1940: 103).

Another grave was found when local people in 1863 dug up a farm-yard at Clibberswick on Unst. Seemingly the objects were not all registered in situ but some of the relics were found in a layer of black soil on top of the rock. From this grave came two bronze tortoise brooches, a bronze trefoil brooch, an armlet of silver and two glass beads (Grieg 1940: 103-105). The character of the items indicates that this, too, was a female grave.

In South Whiteness churchyard a grave-digger in 1938 found an iron axe of Viking type in a stone-lined grave [fig. 6].[2] The location is the site of the ancient church dedicated to St. Ola, which may in origin have been pre-Norse.

The axe was found in association with bones but no other artifact. The

---

2. Shetland Museum. ARC 65381.

axe belongs to Jan Petersen's type E, which he dates mainly to the second half of the 9th or early tenth century, although he mentions that some variants may be dated to later in the 10th century (Petersen 1919: 41-42). It can thus be rather difficult to give a more exact date of the burial itself, but certainly it must be referred to the Viking Age. Viking warrior graves, i.e. graves with weapons as grave-goods, are common throughout the Viking Age in Scandinavia. In Denmark, however, only a few weapon graves are dated to the 9th or the 11th centuries. While low-rank warriors throughout the Viking Age were typically buried in rather poor graves with an axe to announce their warrior status, the political and wealthy elite among the warriors were buried in richly furnished graves until around 970AD, when the Christianisation of the upper stratum of Danish society took place. After that period all warriors, rich or poor, seem to have been buried with the axe as the only weapon (Näsman 1991: 163ff).

If the grave from South Whiteness has to be dated to the late 9th or early 10th century, it probably represents a low rank warrior, but why then was he buried in a Christian burial ground? On the other hand, if the grave has to be dated to the late 10th century, a time where the pagan tradition of richly furnished warrior graves was no more accepted, it may well represent a Christian burial of a rather high ranking warrior. So far the grave is unique in a Shetland and Faroe context, and we can only hope that other weapon graves will turn up soon.

Fig. 6. Iron Axe found in a stonelined grave at the churchyard at South Whiteness, Shetland. Photo: Shetland Museum.

Fig. 7. **Bronze tortoise brooch from the Viking period found at Wardhill near Sumburgh. The object measures 102 x 71 x 26 mm. Photo: Shetland Museum.**

In the Faroe Islands a Viking graveyard was localized and excavated in the second half of the 1950s at the site known as 'Yviri í Trøð' in Tjørnuvík on Stremoy. Here twelve poorly furnished and sparsely equipped graves were excavated, one of which contained a bronze ringed pin of Hiberno-Norse type. The graves can be dated to the 10th century (Dahl & Rasmussen 1956). These were until a few years ago the only known Viking graves in the Faroes.

In 1989 another Viking graveyard was found at the site 'Við Kirkjugarð' in Sandur on Sandoy (Arge & Hartmann 1992). Here at least twelve east-west orientated graves were excavated. Very little skeleton material was preserved and the graves, like those in Tjørnuvík, were in general rather poorly equipped with grave-goods. The excavators are very reluctant to give any firm date or to venture to say whether the graves represent a Christian or a heathen population (Arge & Hartmann 1992: 20).

Shetland differs from the Faroes in having a rather large collection of stray finds. Some of these certainly indicate settlement sites, while others indicate disturbed graves. One example is a bronze tortoise brooch found at Ward Hill north of Sumburgh on Mainland during the Second World War, when trenches were being dug [fig. 7].[3] The brooch, which has the imprint of cloth on the reverse, can be dated to the 9th century. Objects like these normally occur in female graves, and it might therefore derive from a destroyed burial.

---

3. Shetland Museum. ARC 81151.

The evidence of archaeological finds in Shetland and Faroe

While the material from burials and stray finds is sparse and thus of limited value at the moment, the archaeological material from settlements is varied and quite extensive. The archaeological material from Faroese and Shetland settlement sites is in many respects of identical character and gives evidence about daily life and the economy. One rather important aspect, which seems to have attracted rather little attention in previous works, is that of communication and trade as reflected in these objects. In the following, focus on this aspect will be based on a presentation of some of the main groups of archaeological assemblages from the settlement sites in Shetland and Faroe.

Stone objects

In both areas sherds of *steatite* vessels are very common on settlement sites from the Viking Age. In fact, the Viking Age in the North Atlantic is considered to be aceramic, as steatite vessels seem to replace clay vessels. In Shetland the Viking-Age phases at Jarlshof as well as Underhoull are characterized by aceramic assemblages and in the Faroe Islands the Viking-Age sites in Kvívík, Fuglafjørður and Leirvík all seem to be aceramic (Crawford 1979: 40; Hansen 1988: 75). It is obvious that the Norse settlers were very fond of steatite and it is very common for sherds from broken vessels to be reused for other purposes — for instance spindle-whorls, net- and line-sinkers, weights etc.

In the Faroe Islands there is no doubt that objects of steatite were imported since steatite is not found here. It has normally been accepted that the steatite in the Faroes was brought from Norway, either as imports obtained by trade or as part of an initial cargo at the time of the original settlement. The situation is different in Shetland, as steatite is part of the geology of that area, and it has been documented through the location of quarries that steatite was exploited for the manufacturing of vessels during the Norse period (Hamilton 1956: 206pp; Buttler 1989).

It is interesting to note that most of the steatite sherds from Toftanes have been secondarily worked; many of them into spindle-whorls. The same feature was characteristic for the earliest Norse phase at Jarlshof (Hamilton 1956: 207), which might indicate that the vessels from this phase were imported (Hamilton 1956: 130). At the same time the equally extensive number of sherds from Underhoull show only to a very limited degree any signs of having been secondarily worked. This might reflect either that steatite was not as easily available to the Norse settlers in the Faroes as it was in Shetland, where natural sources were abundant, or that the Shetland steatite-industry was established by then and could easily provide the rural settlements with all the items that they required.

The exploitation of steatite in Shetland may have been different from that in Norway, as the industry in Norway may have served large markets in the towns of Viking Scandinavia, while Shetland remained a wholly rural

126

society throughout the Norse period (Buttler 1989: 204). This does not, however, exclude the possibility that the steatite-industry in Shetland may have served other rural societies in the North Atlantic - for instance the Faroe Islands. Unfortunately all attempts so far to determine at which quarry a given object was produced have been fruitless (Buttler 1989: 204).

Another type of stone that was necessary for daily life was *schist*. It was used for hones and quern stones, which occur at all Viking-Age settlement sites. Schist occurs in Shetland but not in the Faroes, which means that without any doubt, as in the case of steatite, the Faroese finds must be imported. The schist used for hones is of at least two different types, since both a light, coarse-grained type and a more fine-grained, dark schist are represented. The resource of the first type has been identified as Eidsborg in Norway (Myrvoll 1985; Mitchell et al. 1984). The origin of the dark schist, however, has not been established yet. Although it cannot be said for certain, there is good reason to suggest that a lot of the hones of the light schist found on North Atlantic sites do originate from Eidsborg, thus reflecting links of communication and exchange between Norway and the colonies in the North Atlantic.

Querns of schist have been found both at Jarlshof and at Toftanes. One of the two intact pieces from Toftanes was furnished with a groove for the insertion of iron-bars in the undersurface and a collar around the central hole on the uppersurface [fig. 8]. This feature seems to be common in the western part of the Viking world, as it occurs in for instance Shetland (Hamilton 1956: pl. XXXV:10-11) and Greenland (Krogh 1982: 105). To the author's knowledge it is not evidenced in Scandinavia during the Viking Age. The origin of this object therefore is probably to be sought for in the south. The best parallel so far identified actually derives from Dunadd in Argyll [fig. 9][4].

At Toftanes a fragment of an armlet of *jet* or *lignite* was found [fig. 10]. Similar armlets have previously been found in Viking-Age graves in Iceland (Eldjarn 1956: 332, fig. 148), Orkney (Grieg 1940: 86, fig. 47) and Castletown, Caithness on the Scottish Mainland (Grieg 1940: 24, fig. 8). Fragments of armlets were found at the settlement sites Brough of Birsay, Orkney (Curle 1982: 66f) and possibly at Jarlshof, Shetland (Hamilton 1956: fig. 56:7). Huge amounts of jet armlets, finger-rings and raw material have been unearthed during the excavations in Viking Dublin (Wallace & Ó Floinn 1988: 22f)[5]. Although jet originates from deposits in Whitby near York, there is good reason to suggest that these armlets turning up at different sites in the North Atlantic were actually produced in Dublin (Hansen 1993: 481ff). Jet

---

4. National Museum, Edinburgh. GP 324. I am grateful to Dr. Alison Sheridan for her kind assistance during my visits to the National Museum.

5. The author had the opportunity to study the unpublished jet-material in the National Museum of Ireland during a visit in 1990. I am grateful to Dr. Patrick F. Wallace and Debbie Caulfield for help and assistance during my visit.

Fig. 8. Quern-stone of schist from Toftanes, Faroe Islands. Photo: Føroya Fornmin-nissavn.

Fig. 9. Quern-stone of schist from Dunadd, Argyll. Photo: National Museum, Edinburgh.

128

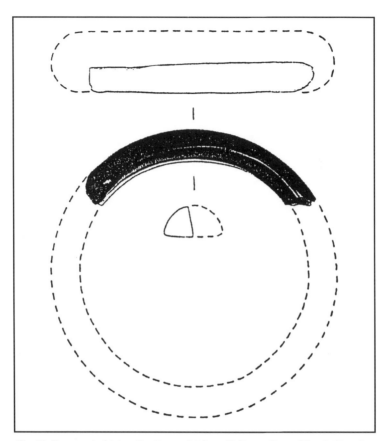

Fig. 10. Fragment of jet or lignite armlet from Toftanes, Faroe Islands (drawing Aa. Andersen).

objects have also been found in Norway, where they concentrate in the southwestern parts (Shetelig 1946: 9). The Norwegian finds seem in general to be earlier than the finds in the North Atlantic.

Another interesting object from Toftanes is a rather big block of *sandstone* that was found standing on the floor in the hall of the farmstead [fig. 11]. The stone, which had probably been used as a hone, possibly originates from an area to the south of the Faroes, for instance Shetland.[6] It could have been brought to the Faroes as ballast in a ship, but on the other hand the real reason for its import to the Faroes is probably that it was required as a hone.

---

6. Personal communication from Dr. Lars Clemmensen, Institute of Geology, University of Copenhagen.

129

Fig. 11. Block of sandstone (hone?) from Toftanes, Faroe Islands. Photo: Steffen Stummann Hansen/Føroya Fornminnissavn.

Metalwork

The amount and variety of metalwork is rather poor in general. As mentioned above, the graves in the Faroes are poorly equipped with grave-goods, and except at Jarlshof metalwork only occurs in small quantities on settlement sites. One type, however, is represented on several sites and this is ringed pins of Hiberno-Norse type. These have been found at Jarlshof in Shetland (Hamilton 1956: Pl. XXIX:4), at Toftanes, Faroe Islands (Hansen 1988: 69f, fig. 9; Hansen 1991: 49, fig. 9; Hansen 1993: 479f), Argisbrekka, Faroe Islands (Mahler 1991: 66) and Tjørnuvík in the Faroes (Dahl & Rasmussen 1956: 162ff). Most of these pins belong to the polyhedral headed type, whose distribution is linked to the western part of the Viking world, as they have virtually only been found in Ireland, the Isle of Man, Scotland, the Western Isles, Orkney, Shetland, the Faroe Islands, Iceland and Newfoundland (Fanning 1983, 1988). Their distribution seems to be identical to that of the jet objects [fig. 12].

Glass

Beads are rather common in graves and settlements from the Viking-Age. They have been found in Jarlshof and they are also represented at Viking-Age sites such as niðri á Toft and Toftanes in the Faroes. These beads, which are mostly made of glass, must be regarded as imports. Some of the beads from the Faroes are of a type (Callmer's type E) that is regarded as originating from the Mediterranean (Callmer 1977: 94ff). In the case of many of them, however, it is impossible to say whether they have entered the North Atlantic via the eastern part of the Viking world (i.e. for instance via Viking towns in Scandinavia, Northern Germany or Eastern England), or whether they entered from the western part of the Viking world (for instance Ireland), since many of them have a Pan-European distribution (Callmer 1977: 94ff).

Wood

One very important body of material is wood. While the conditions for survival of wooden objects seem to be very bad in Shetland, they seem on the other hand to be optimal in the Faroes. The Viking-Age sites in niðri á Toft,

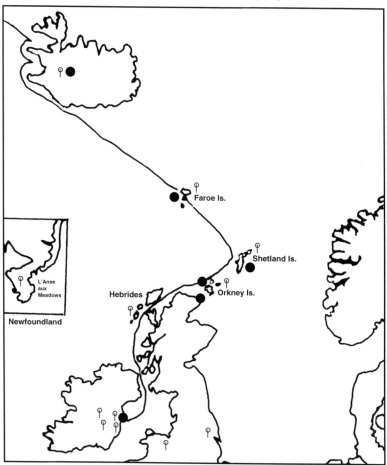

Fig. 12. The distribution of polyhedral headed ringed pins and armlets of jet or lignite in the North Atlantic area. Thomas Fanning 1983 and Steffen Stummann Hansen.

131

við Gjogvará, Argisbrekka and Toftanes have all yielded large amounts of wooden objects. Much of this wood is normally accepted as being driftwood from Siberia, but at the same time there is no doubt that timber and wooden objects were imported and traded in the North Atlantic. Normally one would think that timber came from Norway. On the other hand, however, saga-sources actually suggest, as already mentioned by Small, that timber was imported from Scotland and the Western Isles (Small 1970: 181).

The recent fortunate development of dendrochronology has led to the establishment of chronologies for not only the areas around the Baltic Sea but also Belfast, Dublin, Exeter, London and the East Midlands, as well as one master-chronology for England and South-Central Scotland (Bonde & Crumlin-Pedersen 1990: 5). It was this fact that made it possible not only to determine that Wreck 2 from Skuldelev in Denmark was built in the second half of the 11th century but also that it had been built in the region of the Irish Sea, and probably Dublin (Bonde & Crumlin-Pedersen 1990: 5).

The establishing of the regional curves for dendrochronology provides us with new perspectives on the wooden material from the Faroese sites from the Viking Age. It is thus hoped that the Faroese material will be of such a quality that determinations of planks and other objects of oak may fit into the already established curves. In this case it is hoped that in due time we shall be able to say whether timber and wooden objects were imported from Norway or from areas to the south, thus again reflecting lines of communication and trade.

Shetland and Faroe in a North Atlantic context

There are very strong traditions in Norse archaeology about the origins of the Norse settlers. One tradition has it that the settlers of the Faroe Islands and Shetland came from southwestern Norway during the reign of Harald Fairhair in the late 9th century. This could be termed the 'Norwegian link' (MacGregor 1986: 84; Small 1970: 179). The other tradition has it that a significant part of the settlers came from the south — i.e. the Western Isles. This tradition is largely based on the evidence from written sources such as the Ulster Annals and the Norse sagas, as well as place- and personal names that Norse settlers in Scotland and the Western Isles were forced up into the North Atlantic in the late 9th century. These Hiberno-Norse people — the Gall Gaedhil — thus represent a southern, Scottish influence to the Viking-Age rural communities further up in the North Atlantic. (Crawford 1987: 127; Smyth 1984: 161ff). This tradition could be termed the 'Scottish link'.

Interpretations based on slender archaeological and historical evidence can be very dangerous. Concerning the archaeological finds we still have a rather limited material which needs further investigation and is difficult to quantify. Thus we cannot say whether the distribution of artifacts reflects lines of communication, exchange and trade or actually reflects the movement of people and families. It is still generally accepted that the

Viking-Age history of the North Atlantic reflects an amalgam of processes and events and that the sea was carrying a great deal of traffic.

There is no doubt that the excavations in Viking Dublin and the subsequent studies of the material have already indicated that Dublin must have played a rather important role in the development of the Viking-Age communities in the North Atlantic. On the basis of our present knowledge it is very hard to say to what extent the rural Norse communities in the Faroe Islands and Shetland became integrated links in trading systems and networks or how their cultural identities were established. It is, however, interesting to note that quite a few groups of finds seem to enter the rural communities of the North Atlantic from the south — i.e. jet armlets, ringed pins, quernstones. Other items probably came from Norway, but we still have problems about the origin of steatite, schist and wood, and in all cases there is the possibility that at least some of them, too, came from the south.

What is badly needed today when dealing with the Norse settlement in the Faroes and Shetland is, of course, large-scale excavations on primarily Viking-Age settlements. Excavations of Viking burials would certainly be valuable too, as they normally contain objects whose origin can be determined. A detailed study of the archaeological objects from earlier excavations in both Shetland and the Faroe Islands may also be able to yield information that can help us to understand the patterns of trade and communication.

On the environmental side, a major project is badly needed on the steatite outcrops of the whole Viking world so that steatite objects from farm sites can be analysed and traced back to the appropriate geological outcrop. This could, as already pointed out by Small, in turn lead to a statistical determination of trade patterns in the North Atlantic Norse area (Small 1970:183).

Also, as indicated above, developments in dendrochronology may now give us important information on the origins of wooden objects and timbers.

Another problem is that very few and hardly published Viking-Age sites are known from the Western Isles and North-Western Scotland. Although some Viking graves are known from these areas, we still badly need the settlements. Localization and excavations of Viking-Age settlements on the north- and west-coast of Scotland and in the Western Isles would undoubtedly shed new light on the importance of the 'Scottish link' in the North Atlantic.

Acknowledgements

The author wants to thank Shetland Museum for help and information during my visits there and for kindly providing me with photographs of objects. Further I want to thank Gillian Fellows-Jensen, Institute of Name Research, University of Copenhagen, for her critical comments on this paper.

Bibliography

Arge, S.V. & Hartmann, N., 1992: 'The burial site of við Kirkjugarð in the village of Sandur, Sandoy'. *Fróðskaparrit* 38-39 (1989-90), 5-21.

Bigelow, G.F., 1992: 'Issues and Prospects in Shetland Norse Archaeology'. In: C.D. Morris & D.J. Rackham (eds.), *Norse and later Settlement and Subsistence in the North Atlantic*, Glasgow, 9 -32.

Bonde, N. & Crumlin-Pedersen, O., 1990: 'The dating of Wreck 2, the Longship, from Skuldelev, Denmark. A preliminary announcement'. *NewsWarp* 1990:7, 3-6.

Buttler, S., 1989: 'Steatite in Norse Shetland'. *Hikuin* 15, 193-206.

Callmer, J., 1977: 'Trade Beads and Bead Trade in Scandinavia ca. 800-1000 A.D'. *Acta Archaeologica Lundensia* 11. Lund.

Crawford, B., 1987: *Scandinavian Scotland. Scotland in the Early Middle Ages 2*. Leicester.

Curle, C.L., 1982: 'Pictish and Norse Finds from the Brough of Birsay'. *Society of Antiquaries of Scotland Monograph Series 1*. Edinburgh.

Dahl, S., 1971A: 'The Norse settlement of the Faroe Islands'. *Medieval Archaeology* 14, 60-73.

Dahl, S., 1971B: 'Recent Excavations on Viking Age Sites in the Faroes'. In: P. Foote & D. Strömbäck (eds.), *Proceedings of the Sixth Viking Congress*, Uppsala, 45-56.

Dahl, S.& Rasmussen, J., 1956: 'Víkingaaldargrøv í Tjørnuvík'. *Fróðskaparrit* 5, 153-167.

Eldjárn, K., 1956: *Kuml og haugfé úr heiðnum sið á Íslandi*. Akureyri.

Fanning, T., 1983: 'Some Aspects of the Bronze Ringed Pin in Scotland'. In: A. O'Connor & D.V. Clarke (eds.), *From the Stone Age to the Forty-Five*, Edinburgh, 324-42.

Fanning, T., 1988: 'Three Ringed Pins from Viking Dublin and their Significance'. In: J. Bradley (ed.), *Settlement and Society in Medieval Ireland*, Kilkenny, 161-75.

Grieg, S. (ed.), 1940: 'Viking Antiquities in Scotland'. In: H. Shetelig, *Viking Antiquities in Great Britain and Ireland* II. Oslo.

Hamilton, J.R.C., 1956: *Excavations at Jarlshof, Shetland*. Edinburgh.

Hansen, S. Stummann, 1988: 'The Norse Landnam in the Faroe Islands in the Light of recent Excavations at Toftanes, Leirvík'. *Northern Studies* 25, 58-84.

Hansen, S. Stummann, 1989: 'Toftanes - en færøsk landnamsgård fra 9.-10. århundrede'. *Hikuin* 15, 129-146.

Hansen, S. Stummann, 1991: 'Toftanes: A Faroese Viking Age Farmstead from the 9-10th Centuries AD'. *Acta Archaeologica* 61, 44-53.

Hansen, S. Stummann, 1993: 'Viking Age Faroe Islands and their Southern Links. In the Light of Recent Finds at Toftanes, Leirvík'. In: C. Batey, J. Jesch & C.D. Morris (eds.), *Proceedings of the Eleventh Viking Congress*, Edinburgh, 473-486.

Jóhansen, J., 1971: 'A Palaeobotanical Study Indicating a Previking Settlement in Tjørnuvík, Faroe Islands''. *Fróðskaparrit* 19: 147-157.

Jóhansen, J., 1985: 'Studies in the vegetational history of the Faroe and Shetland Islands'. *Annales societatis scientiarum Færoensis supplementum* XI. Tórshavn.

Krogh, K.J., 1982: *Erik den Rødes Grønland*. København.

Larsen, A-C., 1991: 'Norsemen's Use of Juniper in Viking Age Faroe Islands'. *Acta Archaeologica* 61, 54-59.

MacGregor, L., 1984: 'Sources for a Study of Norse Settlement in Shetland and Faroe'. In: B.E. Crawford (ed.), *Essays in Shetland History*, Lerwick, 1-17.

MacGregor, L., 1986: 'Norse naming elements in Shetland and Faroe. A comparative study'. *Northern Studies* 23, 84-101.

Mahler, D.L.D., 1991: 'Argisbrekka: New Evidence of Shielings in the Faroe Islands'. *Acta Archaeologica* 61, 60-72.

Mitchell, J.G., Askvik, H. & Resi, H.G., 1984: 'Potassium-argon Ages of Schist Honestones from the Viking Sites at Kaupang (Norway), Aggersborg (Denmark), Hedeby (West Germany) and Wollin (Poland), and their archaeological Implications'. *Journal of Archaeological Science* 11, 171-176.

134

Myrvoll, S., 1985: 'The Trade of Eidsborg hones over Skien in the Medieval Period'. *ISKOS* 5, 31-47.

Näsmann, U., 1991: 'Grav og økse. Mammen og den danske vikingetids våbengrave (English summary: Grave and axe. Mammen and the weapon graves of the Danish Viking Age)'. In: M. Iversen (ed.), *Mammen. Grav, kunst og samfund i vikingetid*, Højbjerg, 163-180.

Petersen, J., 1919: De norske Vikingsverd. *En typologisk-kronologisk Studie over Vikingetidens Vaaben*. Kristania.

Shetelig, H., 1946: 'Smykker av jet I norske vikingefunn'. *Bergens Museums Årbok* 1944, 3-14.

Small, A., 1967: 'Excavations at Underhoull, Unst, Shetland'. *Proceedings of the Society of Antiquaries of Scotland* XCVIII, 225-248.

Small, A., 1968A: 'The Historical Geography of the Norse Viking Colonization of the Scottish Highlands'. *Norsk Geografisk Tidsskrift* 22, 1-16.

Small, A., 1968B: 'A Viking Longhouse in Unst, Shetland'. In B. Niclasen (ed.), *The Fifth Viking Congress*, Tórshavn, 62-70.

Small, A., 1969: 'The distribution of settlement in Shetland and Faroe in Viking times'. *Saga-book of the Viking Society* 1967-1968, 145-155.

Small, A., 1970: 'Viking Shetland. A Review'. *Inter Nord. Revue internationale d'études arctiques et nordiques* 1970:11, 178-183.

Small, A., 1992: 'The Juniper decline during the Norse landnam in the Faroe Islands'. *Acta Borealia* 1992:1, 3-7.

Smyth, A.P., 1984: *Warlords and Holy Men. Scotland AD 80-1000*. London.

Thorsteinsson, A., 1978: 'Forn búseting í Føroyum'. *Fróðskaparrit* 26, 54-80.

Thorsteinsson, A., 1981: 'On the development of Faroese settlements'. In: H. Bekker-Nielsen et al. (eds.), Proceedings of the Eighth Viking Congress, *Medieval Scandinavia Supplements* 2, Odense, 189-202.

Wallace, P.F. & Ó Floinn, R., 1988: Dublin 1000. *Discovery and Excavation in Dublin, 1842-1981*. Dublin.

THE EXCAVATION OF A WOODEN BUILDING AT THE BIGGINGS, PAPA STOUR, SHETLAND

Barbara E. Crawford

Introduction

The events which took place on Papa Stour in the spring of 1299 have provided a rich source of research material for me in many respects; the role of the Norwegian tax-collector in Shetland society, the status of women in Norse society, the economics of land assessment and the functioning of the Lawthing to name but a few (Crawford 1984, 1985, 1992). But of all the unexpected avenues which have opened up as a result of my investigations into the first document in Shetland's history, the study of the development of wooden architecture has been the most surprising — and in some respects the most rewarding. I have learned to appreciate the Norwegian heritage of wooden buildings, and to understand something of the principles of their construction. I have also grown to love the atmosphere and warmth of wooden houses, and to regret the total disappearance of this element of our Norwegian heritage in the Northern Isles. It is difficult now to imagine that the bare landscapes of Orkney and Shetland once had substantial wooden houses nestling among the familiar stone buildings; this feature of the Faeroese and Norwegian countryside is what strikes the visiting Scot to the neighbouring North Sea countries more forcibly than any other indigenous element of those Scandinavian societies.

A piece of incidental information in the 1299 document, combined with a progamme of excavation at the Biggings, Papa Stour, has brought out the former importance of wooden buildings in Shetland, and increased our awareness of the significance of a particular type of wooden building in Scandinavian house architecture. The documentary evidence has been set out by me several times before, but will be briefly rehearsed again. In the late thirteenth century Shetland was under the control of Duke Håkon Magnusson, brother of the ruling king Erik Magnusson whom he succeeded on the throne in the year 1299. This royal prince had been given the German title of 'hertog' (duke), along with a large 'appanage' commensurate with his dignity, which included the 'skattlands' of Shetland and Faeroe. It is with his ducal rule, which seems to have been modelled on the feudal power of kings and dukes in the kingdoms of Germany, France and England, that the first documentary sources of information about society and government in the Atlantic islands appear. This was because of the central control exercised over lands and fiscal rights which were an automatic adjunct to a grant of this kind to a powerful member of the royal family, and which resulted in the preservation of record material in the central government archives. One of the documents which still survives is an account of the row over ducal rents and taxes in Papa Stour which gives us such illuminating information about the political, social and economic situation in Shetland at the very end of the thirteenth century (*DN* 1: 89; *Reg.Norv.* II: 978; Clouston 1914: 67; *OSR*: 38). The row was between the ducal rent collector — or 'sysselman' to give him his formal Norwegian title — Thorvald Thoresson, a figure whose role in Shetland at the time was clearly a very powerful one (Crawford 1984: 50; 1992: 76-78); and Ragnhild Simunsdatter, a resident on Papa Stour, and probably a land-holder, who was complaining about sharp practice, or worse, by the sysselman himself. Her accusations must have had some basis in fact, for Thorvald was concerned to refute them, and had a record of the altercation drawn up at the Shetland Lawthing with a rebuttal of her accusations, for transmitting to Duke Håkon in Norway. We do not know the result of this dispute, but Thorvald's powerful position was clearly not undermined for we find him a few years later acting in a high-handed manner in a judicial case concerning another woman, in the island of Yell (Crawford 1992: 81).

All this is incidental (but fascinating) information to the particular piece of evidence given in the document about a building on the ducal farm on Papa Stour, called a *stofa*, where the first confrontation took place between Thorvald and Ragnhild. This name signified a particular kind of building and is a term that I have discussed in detail before (1985: 131-2), and analyse further below (pp.144-145). It was the stimulus to a research excavation which was conducted at the Biggings on the island of Papa Stour through the late 1970s and 1980s, the results of which are nearing completion. The reasons for deciding to excavate at the Biggings rested on a study of the settlement geography of the island and its farm-names (Crawford 1985: 136-141). The discoveries showed what possibilities exist for a research excavation in the heart of a Shetland crofting township, and also what problems (Crawford 1991: 36-43). We were fortunate to be able to excavate in a locality which had been central to settlement, but which had become available for excavation due to a combination of particular circumstances. However, the problems which intensive settlement produce for understanding the archaeological sequence should not be under-estimated. Parts of the site will never be fully understood due to the destruction of the houses in that locality in the 19th century. Fortunately, however, one of the Norse buildings in the yard at the Biggings had been preserved far better because a house was built over it in the mid 19th century and then abandoned in the early 20th century. It is that building sequence which has preserved the remains of what we are interpreting as a *stofa*, and possibly the *stofa* where Thorvald and Ragnhild clashed over the rents and taxes which were due to be paid from the island to Duke Håkon in 1299.

The purpose of this particular paper is to explain what we understand by the name *stofa*, to give a brief survey of architectural investigations of such buildings in Norway, and to present a preliminary description of the late Norse house — or sequence of houses — uncovered at the Biggings which

137

appear to fit into this particular context of medieval Scandinavian house development. The results of this combined historical and archaeological research project are going to add a completely new dimension to our knowledge of the Scandinavian inheritance of the Northern Isles.

1. Building Developments in Medieval Scandinavia

The longhouse was the normal housing structure throughout the European Iron Age in Scandinavia where excavations have uncovered the impressive long halls of Iron Age chieftains at Leire in Denmark (Christensen 1981), Ullandhaug near Stavanger (Myhre 1980), and Vågen, Lofoten, North Norway. The longhouse encompassed all dwelling rooms under one roof and very often the animal house (byre) as well. The latter form was a dominant feature

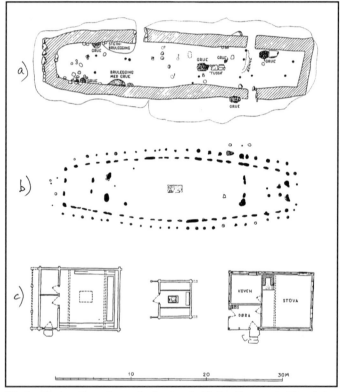

Fig. 1. Contrasting plans of a) stone-built longhouse at Storrsheia, Bjerkreim, Rogaland; b) Stave-built barracks house at Trelleborg, Zealand; and c) log-timbered 'stova'. (From: *Gilde og Gjestebod*, ed. J. Landsverk, Norsk Kultur Arv. 1967)

of Scottish vernacular building history throughout the Lowlands, Highlands and Islands from the medieval period up to modern times.

During the early Middle Ages in Scandinavia there was a move away from these long rectangular structures with parallel rows of load-bearing posts down the middle of the living space, and broad benches along the side walls, to a totally new kind of building. This change was determined by the introduction of the technique of log-timbering or 'lafting' (see fig. 2a) in which the roof rested on the outer timber walls, and the length of the timbers dictated the size of the building. The verb *å lafte*, noun *lafteteknikk*, is used in Norwegian of the technique of jointing the timbers at the corners of the structure. This technique is sometimes called in English 'notched log', but the Norwegian word will be adopted as 'lafted', as by Fett and Sørheim in their English translation of the Gamlebyen report (see 1989: 91). This led to the

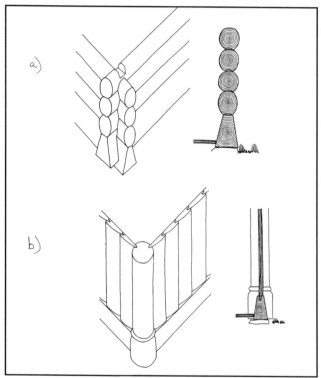

Fig. 2. Sketches showing different methods of wooden house construction: a) 'Lafted' timber in which the walls are made of horizontal logs notched at the corners. b) Stave-built walls, in which the vertical planks are slotted into a sill beam which connects with large corner posts. (From: H. Christie, *Middelalderen Bygger i Tre*, Universitetsforlaget, 1974)

139

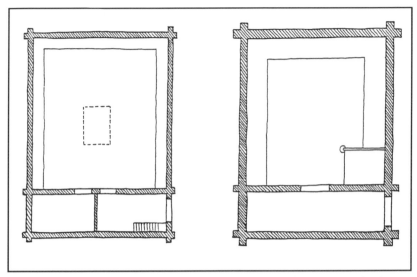

Fig. 3.   Left, typical three-room plan (Raulandstua). Right, typical two-room plan (reconstruction based on several buildings). Not to scale. (From: T.M. Fett, 'Bygninger og
Bygningsdetaljer' fig. 102 in *De Arkeologiske Utgravninger i Gamlebyen, Oslo*, bd.
6, ed. E. Schia, 1989)

establishment of smaller, squarer, totally wooden buildings which had
separate functions rather than the long-house where all the functions were
carried on under the one roof (see fig.1). It is not known exactly why and
when this new technique was introduced into Scandinavia but it seems likely
to have been copied from eastern Europe and Russia where such houses have
been found at Novgorod dating from the 10th century (Brisbane 1992: 136ff).

Urban excavations have produced the earliest evidence for such timber
buildings in Norway. At Trondheim they were being built in the second half
of the 10th century (Christophersen 1992: 73). At Oslo the oldest settlement
goes back to the early 11th century but the standard type of timber building
develops c.1100-a two-room structure with an almost square main room, and
an ante-room (*forstue*) through which the building was entered (fig.3). The
whole measured on average 7.3m x 5.3m or 34.4m^2 (Fett 1989: 29). The
majority of such houses in Oslo were 'lafted' whereas most of the wooden
buildings excavated at Bryggen, Bergen, were of stave construction (post and
beam), with strong upright posts and sill-beams into which were slotted
upright planks (fig.2b). This series of structures starts in the late 12th century,
and they appear to have been mostly warehouses (Herteig 1991: 114).

Stave construction symbolises a rather different tradition of building
and one particularly associated with Church architecture. It was also used for
housing in West Norway, although 'lafted' timber buildings were commonly

140

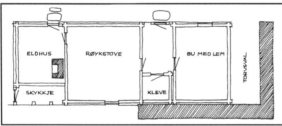

Fig. 4. Surviving wooden house of the 'longhouse' type at Risa, Lindås, Nordhordaland, with the kitchen (*eldhus*), living-room (*røykstova*), and store (*bu*) interconnected in a row, with one end protected by a large stone-built wall. (From: O.D. Laerum and N.G. Brekke, *Røykstova-Bustad Gjennom to Tusen Ar*, fig. 6.8)

constructed as well, which might be of *sleppverk* (= horizontal wall planking slotted into upright posts).

1.1. Introduction of the *stofa*

Dwelling-houses of this kind, that is of timber framing, without central posts, which appear in the towns of Norway in the 11th century, were known by the ON word *stofa*. This is a difficult term to translate — 'living-room' seems rather inadequate — and it has little meaning in the English language, except that our word 'stove' is probably of the same origin. Certainly the concept of an enclosed form of fireplace had something to do with such a room originally (Stoklund 1984: 101; 1993: 211). At Oslo the majority of these buildings were furnished with a corner fireplace rather than a central hearth

141

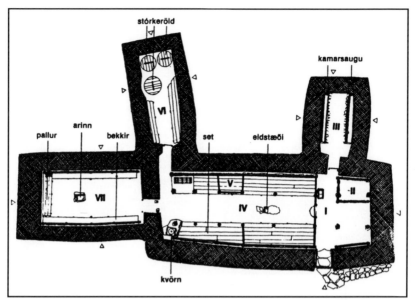

Fig. 5. Plan of reconstructed 12th century farm at Stöng, Þjorsadalur, Iceland. The original 'skali' (IV) is on the right, with the 'stofa' (VII) added onto the left gable. Note the central hearth (*arinn*) and benches (*bekkir*). (From: site guide book by H. Agustsson)

(Sørheim 1989: fig. 1) although this was not the case in rural areas. The term *stofa* (*stova, stua*) came to be used for the main dwelling house in all medieval Norwegian settlements, whether urban or rural, and the word *røykstova* ('smoky stofa') was the usual word for the central building in the community right up to the twentieth century, deriving from the permanent smoke haze which permeated these buildings from the open hearth in the centre of the floor (Laerum and Brekke 1990).

This dark, smoky, moderately-sized wooden building was the hub of the family's existence, where a number of domestic activities were carried on, including light work and eating, and where people gathered in the evenings. Possibly it was used for sleeping also, and at a later date fixed beds were built along the sides. The heavier domestic activity of the baking, brewing, steeping kind was confined to the firehouse or kitchen (*eldhus*) where the larger cooking fireplaces and ovens were found. There would also be another domestic building called the *bu* (store), where food was kept, and which was raised up on stone slabs to discourage vermin (*stabbur*). The separation of these three buildings was usual in east Norway, where they are often rather far apart from each other perhaps because of the danger of fire spreading from one to another. The three terms *stova, eldhus* and *bu* are referred to in medieval documents, although it is not always clear that they were separate

142

Fig. 6. Reconstruction of a Medieval house excavated on Lurekalven in North Hordaland. It consisted of *eldhus* (kitchen), *stove* (living-room), *bu* (store) and *loe* (byre) in a *rekkjetun* or longhouse construction. Note the variety of horizontal and vertical walling depicted. (Drawing by N.G. Brekke)

units; they might have been separate rooms but under one roof- especially in west Norway (fig. 4).

In west Norway the building of 'lafted' timber structures was less common, but nonethess the *stofa* was of wooden construction. Was the *stofa* separated off from the end of the old Viking-Age longhouse (*skali*) or was it added on to it, as was apparently the case in Iceland, where the excavations of the house at Stöng clearly show the *stofa* as an additional element? (Stenberger 1943): (fig. 5). The house-building tradition in historic times in west Norway — which is what we should be looking at, as far as Shetland is concerned — was for the different rooms of the house to be built together in a row (*rekkjatun*). But is this a direct continuity from the Viking-Age longhouse or is it the development of a different kind of house construction, in which each building is a separate unit, although lying contiguous to each other along the same alignment? Architectural historians have differing ideas about this house development. Berg declares that all that is known about wooden buildings from the Middle Ages is of separate, free-standing structures (Berg 1982: 190; 1992: 148). But there is a growing body of opinion which argues for the persistence of the longhouse tradition through the medieval period in west Norway (Myrhe 1982: 195-217; Stoklund; Brekke). The problem is that there are so few excavated medieval sites in Norway that the archaeological evidence is not abundant. Lurekalven, near Bergen, is one of the few medieval farmhouses which have been excavated and it is apparently constructed in the longhouse tradition, with the *stove* in the middle, *bu* at one end and *eldhus* at the other (fig. 6) (although the function of the different rooms is not absolutely clear from the existing publication: Kaland 1985: 186). The building appears to have been constructed in a mixture of lafted and stave-built wooden structures on stone foundations. All these problems are exceedingly pertinent to the Biggings site as will be discussed.

1.2 Excavations of *stofa* buildings in urban locations

There is in the first place the problem of recognising wooden buildings archaeologically, because of the non-survival of wood in certain conditions, or because of the removal of wooden walls for re-use. Sometimes the recognisable foundations of such walls may consist only of corner stones for log-timbering to rest on, or sill stones in a row for the ground beam of stave-built structures. The good survival of wooden foundation beams in Gamlebyen (Oslo), Bryggen (Bergen) and at Trondheim is due to the fires which took place in these towns and the rebuilding on top of the rubble. The absence of stone foundations to the wooden walls at the Biggings made it very difficult to interpret the house plan, and this was a factor in under-standing the site which we were very slow to come to terms with.

Wooden floors may be less easily re-used and therefore survive in the archaeological record (if conditions are right). In the case of the Biggings

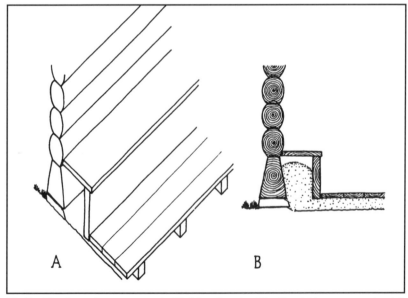

Fig. 7. Sketches of narrow, earth-filled benches (*moldbenk*) which were constructed against two or three of the outer walls of the medieval 'stofa' buildings in Scandinavia. (From: H. Christie, *Middelalderen Bygger i Tre*, fig. 8)

wooden floor its survival must have been because it was in such poor condition and so old that it was not worth attempting to re-use and was covered by clay which formed a new anaerobic floor layer. Evidence from the urban excavations shows that wooden floors could be either laid on the earth or carried on joists-which was the most usual in the two-roomed *stofa* at Gamlebyen. They could be constructed so that they had no connection with the side walls (*flyttende* or 'floating') or they could be joined in to the wall

Fig. 8. Årestova from Vågå, Gudbrandsdal (now in Maihaugen Open-Air Museum, Lillehammer). Note the *blekkjarstein* in front of the hearth to protect the fire from draughts (Fig. 4.1 from Laerum and Brekke, 1990: De Sandvigske Samlingen)

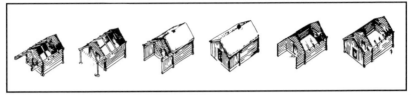

Fig. 9. Sketches showing the development of a single-roomed *stofa* (on left) to a three-roomed one by means of a gable extension. Note that the extension could be either stave-built (on left) or constructed with horizontal timbers (on right). (From: A. Berg, *Norske Tømmerhus fra Mellomalderen*).

(fast). Nailing the floor to the joists was the most usual way of securing it. The distance between the joists varied from 1.3m-3.3m. The earliest floors in Oslo were not planked, but made of beaten earth, and these buildings were probably dwelling-houses because they also had hearths (Fett 1989: 44-5).

One distinctive feature of the excavated urban timber buildings was the existence of wall benches along one, two or three sides of the interior of the room, called *moldbenk*. They were made of wooden planks constructed against and over an earthen core (see fig.7). Such benches are known in the oldest standing timber buildings of Norway such as Raulandstua (Bygdøy Folk Museum dated c.1200), and they are presumed to have existed in many of the urban houses where there now can be seen a gap between the edge of the floor and the outer wall of 50-80 cms. Sometimes there are remnants of the board which was set on edge against the front of the earthen bank. In one case in Gamlebyen the cross cleats (*oker*) which supported the upright plank and were secured to the wall beam had survived. The *moldbenk* was probably about 40 cms. high (at Trondheim 25 cms.) and it appears that sometimes the floor level could be somewhat lower than the outside wall foundations. The purpose of such wall-benches seems to have been to insulate the house against draughts coming through the timber wall. They could hardly have been used for sleeping on, as the wide benches found in Viking-Age houses are thought to have been. In later log-built houses wooden sleeping-platforms/beds were built up against the walls of the *stofa*.

In the town houses excavated in Gamlebyen *moldbenker* are always found in association with a corner hearth. But this is not necessarily the case with *stua* in the country districts. In fact there are some famous old timber buildings in Norway called *årestua*, and the *åre* is the stone hearth set centrally in the floor (as in the *røykstova*). It often had a large stone set at the back of the fire to divert draughts coming in the door, called a *blekkjarstein*, just as is known in the older Orkney farmhouses (fig.8). The corner fireplace (*hjørneildsted*) is said not to have really taken on in the country districts until the end of the Middle Ages (Berg 1992: 150). It is quite a distinguishing feature of the excavated houses at Gamlebyen that the corner fireplace took over from the central hearth in the 12th century (fig.3); the two-roomed house

146

with a corner fireplace against the dividing wall of *stua* and *forstua* was then the standard type of dwelling-house until the 13th century when other changes start to take place in the dwelling-house plan, and fireplaces disappear altogether from the urban archaeological record (probably because they came to be located on an upper floor).

The single-roomed timber house (*einromstua*) was particularly predominant in west Norway (Berg 1992: 153) and likely to have been the usual type before the problems of the later 14th century (when the Black Death hit Norway very badly). It was usually 5m x 5m, had the entrance door mid-way in the gable which was sometimes covered with a porch. This is called the 'megaron' plan and the walls extending forward from the house itself which formed the porch, could be stave-built, or 'lafted' (see fig. 9). This porch was eventually enclosed and formed a second room, or was divided and the classic three-roomed building (*treromstua*) came into existence.

1.3. The Northern Isles

The few published excavations which have taken place on Viking and Norse sites in the Northern Isles have revealed nothing of such buildings as those described above and very little of the features which are standard in them,

Fig. 10. *Røykstova*, **Kirkjuboer, Faeroe Islands. This remarkable 'lafted' timber structure is thought to date from the 12th century. (Photo: author)**

such as wooden floors, corner hearths or narrow wall benches. The survival of wooden structures has never in fact been noted. Yet there must have been wooden houses and there must have been plenty of wooden fittings in them as in stone-built ones. The significance of the place-name 'Stove' was not appreciated until the research project into the 1299 document and associated excavations at the Biggings got under way in the 1970s (Crawford 1985: 131-2). Such place-names tell us that wooden buildings of the type described must have existed at those places in the islands. There are five farms called Stove in Orkney and a good few more incorporate the 'stove' element in Shetland: about 19 (Stewart 1990: 198). Indeed the technical term 'stock-stove' for pre-fabricated wooden buildings imported from Norway survived in Shetland into the early modern period (Smith 1980). Nothing has survived in Orkney or Shetland like the famous Røykstova at Kirkjuboer in the Faeroes (fig.10), which still stands as a dramatic witness to the contacts with the home country of Norway, and as proof of the use of timber construction techniques in the Atlantic islands. This is of course at the seat of the bishop and evidence of the wealth and status of the most powerful members of the medieval church. It would clearly only be the wealthiest in Faeroese society who could afford to import and live in such a home.

All excavated sites in Shetland from the Norse period have revealed a traditional method of house structure and of internal lay-out. The early longhouse (*skali*) with one large open room, heated by the *langeld* (= 'long hearth') in the centre of the floor and with the roof supported on double rows of internal load-bearing posts seems to give way to a true longhouse plan in which the animals were housed under the same roof as the living quarters. Further changes have been recorded in the excavations at Sandwick in Unst where the reorganisation of living space entailed the abandonment of the central hearth and its replacement by an oven-like hearth placed in the room corner; the construction of a large bench or dais at one gable end; and the addition of small outshot rooms along the south wall (Bigelow 1987: 29). These changes took place in the 13th or 14th centuries and the living room of the later Sandwick house certainly developed more 'stofa-like' features; it was reduced in width and length (new dimensions 8 x 4m); its only entrance was through the internal dividing wall next to the central passage and the entrance near the gable wall was blocked; it may even have been provided with internal wooden panelling for there are signs of sill stones running along the longwalls. House I at Jarlshof was a longhouse, but with many alterations at both ends, and although recent reconstructions show it with wall panelling this is pure assumption. There is a total lack of any wooden features recorded from either Jarlshof or Sandwick or Underhoull, another Unst site (Small 1964-6) . There is certainly no trace of any wooden floors ever having existed at any of these sites — or of *moldbenk*, the other standard feature of the Norwegian *stofa*. Sandwick remains a stone-built house of the old Viking kind with a few re-arrangements of internal features.

148

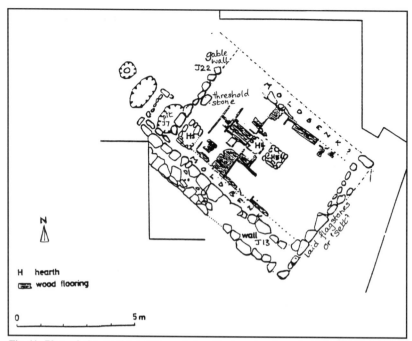

Fig. 11. Plan of the 'stofa' building at the Biggings in phase 3 (12th-13th centuries), showing the extent of the surviving wooden floor, central and corner hearths, and protective stone wall (J13)

2. Consideration of the Biggings *stofa*

The discovery of the wooden floor in the south-eastern half of the site (fig. 11) immediately marked the Biggings out as different from all previous excavated Viking or late Norse houses in the Northern Isles, or anywhere else in Scotland. The lack of suitable timber within Shetland has meant that all building wood has had to be imported throughout historic times. This was not an insuperable problem for the Norse settlers in the Atlantic islands, as we have seen from evidence for the importation of building timbers in the Faeroes. The total disappearance of all former wooden buildings in Shetland means however that there is no precedent to help in our interpretation of the Biggings site, and no experience of the *stofa*-type building which has formed such an important part of Scandinavian domestic architecture. The fact that such a feature was exactly what was mentioned in the documentary evidence still made it no easier to come to terms with the implications of this building tradition. The evidence uncovered was of quite a different kind from what was known of Viking settlement archaeology from excavations previously carried out in the Northern Isles, and it was with difficulty that we adjusted to

149

the new and different circumstances of wooden structures. Our understanding of wooden construction still remains quite inferior to the expertise of Scandinavian archaeologists and historians in these matters.

2.1. Description

The wooden floor, and its dimensions, indicate that we are dealing with a structure of the *stofa* type and it will therefore be referred to as the *stofa* in discussion. This building was at the eastern end of the Biggings yard and aligned NW-SE, (although the four sides of the building will be referred to as north, south, east and west).[1] It would appear that the dimensions of this building changed little from its initial foundation in the 11th century through to the mid 19th century when the whole Biggings township was laid out anew, and all the existing buildings were destroyed at that time. New croft houses were then constructed, one of which was built diametrically across the previous alignment of the *stofa* (SW-NE) but using the remains of the *stofa* itself as a foundation. These remains were thus preserved underneath the 19th century building which was then abandoned in the 1930s, providing the opportunity for excavation to take place.

This remarkable continuity of residence on the same alignment is quite clear from the evidence of the floor area which changed little in width — and only slightly in length — throughout the history of the site until the destruction of the mid 19th century. Measuring from the southernmost plank of the wooden floor to the ? sill beam at the north side the internal width was 4.4m, while the length was just under 7m from the east gablestones to cross-wall J22 (there was some evidence for an earlier floor having extended slightly west of J22). If the width of the earth bench (presumed *moldbenk*) along the south wall is added (40cm) and if a corresponding *moldbenk* on the north wall is assumed, then the building's internal width would have been 4.6m-the normal average width of many timber *stue* in Norway.[2]

2.2. Structure of the *stofa*

Although stone walls exist on the site and will be discussed next the present interpretation of this building is that it was of wooden construction. This was not the original assumption; in 1986 the *stofa* was described as being one room in a stone building, because it never occurred to us that it could have

---

1. The remaining excavated structures are not discussed here: they include the *eldhus* and possibly the *bu* also.
2. Width of two-roomed *stue* in Gamlebyen range from 3.8m to 6.1m; at Bryggen from 3.8m at 5.5m. Length of the *stue* alone at Gamlebyen range from 4.2 to 6.6m; at Bryggen from 4.0 to 7.8m (9.9) The Borgund *årestua* measured 11 x 5m but it must have been of more than normal domestic size.

been anything else. The baffling absence of stone house walls was put down to destruction. Moreover there existed the feature of stone wall J13 (fig. 12) on the south side of the wooden floor, which appeared in upper levels and which has remained as a permanent feature throughout the excavation. Its construction and dimensions are impressive, for although its full length is only 8m it is massively made, and in its best-preserved section has a width of 1-1.4m. The inner and outer faces are made of carefully chosen stones which give a level surface and the central infill is of hard-packed earth with some smaller stones. This is a similar method of construction to the walls of the Jarlshof houses which are however somewhat narrower. Where this wall J13 ran underneath the later croft house it was disturbed and only the lower foundation stones of rhyolite boulders survive. The two or three surviving upper courses are well-laid slabs of sandstone beach boulders.

Wall J13 runs the length of the wooden floor and extends a little beyond the cross-wall (J22) so that it had never formed a corner with that cross-wall, which was probably the foundation of the west gable (fig.11). It was assumed during excavation that Wall J13 must at one time have continued further west to form the full long wall of a long-house structure, but this now seems unlikely. It was probably never any longer and appears to have been a detached piece of walling the purpose of which was to provide protection for the timber wall of the *stofa* (a feature found in the coastal parts of west Norway) and it had no integral connection with the wooden construction (see later discussion). The possibility that it may have formed the stone foundation for a timber superstructure has been discounted.

Turning to the crosswall J22 at the west end of the *stofa* we have another very significant part of the building's construction which also formed an important element in the excavation of the site. This cross-wall extends right across the width of the building from Wall J13 to the north side of the floor. Although formed of only a single line of stone these were large and well-laid blocks and this wall had been part of a significant addition to the building at some point in its history. Wall J22 was contemporary with the second wooden floor as fragments of the first wooden floor were found underlying some of the stones. As this single line of stones must have supported a timber superstructure (probably of upright panelling) cross-wall J22 can fairly certainly be interpreted as the foundation of the west gable wooden wall. As it did not replace an earlier stone foundation it would appear that the original west gable cannot have rested on stones but must have been constructed of horizontal logs. If it had been stave-built the post holes would have survived (in this respect it is interesting to note that a line of post-holes was found where the original west gable of the primary house at Jarlshof had been before it was extended: Hamilton 1956: 107). Some stake-holes were found along this alignment underneath the cross-wall from phase 2 (see below pp.156-157 for phasing) but these were not substantial enough to have been connected with a stave-built wall.

Cross-wall J22 in fact provides some good evidence of wooden construction, for single lines of stones are clearly used as foundation sills for timber walls in both Norway and Iceland (Stenberger 1943: 85). The size and permanency of the stones does not suggest that they were the foundation for an internal dividing wall (although this possibility has been very carefully considered). The lack of evidence for any flooring immediately west of this line suggests that cross-wall J22 must have been the end of the *stofa* building and this has important implications for the question of whether the *stofa* was part of a longhouse structure or whether it was an independently constructed building.

Several features point to the main entrance having been located in the centre of this west gable. In the first place the corner hearth inside the *stofa* lies in the corner formed by the south side wall and the west gable wall (see fig.11), which corresponds exactly to the position of such corner hearths in Norwegian *stue* which were always placed next to the wall where the entrance lay. Secondly, a large level slabstone (no.86) located inside and mid-way along the gable wall is ideally placed to be an internal threshold stone. This area is the least disturbed part of the Norse building phases and we do have some confidence that the main entrance into the *stofa* was located here, as it should have been.

However the destruction on the north and east of the site had been such that we are far less confident in interpreting the walling structures on these sides. The south-east gable had been very badly disturbed and the alignment altered with a later structure of rhyolite blocks inserted. They were certainly not forming a sill foundation, and may be better interpreted as a protective outer wall to an inner timber wall, as J13. Outside these stones a well-constructed row of flag-stones ran the length of the east gable. These had been re-used when the Gørl was constructed to form a 'sett', an area of paving which was traditional in Shetland crofts, particularly near the entrance. They probably relate to a later phase of the building sequences. No such exterior paving was found anywhere else on the site . The north side of the *stofa* is even more problematical. Here the ground falls away, and this area formed the main entrance into the Biggings yard which may account for the hollowing effect from its frequent use by farm traffic. Whatever walling had existed on this side of the *stofa* had been completely masked by later activity.

This baffling picture of stone walls which had little connection or relationship with each other became more explicable once it was appreciated that we were dealing with a wooden building. This has helped to provide an explanation for the absence of walls, and the disconnected type of walling discovered on the site. Stone walls are encountered in the excavation of wooden buildings in Norway (although rarely in the towns) and where they do occur they are sometimes interpreted as providing a stone foundation for a timber superstructure which has usually totally vanished. At Bryggen such walls average only 85cms. in width. In rural areas detached pieces of stone walling could however serve another purpose around a timber building — and are seen today in exposed parts of coastal Norway where they are built on the south or west sides of the house to form a protective skin against the prevailing Atlantic weather. They were not integral to the building which existed as a timber structure totally unconnected with the stone wall (see fig. 4). These walls were moreover quite substantial structures, usually as high as the roof line, with a double facing of stone. In south Norway the Jaeren house was constructed as a timber building but entirely surrounded by stone walls with a passageway between the timber walls and the stone surrounding wall (Stoklund 1983-4: 216-7). They seem also to feature at the medieval house sites excavated on Lurekalven and Høybøen (Kaland 1987: 186). Such protective stone walls have also been recognised in Iron Age houses at Ullandhaug (Myhre 1982). There is no doubt about their existence in the Faeroe Islands where they were a feature of the houses until modern times (Stoklund 1984, 106) and have been discovered round the north and south sides of the medieval timber churches recognised at Sand (nos.2-5) while church no. 2 had a wall running round the eastern chancel also (Krogh 1975: 52-3). However, the log-timbered Røykstova at Kirkjuboer does not appear to have been provided with such a feature.

Wall J13 at the Biggings would seem to compare with such protective stone walls and the present conclusion is therefore that Wall J13 was constructed in phase 3 as an outer skin for protecting the wooden *stofa* on its south-west side. Whether the *stofa* was built of lafted timber or was of stave construction is not yet fully determined, but it seems as if different methods of construction were used in the different phases, and possibly even combined in the one building, so that the side walls could have been of horizontal timber and the gables of upright panelling (see fig. 6).

2.3. Building Periods

Phase 2

The first wooden building was furnished with a central fire-pit (J105) and a wall-hearth (J108). These appear to be contemporary. The floor was earth and flag-laid. There was no evidence of any stone walls and it is thought that this must therefore have been a wooden building with *moldbenker*. Dating evidence suggests 11th-12th century .

Phase 3

The central fire-pit and wall-hearth went out of use and the former was covered with peat ash when the wooden floor was laid in the 12th century. This remodelling was along classical *stofa* lines according to current Norwegian fashion, with a corner hearth (J27) located and styled on the pattern of such hearths at Gamlebyen, Oslo (fig.13). It was a slightly larger

Fig. 12. View of the west end of the 'stofa' with the joists and planks of the wooden floor just showing (top centre) and underneath the 19th century crofthouse wall. The corner hearth J27 (*hjørneildsted*) can be seen abutting against the earth bank of the *moldbenk*. Stone setting and threshhold stone bottom centre

wooden house than in phase 2 (6.4m long x 4.8m wide between the walls). A central hearth of the *åre* type (with a flat stone-flagged base and kerb) was placed in the middle of the wooden floor, perhaps in a later part of this phase. It was during this phase that the stones for the north-west gable wall (J22) were laid and the protective wall J13 probably constructed, although this has proved impossible to date.

An additional feature was added on to the north-west gable wall built around a large pit (J7). The sill stones for its walls have survived and indicate that a small annexe with a soakaway served some ablutionary purpose (perhaps as a latrine). The protective wall J13 was extended far enough to preserve the timber walls of this annexe from the effects of the south-west gales.

Later phases.

Evidence suggests that the *stofa* underwent a change of use in the later medieval period, and that it was indeed at some point destroyed by fire. The large number of pits of different kinds dug in and around the building indicate that activities of a domestic industrial kind were carried on within it.

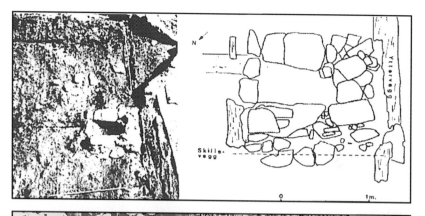

Fig. 13. Corner hearth J27 at the Biggings with protective wall J13 behind, and (top) corner hearth K62 at Gamlebyen, Oslo. (From Sørheim, 1989, fig. 13)

Conclusion

This present brief survey of the chronological development cannot give details of the finds assemblage or of dating evidence to elaborate on the phasing. Dating evidence indicates that the wooden floor discovered at the Biggings came from a *stofa* which must have been old at the time that Thorvald Thoresson held his meeting with Ragnhild Simunsdatter in 1299. It had been laid some time before and within a *stofa* building which was already in existence. This was in the period before any documentary evidence exists to tell us by whom it was laid, whether the llth century kings, or possibly the earls of Orkney. Closest parallels for such wooden buildings and their internal furnishings have been found in the urban excavations of Oslo, Bergen and Trondheim. These similarities tell us that the builders of the Biggings *stofa* were fully in touch with developments in the urban centres of Norway. The likelihood is of course that the materials were imported from Norway ready for erection — as they were later, in the period when historical evidence exists for such trade. Pieces of birch bark found in the debris lying on top of the wooden floor were remains of the roof covering which had certainly been imported from Norway. Birch bark was the normal means of providing an impermeable layer underneath the turf roof of Norwegian farmhouses right up to this century, and it was imported into Faeroe for this purpose. Birch bark, wooden floors, corner hearths, *moldbenker* are all standard features of houses in Norway and the islands of the north Atlantic in the middle ages. The wooden houses at the Biggings provide us with tangible evidence of Shetland's place in that Norse world of the North Atlantic and they help us to re-create that world in the historical imagination.

Acknowledgements

The post-excavation research has been carried out in conjunction with Beverley Ballin Smith, on whose analysis the above phasing is based. The final excavation report will be published with her, possibly in Norway.

Bibliography

Berg, A., 1982: 'Samansetjing av enkelthus til lån i Vest-Noreg'. In: Myrhe et al. (eds.), 186-93.

Berg, A., 1989: *Norske Tømmerhus fra Mellomalderen*, I, Norske Minnesmerker. Oslo.

Bigelow, G., 1987: 'Domestic Architecture in Medieval Shetland'. *Review of Scottish Culture 3*, 23-38.

Brekke, N.G., 1975: *Bygeskikk i Nordhordland*. Bergen.

Brisbane, M.A. (ed.), 1992: *The Archaeology of Novgorod, Russia*. Society for Medieval Archaeology, monograph no.13.

Christensen, T., 1991: *Leire-Syn og Sagn*.

Christophersen, A. 1992: 'Royal Authority and Early Urbanisation in Trondheim during the transition to the historical period'. In: *Archaeology and the Urban Economy*, 'Festskrift' til A. Herteig, Arkeologiske Skrifter Historisk Museum Bergen, 5, 91-130.

Clouston, J.S., 1914: *Records of the Earldom of Orkney*. SHS, 2nd series vol. VII.

Crawford, B.E., 1984: 'Papa Stour: Survival, Continuity and Change in One Shetland Island'. In: Fenton and Pálsson (eds.), 40-58.

Crawford, B.E., 1985: 'The Biggings, Papa Stour — a multi-disciplinary investigation'. In: Brian Smith (ed.), *Shetland Archaeology*, Lerwick, 128-58.

Crawford, B.E., 1991: 'Excavations at the Biggings, Papa Stour, Shetland'. In: G. Bigelow (ed.), *The Norse of the North Atlantic*, Acta Archaeologica, 61, 1990, 36-43.

Crawford, B.E., 1992: 'Thorvald Thoresson, Duke Håkon and Shetland'. In: *Kongsmen og Krossmen, festskrift til Grethe Authen Blom*, Det Kongelige Norske Videnskabers Selskab, Skrifter 1, 69-89.

Curle, A.O., 1934-5: 'Excavation of a Dwelling of the Viking Period at Jarlshof'. *PSAS*, LXIX, 85-108.

DN = Diplomatarium Norvegicum, Christiania, 1849-.

Fenton, A. and Pálsson, H., (eds.), 1984: *The Northern and Western Isles in the Viking World*. Edinburgh.

Fett, T.M., 1989: 'Bygninger og Bygningsdetaljer'. In: *De Arkeologiske Utgravninger i Gamlebyen, Oslo*, bd.6 *Hus og Gjerder.*

Hamilton, J., 1956: *Excavations at Jarlshof, Shetland*. HMSO. Edinburgh.

Herteig, A., 1991: *The Bryggen Papers* vol.3, pt.2. *The Buildings at Bryggen. Their Topographical and Chronological Development*. Norwegian University Press.

Kaland, Sigrid, H.H., 1987: 'Viking/Medieval Settlement in the Heathland Area of Nordhordland'. *Tenth Viking Congress*, Universitetets Oldsaksamlings Skrifter, Ny rekke nr.9, 171-90.

Krogh, K., 1975: 'Seks Kirkjur heima á Sandi', *Mondul* 2, 21-54.

Laerum O.D. & Brekke, N.G., 1990: *Røykstova-Bustad Gjennom To tusen År.*

Murray, H., 1983: *Viking and Early Medieval Buildings in Dublin*. BAR 119.

Myhre, B., 1980: *Gårdsanlegget pa Ullandshaug. Gårdshus i Jernalder og tidlig Middelalder*. Ark.Mus. i Stavanger, Skrifter 4.

Myrhe, B., 1982: 'Synspunkter på huskonstruksjon i sørvestnorske gårdshus fra jernalder og middelalderen'. In: Myrhe et al., 98-118.

Myrhe, B. et al. (eds.), 1982: *Vestnorske Byggeskikk gjennom to tusen år.* AmS, Skrifter 7.

OSR = Orkney and Shetland Records, A. and A.W. Johnston (eds.), 1907-42.

Small, A., 1964-5: 'Excavations at Underhoull, Shetland'. *PSAS*, XCVIII, 225-49.

Smith, B., 1980: 'Stockstove Houses'. *Shetland Folk Book*, VII, 22-27.

Stenberger, M., 1943: *Forntida gårdar i Island*. Copenhagen.

Stoklund, B., 1983-4: 'Kove, Svale og Skot'. *By og Bygd*, xxx, 215-30.

Stoklund, B., 1984: 'Building Traditions in the Northern World'. In: Fenton and Pálsson (eds.), 96-115.

Stoklund, B., 1993: 'On the concept of 'eldhus' and 'stova': the Faeroese evidence'. In: H. Cheape (ed.), *Tools and Traditions. Studies in European Ethnology presented to Alexander Fenton*, Edinburgh, 211-17.

Sørheim, H., 1989: 'Ildsteder'. In: *De Arkeologiske Utgravninger i Gamlebyen, Oslo*, bd.6 *Hus og Gjerder.*

Thorsteinsson, A., 1976: 'The Testimony of Ancient Architecture'. *Faroe Isles Review*, 1.

THE MEDIEVAL CHURCH IN SHETLAND: ORGANISATION AND BUILDINGS

Ronald G. Cant

Christian Origins

Among the exhibits in the Shetland Museum in Lerwick one of the most remarkable is what has come to be known as 'the Monks' Stone', discovered at the early ecclesiastical centre of Papil on West Burra Isle in 1943. Apparently designed as the principal component of a 'box shrine' character- istic of the eighth century, it depicts a sequence of hooded figures equipped with croziers and book-satchels advancing over the waves of the ocean towards a free-standing cross — apparently commemorating the coming of Christianity to the islands. These ecclesiastics — one mounted and clearly of greater authority — were almost certainly the *papar* identified by the Norse invaders of the ninth century at various settlements throughout the islands by designations such as Papil or the prefix Papa, indicative of a parental concern towards their communities in contrast to the hermits on isolated cliff-tops or stacks elsewhere (Crawford 1987: 164-7; Lamb 1974).

While some of the hermits may have been of Irish derivation (like others in comparable locations in the north Atlantic) the *papar* were more probably of Pictish origin, completing in the early eighth century an enterprise begun some three hundred years before at Whithorn in Galloway. Thus it was appropriate that what might well have been the initial centre of

Fig. 1. Papar in procession.

159

Christian activity in Shetland should have acquired (though probably at a somewhat later date) the name of St Ninian's Isle.

Ninian was a Roman Briton, citizen of one of the latest and most remote provinces of an empire then reaching its end in western Europe but which, through its latter acceptance of Christianity (however limited) and the initiative of 'missionary saints' like Ninian and his successors, would transmit a notable legacy to the peoples of the more remote regions of the British Isles. With the details of that enterprise this study is not concerned save to note that it was of a highly complex character, involving Britons of Strathclyde, Scots from Northern Ireland settled in 'Dalriada' or Argyll to the west of the great area occupied by the 'Pictish Confederation' north of Forth and latterly at least extending to Orkney and Shetland.

From such evidence as is available it would seem that the ecclesiastical organisation of Shetland in this initial period was of the monastic form characteristic of the Celtic church. Under this — unlike most of their medieval successors — the monks did not live apart from ordinary society but held a central position in the life of their neighbourhood, their abbot or other senior ecclesiastic working in close co-operation with the chief 'secular dignitary' of the locality. On St Ninian's Isle the excavations of 1955-59 revealed beneath the visible ecclesiastical remains evidence of an earlier church within which the famous 'treasure' had been deposited, also fragments of shrines and small cross-slabs. The opportunity was also taken to extend the investigation to Papil on West Burra where a large vertical cross-slab ('the Papil stone') had been identified in 1877 — similar in character to 'the Bressay stone' identified in 1864 — also 'the Monks' stone' found in 1943.

On these matters space does not allow for more than a few brief observations, first, that although there was clearly a church on St Ninian's Isle and almost certainly at Papil, these would be relatively small buildings with space for no more than the most important items, such as the 'box shrines'. The large vertical stones would stand in the adjacent kirkyard where they might serve as 'preaching crosses' like those in the northern Scottish mainland from which Orkney and Shetland were most probably converted — with others at more remote centres where there might be no church. After the Norwegian settlement these cross-slabs seem to have been adapted to serve as personal memorials, but although the additions include elements of Pictish provenance there are others of even more emphatic Norse character.

Norse initiatives

By the end of the ninth century the incoming Norwegians had probably achieved an ascendancy in most parts of Shetland. And despite evidence from certain locations in the Western Isles that — initially at least — the new settlers lived apart from the old, here they seem to have absorbed them in their own communities. Again, while they clearly held the *papar* in some respect, it may be doubted whether the Shetland church had the resources itself, or the kind of external contacts to enable it to maintain an effective and continuous Christian influence.[1]

In 994, however, King Olaf Tryggvason of Norway, on a visit to King Ethelred of England, announced his conversion to Christianity and in the course of his homeward voyage secured that of Sigurd, Jarl or Earl of Orkney c.985-1014 whose rule also extended to Shetland. But even if Sigurd acquired the services of one or more of the royal chaplains, as his successor Earl Thorfinn may also have done in the course of a visit in 1034 to King Olaf Haraldsson (the later St Olaf), there could be no continuous priesthood in the islands without a resident bishop. Thus although a Bishop of Orkney (of Anglo-Danish provenance) is mentioned about this time, some fifteen years later Archbishop Adalbert of Bremen, whose province had come to include the entire Scandinavian north, received a request from Orcadian envoys to send preachers to the islands.

The request — which confirms that Christianity in the northern isles was still at a relatively early stage of development — was reinforced by a personal visit by Earl Thorfinn himself (c.1050) to a remarkable range of European dignitaries (culminating in the Pope). Returning thereafter to his principal residence of Birsay, he built 'Christ's Kirk, a stately minster' subsequently consecrated by Bishop Thorolf (probably a Norwegian), 'and here the episcopal seat in the Orkneys was first established' (Cant 1974: 2).[2]

While there is still uncertainty regarding the identity of Earl Thorfinn's 'minster',[3] there are considerations for thinking that it is most likely to have been the ecclesiastical structure adjacent to his own residence on the Brough, embodying as it does work of two periods corresponding to two phases in the development of the bishopric (Cant 1993: 11-12). The earlier (c.1055) would seem to have comprised no more than the nave and chancel, the later (c.1110) involving the addition of a semi-circular apse to the chancel or choir, and the remodelling of the arch between choir and nave to allow for the insertion of 'altar-niches' in the eastern corners of the latter. In the external composition these might well have been carried up as cylindrical towers as in the

---

1. For a more detailed discussion of this problem see Crawford 1987: 164-9, also Lamb 1995.
2. By 'the Orkneys' was implied all the territories under the control of the Earl — at the time in question including Caithness and some of the more northerly Western Isles, as well as Shetland, which came to be included in the full official title of the bishopric, though generally omitted in common usage.
3. Two different locations have been suggested for the Birsay 'minster': (a) on the Brough, (b) on the mainland, on a site occupied by the parish church. The former is followed in R.C.A.H.M.S., 1946: Orkney, No. I, also by Radford in Wainwright (ed.), 1962: *The Northern Isles*, 174-180, and by the present writer. The latter location is followed by Lamb in *Proc. Soc. Antiq. Scot.*, CV, 200-205. A helpful analysis of the problem is provided by Crawford 1987: *Scandinavian Scotland*, 184-190.

remarkable church at Deerness (of slightly later date). At Birsay there are also indications of an intended 'west-work', perhaps like that at Stenness and certain Norwegian churches of this period (Cant 1993: 13, 19).

Two matters fall to be considered at this point, the first concerning the provision made in this initial phase of the bishopric for the maintenance of episcopal authority in Shetland, the second what evidence there may be of local churches or chapels in both island groups before the creation of a comprehensive 'parochial organisation' in the succeeding period. On the first, if the ruined structure on St Ninian's Isle is examined it will be found that the western element, built over the pristine church within which the famous 'treasure' was found, is the earlier, and the eastern an addition in the form of a simplified version of the Birsay minster in its second phase. While the evidence is not conclusive, it seems reasonable to attribute the western element to Bishop Thorolf or one of his successors in the late eleventh century and the eastern to Bishop William 'the old' shortly after the remodelling of the Birsay minster, perhaps in the early 1120s (Cant 1993: 13).

Towards the medieval church order

In 'Nordic Europe', and to a special degree in Norway and its dominions 'west-over-sea', the creation of the definitive medieval church order was predominantly an achievement of the twelfth century. In 1104 the Birsay bishopric acquired a more appropriate constitutional position (than that contested between York and Bremen) within a Scandinavian province of Lund (itself then in Denmark) and in 1154 was included in an explicitly Norwegian province of five 'mainland' and six 'island' dioceses under an archbishop of Nidaros or Trondheim (Cant 1974: 4).

The bishop of Orkney and Shetland throughout the greater part of this period was William, later to be known as 'the old' to distinguish him from a successor of the same name but justifiably so called when he died at a great age in 1168. Almost certainly an Orcadian, he probably owed his appointment (c.1112)[4] to King Sigurd 'the Crusader' who had acted as virtual governor of Orkney and Shetland for his father Magnus 'Barelegs' before he succeeded him on the Norwegian throne from 1103 to 1130. And although in Orkney conflict between rival claimants to the earldom continued throughout most of Bishop William's tenure of the see, he contrived to maintain his authority and can probably be credited with most of the changes effected in the organisation of the diocese at this time.

His initial task was likely to have been the enlargement of his 'episcopal minsters' at Birsay and St Ninian's Isle. In the former case this work was supplemented, on the north, by a residential building with direct access to the church. Sometimes identified as 'the bishop's palace', it may

---

4. See the elucidation of the complicated situation regarding the episcopal succession in this period in Watt 1969: 248-9.

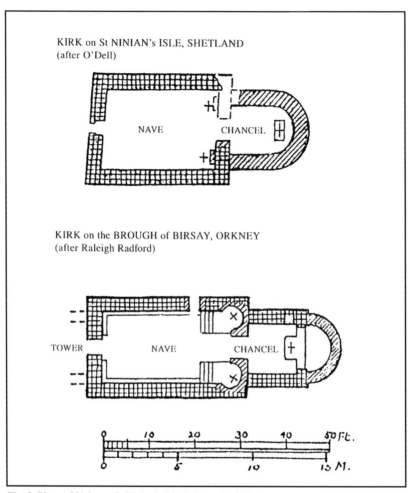

Fig. 2. Plans of kirks on St Ninian's Isle & Brough of Birsay.

well have been so, but it is also likely to have housed the additional clergy (perhaps Benedictines or Augustinians)[5] associated with the minster, and one might expect similar provision at its Shetland counterpart (Cant 1993: 13).

Another Orkney ecclesiastical structure of this period is a fragment of the 'round church' at Orphir, a remarkable creation planned to serve a parochial purpose but otherwise unrepresentative of parochial design of this

---

5. Precise information regarding 'regular clergy' in the Orkney diocese in the medieval period is singularly lacking, but these seem to have been the preferred orders in other island dioceses.

period.[6] More typical, and forming a link with its Shetland counterparts, is the Cross Kirk of Tuquoy, Westray, adjacent to the home of one of the island's principal landholders and quite possibly originating as a 'domestic chapel' for his family and dependants, subsequently enlarged to become one of the two parish churches of Westray (Cant 1993: 15).

In its first form the church was about half the size of Earl Thorfinn's minster and of rougher masonry, but the little chancel was covered by a barrel-vault and linked to the nave by a well-formed arch on inclined jambs characteristic of Irish romanesque work c.1100. While this might perhaps have been introduced when the nave was lengthened for parochial use (c.1130) it is at least conceivable that the original structure might date from the period following Bishop Thorolf's arrival with missionaries assigned for just such a purpose.

The design of Tuquoy church may also have a relevance for Shetland in that the chancel of St Mary's, Sand, in the west mainland, is of similar form, rougher but on a larger scale, the nave 9.5 x 4.5m, the chancel 4.0 x 2.3m. Although often described as a 'chapel' in modern usage, it was in fact the 'head church' of Sandsting, an area associated with a *thing* or regional assembly and law-court in the government of the islands. This in turn had been derived from the way in which the Norse settlements had been effected and developed thereafter (Cant 1984: 69-70).

At the north-east corner of the Shetland archipelago is the sizeable and well-provided island of Unst, likely to have been the Northmen's first landfall and, with the adjacent islands of Yell and Fetlar, the most probable location of the initial settlements. As was observed by Professor O'Dell in his pioneer study of the islands (O'Dell 1939: 264), this area is notable for the number of its *scattalds*, manageable groupings of adjacent settlements forming the basis of social, economic and 'governmental' organisation. In Unst there were twenty-four within which fourteen church or chapel sites have been identified. In Fetlar there were nine, each with a chapel, and at Papil a 'head' or 'parish' church. In Shetland as a whole there might have been some two hundred, in two-thirds of which structural vestiges remain to this day.

While the 'Papil' sites had clear associations with the earliest Christian worship, it is only at St Ninian's Isle that a building of pastoral character has been identified. Some of the others might conceivably be attributed to the period of Bishop Thorolf, but most to that of Bishop William. Many of them may have had a limited existence unless they achieved the status of parish churches (*sognekirker*) maintained by tithes or teinds (*tiundar*) drawn annually from an associated parish (*sogn*).

---

6. Formerly thought to have been built by Earl Håkon on the model of the church of the Holy Sepulchre in Jerusalem on his return from a pilgrimage there in 1120, it may in fact have been derived from Scandinavian prototypes. See Fisher 1993: 375-387.

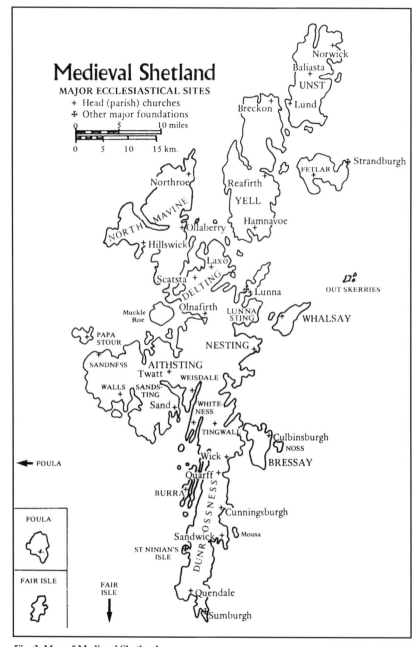

Medieval Shetland

MAJOR ECCLESIASTICAL SITES

+ Head (parish) churches
⊹ Other major foundations

0   5   10 miles

0   5   10   15 km.

Norwick
Baliasta
UNST
Breckon Lund
Strandburgh
FETLAR
Northroe Reafirth
YELL
Hamnavoe
Ollaberry
Hillswick
Laxo
Scatsta
DELTING
Lunna
OUT SKERRIES
Olnafirth LUNNA STING
Muckle Roe WHALSAY
PAPA STOUR
NESTING
SANDNESS AITHSTING
Twatt WEISDALE
WALLS SANDS TING
Sand WHITE-NESS
TINGWALL
Culbinsburgh
NOSS
FOULA
Wick BRESSAY
Quarff
BURRA
Cunningsburgh
FOULA
Sandwick Mousa
ST NINIAN'S ISLE
FAIR ISLE
FAIR ISLE
Quendale
Sumburgh

NORTH MAVINE

DUNROSSNESS

Fig. 3. Map of Medieval Shetland.

Shetland churches and chapels (NE)

St Mary's Sand might well be the earliest head church in Shetland, for although the settlement in which it was located, in the west mainland, might be of later origin than those in the north-east islands, it had closer links with Orkney (continued into recent times) through the latter's north-west islands of Westray and Papa Westray by way of St Ninian's Isle and Burra. In examining the churches of Shetland as a whole, however, it may be most convenient to begin with Unst and proceed thence west and south to Dunrossness and Fair Isle.

As it so happens, Unst provides a representative introduction to the local church organisation of Shetland in that its single parish priest (*sogneprest*) was in charge of three churches grouped in a priest's district (*prestegjeld*) coterminous with the area of a *thing* (regional assembly and law-court) probably already in existence throughout the islands. In Unst these churches were respectively at Norwick for the north, Baliasta for the middle, and Lund for the south. While one might have expected the head-church (*hovedkirke*) and manse (*prestegård*) to be in the most central location at Baliasta, they seem to have been at Norwick.[7] Eleven local chapels have also been identified — one on the adjacent island of Uyea. Of surviving structures St Olaf's church at Lundawick is the most complete, of simple rectangular plan c.12.5 x 4.5m entered by a round-headed west door but perhaps originally of similar form to St John's Norwick with its nave of 8.0 x 4.0m and chancel 5.0 x 2.5m. The Uyea chapel has a nave c.4.6 x 3.5m originally linked to a chancel c.3.0m square by an arch with inclined jambs no more than 0.61m wide (R.C.A.H.M.S. *Shetland*: Nos. 1541, 1536, 1598).

Like Unst, the priest's district of Yell was a 'thing district' with three parish churches — at Breckon for the north, Reafirth for the middle (also the head church) and Hamnavoe for the south, also sixteen chapels — of all of which little remains. By great good fortune, however, St Olaf's Breckon was recorded by Sir Henry Dryden in 1856 when still largely intact (R.C.A.H.M.S. *Shetland*: No. 1712). He shows a nave c.5.8 x 4.1m within and a chancel 3.1 x 3.0m entered by a round-headed arch of identical width like St Mary's Sand but with vertical jambs. In the south wall is a *sedile* for the priest.[8] In Fetlar, with a head church and perhaps ten chapels (Crawford 1987: fig. 68) parish and priest's district, also 'thing district', were one and the same. Disappointingly, however, it retains little of architectural character except possibly parts of the north wall of the church at Papil.

---

7. The likelihood is that the church at Norwick had been established first and was able to maintain its 'primacy' in the later 'definitive organisation' of the diocese. A similar situation may well have prevailed in the cases of Hillswick (Northmavine) and Quendale (Dunrossness).

8. See more detailed description (derived from Sir Henry Dryden) in MacGibbon and Ross 1896-7: I, 151-7.

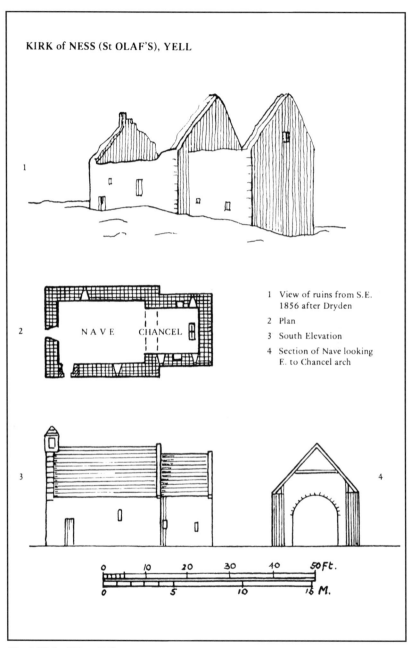

KIRK of NESS (St OLAF'S), YELL

1   View of ruins from S.E.
    1856 after Dryden

2   Plan

3   South Elevation

4   Section of Nave looking
    E. to Chancel arch

NAVE   CHANCEL

0   10   20   30   40   50 Ft.

0   5   10   15 M.

Fig. 4. Kirk of Ness, Yell.

167

In the mainland, the whole peninsula north of Mavis Grind formed the 'thing area' and 'priest's district' of Northmavine, comprising three churches at North Roe, Ollaberry, and Hillswick (the head church, St Gregory's). There were also five chapels and an 'aamos kirk' (pilgrimage church, to be discussed later) but of the others hardly a vestige remains. South of Mavis Grind the area and district of Delting (Dalething) is almost more disappointing. While there is a graveyard at Dale, latterly at least the head church seems to have been at Scatsta (St Paul's) with another church at Laxobigging, both reduced to mere sites. Thus it is only at Olnafirth, within the ruin of its eighteenth century successor, that evidence might be forthcoming of the character of a parish church of Delting. There were also four possible chapel sites on the mainland and one more on the isle of Samphrey in Yell Sound.

To the south-east of Delting are Lunnasting and Nesting — as their names indicate, 'thing areas' and in the medieval period separate priests' districts. The first had a head church now of particular interest as the only example of a (partly) medieval structure still in use, also two chapels. The Nesting district, with its head church and manse in a remarkably bleak situation at Kirkabister, also contained a second parish embracing the large island of Whalsay and the Skerries beyond, its church at Kirkaness. There were two chapels on the mainland and four more on the islands, that on the Inner Holm of Skaw with ruins of some extent. Further examination of these two churches might be worthwhile.

Shetland churches and chapels (SW)

Moving to the western mainland, it has already been noted that St Mary's church at Sand was one of the earliest of its kind in Shetland. The title of the area it served, 'Sandsting', and that of its northern neighbour 'Aithsting', together with other evidence regarding their clergy, indicate that in the medieval period (like Lunnasting) they ranked as priests' districts with two or three chapels respectively. By contrast, their western neighbour — of Walls and Sandness — had as arduous responsibilities as any in Shetland, the priest of its head church of St Paul and its five parochial chapels being also responsible for the parish church (and a chapel) at Sandness, together with the church on Papa Stour and another (with a chapel) on Foula. Further careful examination of these two churches might be worthwhile.

While there are vestiges of some of these buildings, those most likely to contain work of medieval provenance might be the island churches of Papa Stour and Foula. While it is known that the former was re-built in 1807, it stands in the medieval kirkyard and, like Baliasta church in Unst when it was enlarged for more general use in 1764, might have incorporated the north wall and gables of its medieval predecessor. On Foula the structure in the old kirkyard at Hametoun, though lacking details for precise dating, has a form and character consistent with a medieval origin.

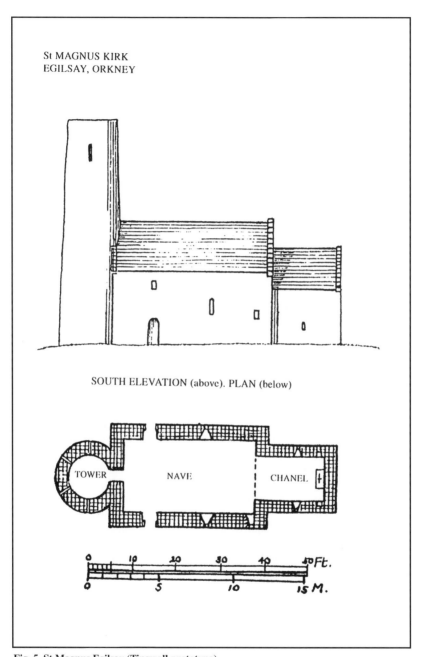

St MAGNUS KIRK
EGILSAY, ORKNEY

SOUTH ELEVATION (above). PLAN (below)

TOWER   NAVE   CHANEL

Fig. 5. St Magnus Egilsay (Tingwall prototype).

169

On an elevated central site on the mainland appropriate to its status was the head church of Tingwall (meeting place of the *Lagthing* — supreme court and legislative assembly for the whole of Shetland) which was the largest and most impressive of the medieval period here. Dedicated to St Magnus, its design was clearly inspired by that of the church erected to his memory (probably about 1136) on the island of Egilsay in Orkney.[9] But while this, despite its prestige, held no place in the administrative structure of the diocese, the church of Tingwall was not only the head church of its district but of the whole island group through its association with the Archdeacon of Shetland. In the medieval church order this functionary was the administrative deputy of the bishop, and in a large diocese there might be more than one, each in charge of a particular area. As might be expected, this came to be the case in Orkney and Shetland, and although there is no mention of an Archdeacon of Shetland until 1215 — and of Orkney even later — they were almost certainly envisaged in the constitution of the Norwegian church in 1154 and, in Shetland, quite possibly introduced by Bishop William.

In design the church on Egilsay (Fernie 1988) comprised a chancel, nave, and cylindrical western tower, as did that of Tingwall, but on an appreciably larger scale, its nave 15.0 x 5.5m compared with 9.2 x 4.7m. The building actually survived until 1788 when it was replaced by the present structure (Cant 1993: 18). Of its associated churches of Weisdale and Whiteness some foundations survive, also of a chapel at Kebister and another on the isle of Trondra, but of the other five no more than possible sites.

The early centre of Papil on West Burra, location (until 1804) of a 'round-towered' parish church of lesser scale,[10] has now no structure above ground save the ruin of its successor. After the Reformation the parish was linked with that of Bressay in a single 'ministry', an odd arrangement sustained by a 'portage' over the mainland and an associated chapel (one of six such) at Easter Quarff. In the medieval period, however, they seem to have been separate charges. On Bressay the church at Cullingsburgh is of cruciform plan but the 'transepts' date from the seventeenth century (Cant 1978: 24). Of the two chapels — and a third on Noss — little remains, though what might be part of a 'round tower' was discovered near the last in 1994.

South of Quarff the rest of the mainland, and its associated islands, constituted the district of Dunrossness. Comprising three parishes, its head church was the southmost, awkwardly sited near the sea-shore at Quendale, where it was overwhelmed by a sandstorm in the seventeenth century. The two other churches were at Cunningsburgh (for the north) and Sandwick (for the centre) and there also seem to have been nine chapels (one on Fair Isle).

---

9. See Fernie 1998 and Cant 1993: 17-18.

10. So it would seem, though Edmondston 1809: i, 124 speaks of both towers as being 'of hewn stone, between sixty and seventy feet high' — comparable to that of Egilsay when complete (Fernie 1988: 147).

Initially, too, there would be the 'episcopal minster' on St Ninian's Isle, probably of a monastic character and perhaps in being for a relatively short period. On the adjacent coast, at Ireland, was an isolated 'round tower' — of indeterminate function.

In sum, then, the ecclesiastical establishment of Shetland as completed would seem to have comprised fourteen priests' districts, six of these coterminous with a single parish. The others, between them, had twenty-four, making a total of thirty. There may also have been ninety chapels, not all in existence at the same time.

Later developments

By the close of the twelfth century most of the organisation and related structures discussed in the two preceding sections was probably in existence, and one might have expected the ensuing period to be one of consolidation. In a sense this was so, but it was also marked by a departure from some of the basic principles of the new church order as embodied in the Gulathing law-code. In particular, it provided that the tithes or *teinds* — in theory one tenth of the annual 'produce' of each parish — should be divided between the bishop, the priest, the church, and the poor (Kolsrud 1958: 182). At an early stage, however, they began to be claimed by what might be termed the 'ecclesiastical superstructure' — of diocesan and cathedral functionaries.

Principal among these was the Archdeacon of Shetland, first mentioned in 1215 and primarily responsible, under the bishop, for supervision of the parochial clergy of that area. This being so, one might have expected provision to be made for him by an allocation of part of the bishop's share of the teinds. There was, however, a further complication when Bishop Bjarne (1188 x 1192 — 1223), following the example of Bergen, appointed the sole archdeacon of that period, Andrew of Shetland, to preside over the chapter of 'secular canons' by then contemplated for Kirkwall Cathedral instead of the one of monastic character previously envisaged and continued as such despite the emergence of an archdeacon of Orkney c.1309 (Watt 1969: 254-5). Even so, his possession of extensive lands and rentals (in Tingwall in particular) might have provided adequate support for most of his activities.

By 1327-28, however, it becomes clear that provision for 'the canons and prebendaries', previously based, to some extent at least, on *stouks* or land-rentals (Clouston 1926), was now derived, to a great and increasing degree, from the 'appropriation' of parochial teinds (Andersen 1988: 61; Cant 1995a: esp. 108-9). In the case of Shetland, however, it can at least be said that this trend was virtually limited to Tingwall, Whiteness, and Weisdale, assigned to the archdeacon, and one half of the corn teinds of the other parishes (three quarters in the case of Fetlar) to the bishop. The process was doubtless accelerated with the appearance of Scotsmen in possession of both archdeaconries in 1369-72. Thus a century before the diocese of Orkney and Shetland passed to the Scottish Church in 1472 — following the 'pledging' of the civil government to the Scottish monarchy in 1468-69 — every parish had become a *vicarage* retaining only a fraction of its pristine endowment.

During this same period certain developments become apparent in the architectural form of churches and chapels. Hitherto generally of two distinct components (nave and chancel) they now tended to be of a simple rectangular plan. In two cases the buildings were of late date and non-parochial character. The earlier was probably the pilgrimage church of the Holy Cross ('Cross Kirk') at Breckon (Eshaness) Northmavine, some 8.6m x 4.4m in internal dimensions. The other was the collegiate church of Dunrossness, a 'corporate chantry' of the Sinclair family maintained by *stouks* elsewhere in Shetland, perhaps represented by parts of 'the Old House of Sumburgh' at Jarlshof (R.C.A.H.M.S. *Shetland*: No. 1139). Most interesting of all is the parish church of Lunna, a rectangular structure 20.6 x 10.3m within, much altered but retaining parts of the medieval fabric, especially in the massively buttressed south wall. Towards its east end this is pierced by a *squint*, not for lepers but, as in many churches, to enable the priest to supervise the altar from an adjacent sacristy.

At Lunna, being a 'head church', the sacristy would probably lead on to the *prestegård* or manse, this likely to have been a single-storeyed structure but with a *lopt* or loft like that mentioned in a transaction at Sandwick (Unst) in 1328 (Clouston 1912: 14). The group might also include matching farm buildings for the *glebe* or land-holding to which every parish priest was entitled. At other parish churches, at a distance from the head church and manse, overnight accommodation might be provided in a loft within the building. And in connection with these journeys it is important to remember that most of them were likely to be voyages — sometimes involving portages — in the sea-bound environment of Shetland.

Epilogue

Between 1985 and 1987, at Kebister on the east coast of Tingwall parish, a structure was excavated that, from its location and the high quality of its masonry — including a fine carved panel depicting what proved to be the arms of Henry Phancouth, Archdeacon of Shetland 1501-29 — suggested that it might be his official residence. In the outcome, however, it turned out to be a 'teind barn' for the reception and storage of 'payments in kind' of tithes and rents to the archdeaconry, perhaps also to the bishopric (Owen and Smith 1988: 1-20).

Its design and construction — very probably by masons associated with the cathedral of which the archdeacon was the presiding officer (Fawcett, R. in Owen and Smith 1988: 7-10) — are in marked contrast to the buildings discussed in this survey, but it must be emphasised that, for all their austerity, they were commissioned by men well versed in contemporary architectural design and built by others reproducing from the resources of their rugged homeland buildings of the same essential form and character.

Bibliography

Andersen, P.A., 1988: 'The Orkney Church of the Twelfth and Thirteenth Centuries'. In: Barbara Crawford (ed.), 56-71.

Batey, C.E., Jesch, J. and Morris, C.D. (eds.), 1993: *The Viking Age in Caithness, Orkney and the North Atlantic*. Edinburgh.

Berg, Arne, et al. (eds.), 1993: *Kirkearkeologi og Kirkekunst* (Studies in honour of Sigurd and Håkon Christie). Ovre Ervik, Norway.

Cant, R.G., 1972: 'The Church in Orkney and Shetland and its relations with Norway and Scotland in the Middle Ages'. *Northern Scotland* I, 1, 1-18. Aberdeen.

Cant, R.G., 1976: *The Medieval Churches and Chapels of Shetland*. Lerwick.

Cant, R.G., 1984: 'Settlement, Society and Church Organisation in the Northern Isles'. In: Fenton, A. and Pálsson, H. (eds.), *The Northern and Western Isles in the Viking World*, Edinburgh, 169-179.

Cant, R.G., 1986: 'The Medieval Church in the North'. In: Baldwin, J.R. (ed.), *Firthlands of Ross and Sutherland*, Edinburgh, 47-58.

Cant, R.G., 1993: 'Early Church Design in Orkney and Shetland (c.1050-1200)'. In: Berg, Arne *et al.*, (eds.), 1-17.

Cant, R.G., 1995: 'The Constitution of Saint Magnus Cathedral'. In: Crawford, B.E. (ed.), 105-121.

Clouston, J.S. (ed.), 1914: *Records of the Earldom of Orkney*. Scottish History Society, 2nd Series, VII. Edinburgh.

Clouston, J.S. 1926: 'The Old Prebends of Orkney', *Proceedings of the Orkney Antiquarian Society* 4, 31-6.

Crawford, B.E., 1987: *Scandinavian Scotland*. Leicester.

Crawford, B.E. (ed.), 1988: *St Magnus Cathedral and Orkney's Twelfth Century Renaissance*, Aberdeen.

Crawford, B.E. (ed.), 1995: *Northern Isles Connections* (Essays from Orkney and Shetland presented to Per Sveaas Andersen), Kirkwall.

Edmondston, A., 1809: *Historical Antiquities of the Shetland Islands*. 2 Vols. Edinburgh.

Fernie, E., 1988: 'The Church of St Magnus, Egilsay'. In: Crawford, B.E. (ed.), 146-161.

Fisher, I., 1993: 'Orphir Church in its South Scandinavian Context'. In: Batey, C.E. *et al.* (eds.), 375-380.

Goudie, G., 1904: *The Celtic and Scandinavian Antiquities of Shetland*. Edinburgh.

Kolsrud, O., 1958: *Noregs Kyrkjesoga* I: *Millomalderen*. Oslo.

Lamb, R.G., 1972-74: 'The Cathedral of Christchurch and the Monastery of Birsay'. *Proceedings of the Society of Antiquaries of Scotland* 105, Edinburgh, 200- 205.

Lamb, R.G., 1974: 'Coastal Settlements of the North'. *Scottish Archaeological Forum* 5, Edinburgh, 76-98.

Lamb, R.G., 1995: 'Papil, Picts, and Papar'. In: Crawford, B.E. (ed.), 9-27.

MacGibbon, D. and Ross, T., 1896-7: *Ecclesiastical Architecture of Scotland*. Vol. 1, especially sections relating to work of Muir, T.S. (pp.65-100) and Sir Henry Dryden (pp.101-173). Edinburgh.

O'Dell, A.C., 1939: *The Historical Geography of the Shetland Islands*. Lerwick.

Owen, O. and Smith, B., 1988: 'Kebister, Shetland: an armorial stone and an archdeacon's teind barn'. *Post-medieval Archaeology* 22, 1-20.

Radford, C.A.R., 1964: 'Art and Architecture, Celtic and Norse'. In: Wainwright, F.T., 183-7.

R.C.A.H.M.S., 1946: Royal Commission on the Ancient and Historical Monuments of Scotland, *Inventory of the Ancient Monuments of Orkney and Shetland*. 3 Vols.: II, Orkney; III, Shetland.

Sibbald, Sir Robert (ed.), 1845: *Description of the Isles of Orkney and Zetland* (reprint of original 1711 edition). Edinburgh.

Small, A., Thomas, C. and Wilson, D.M., 1956: *St Ninian's Isle and its Treasure*. 2 Vols., especially Vol I, pt.ii. Aberdeen University Studies 152. Oxford.

Wainwright, F.T. (ed. and contrib.), 1962: *The Northern Isles*. Edinburgh.

Watt, D.E.R., 1969: *Fasti Ecclesiae Scoticanae Medii Aevi*. 2nd draft. St Andrews.

173

EARL WILLIAM TO EARL PATRICK: A SURVEY OF THE HISTORY OF ORKNEY AND SHETLAND FROM 1468 TO 1615

Peter Anderson

It is difficult to avoid the word 'transition' when speaking of the period from 1468 to 1615. It is an era which really does seem, at least at first sight, to have a genuine beginning and end. Things are different before and after. There are crises at the start, and at the finish. In the period 1468 to 1472 first the Norwegian royal lands, then those of the Sinclair earldom, and finally those of the bishopric, come to have a Scottish allegiance. At the end of the period 1610-1615 the second Stewart earl is dead, the earldom itself is dead and buried, the castle of Kirkwall — its centre since the late 14th century — has been reduced to rubble, the law has become Scots Law, the royal and bishopric lands have been completely reorganised, and the former have been erected into a stewartry under the crown, which is to exercise for many years thereafter a much stronger control than had ever been possible in the fifteenth and sixteenth centuries.

What happened in between? Was there some identifiable process leading inexorably from the circumstances of 1468 to those of 1615? What is the story — what are the main themes — of the period? The era is one packed with incident, and in such circumstances the search for some all-embracing motive force might find only something so broad as to be meaningless, but it is possible to look for real elements of continuity and evolution. Such as? One is the efforts of the Scottish crown to find some appropriate way of governing Orkney and Shetland. Another is attempts by forces, within the islands and without, to counter the crown's intentions in order to bring power to themselves. The forces involved in these two processes interact, sometimes murderously, with each other; and the whole culminates in the Stewart earldom, its rise and utter collapse. In both cases events become turbulent and complicated, sometimes tediously so; but behind all the mayhem I believe there is a detectable consistency of approach to the peculiar circumstances of time and place.

One might also suggest another theme — the 'Scottification' (Clouston's pejorative term - 1932: 292) of the Northern Isles. In institutional terms the existence of this is difficult to deny. However it could be argued that Scottification, or Scotticisation, had been in progress for centuries before, at least since the succession of Scottish families to the earldom. The same could be said for the political drift of the islands from Norwegian to Scottish hands — that the events of 1468-72 were not a 'crisis' at all, but merely the recognition of a process which had been going on apace. And the 'crisis' of 1610-15 was brought about, not by a sudden Scottish desire for uniformity within the realm — though the notion certainly appealed to James VI — but by the embarrassing and unpardonable behaviour of one man — Earl Patrick. I believe that the period did begin and end with a crisis; that we can trace themes which lead us from the first to the last; and that Scotticisation was a necessary consequence of events. It was natural, and accepted, that the problems of the period should be addressed in a Scottish way.

Let us look first at attempts to govern Orkney and Shetland from Edinburgh. It is clear from the first that the Scots were not unaware of the problems which the Norwegians and Danes had experienced in their time. As Barbara Crawford points out, 'the main theme running through the history of the earldom of Orkney is of the theoretical claims to control by the kings of Norway and the *de facto* independence which the earls seem normally to have possessed' (Crawford 1985: 233). James II and James III were clearly determined that they would not be as powerless as the Danish king had been in the face of William Sinclair's continued refusal to do him homage. William had moreover made a thorough nuisance of himself in Scotland during the attempts by James II to confer with Denmark on the questions of the Annual of Norway and the Northern Isles, and it was clearly felt necessary to curtail, as far as possible, his power with regard to the islands. He was forced to part with his earldom of Orkney, whose lands were then added to the holdings of the kings of Scots as part of the *pro rege* lands (Crawford 1976: 158-167; 1985: 233-9). William Sinclair had already made remarkable preparations to offset this and the prices he exacted were not inconsiderable. The whole story demonstrates the remarkable tenacity of the Sinclair family as a whole in maintaining their position in the islands for seventy years after they ceased to be earls. In particular I shall return presently to the question of earl William's 'conquest lands' — the lands which he and his illegitimate son Sir David Sinclair of Sumburgh acquired independently of the earldom, buying them up from the udal proprietors. These were themselves to form a theme running through much of our period.

The Scottish answer to the problem of who should represent the crown in Orkney and Shetland also shows a consciousness of what had been done before — namely the employment of the bishops. About 1420, Erik of Pomerania had used Thomas Tulloch as his representative in an attempt to put the young William Sinclair in his place; now William Tulloch and then Andrew Pictoris were employed as tacksmen of the *pro rege* lands (Crawford 1976: 159; Anderson 1982: 18-20). And the bishops did more than draw the revenues. The curtain walls of Kirkwall castle, added in the 15th century to the original tower house probably erected by the first Sinclair earl, are said to have borne a stone with arms including a mitre (Barry 1805: 228).

This ascendancy of the bishops was of short duration. The death of William Sinclair and the transfer of Bishop William Tulloch to the see of Moray opened the way for a confrontation — between William Sinclair's grandson Henry, Lord Sinclair, and Bishop Andrew Pictoris. Both were extremely able and noteworthy men. Henry Sinclair's reputation as man of

175

affairs, scholar and soldier, is well-known. Andrew Pictoris (or Schindeler, or Maler, or Dr Andreas) was a fascinating character, who was 'in the forefront ... of James [III]'s supporters during the flash-points of that interesting monarch's career' (Smith 1989). For that reason Henry Sinclair's attempts to achieve power for himself, beginning in the mid 1480s, did not become fully effective until after the king's death ten years later; and even then they were not unconditional.

The picture seems to be that of two royal servants fighting for the royal favour in respect of the 'lordships' (*dominiorum*) of Orkney and Shetland. Henry's interest in these is first noted in the exchequer return of 1484. Significantly, this is the period of James's recovery from his worsting at the hands of the duke of Albany. Admission to the revenues of Orkney and Shetland may have been one of the prices the king felt he had to pay for Henry Sinclair's support. In 1485 Henry's title is effectively described as a subtack from Bishop Andrew, but there then followed a period where the exchequer records are silent as to who is in control. The king, stronger again, may have changed his mind. Henry Sinclair did not finally become tacksman in his own right until May 1489, and even then there are several reasons to suppose that the government of James IV was no more enthusiastic than its predecessor about the advance of the Sinclairs in the Northern Isles.

In 1486, shortly after Henry's first appearance in the exchequer records, Kirkwall was erected into a royal burgh — *blenche ferme*, and with the most unusual grant of the cathedral building, a decision whose effects are still felt today. In 1490 the bishopric was erected into a regality, and five years later bishop Andrew and his successors received the island of Burray and a number of skats formerly due to the earl. This grant was ratified by the king on his declaring himself of perfect age in 1498 and specifically excluded from the earldom lands in the renewal of Henry Sinclair's tack in 1501 and other renewals thereafter. Henry Sinclair's tack of 1489 was for thirteen years, a length of time which suggests the final confirmation of a conventional 19-year tack which had come into effect six years before. It was hedged round with the threat of alternative tacks to the earl of Bothwell, his brother-in-law, and John Hepburn, prior of St Andrews, Bothwell's uncle.

When I first examined this episode in my book *Robert Stewart* (Anderson 1982: 20-1), I took the view that Henry Sinclair had got more-or-less everything he wanted, and the concessions to burgh and bishopric were forlorn attempts by the crown to save something from the wreckage. The rediscovery of Bishop Andrew has forced me to modify this view. The charter of regality makes specific mention of Andrew's service to the king's parents, and he received royal gifts at the same time. Moreover Henry Sinclair was never able to reclaim the skats and rents the bishop had taken from the earldom. Bishop Andrew, for his part, felt safe enough to travel to Europe in 1494 (Smith 1989: 96).

The rivalry between Lord Henry and Bishop Andrew took another form in Shetland. This was the struggle between their respective illegitimate sons, Sir David Sinclair of Sumburgh and Henry Phankouth, archdeacon of Shetland, over the presentation of the latter's successor in office. Sir David Sinclair may well have typified everything that the kings of Scots were seeking to avoid in their governance of the Northern Isles. Like his father, Sir David had been the servant of two masters, the monarchs of Scotland and Denmark, and in the dispute he was probably backed by the king of Denmark. He presented his friend Magnus Harwood to the benefice. James IV sent stern letters to all concerned, confirmed the aged Andrew's charter of regality, and appointed a younger man, Edward Stewart, to take on the practical duties of the see. James was however careful not to overset the balance which had been achieved between Sinclair power in the north and he avoided too obvious a support for the bishop's regality jurisdiction (Smith 1989: 97-8). The old bishop's young understudy did not remain in the north for long after Pictoris died — probably about 1505 — though his arms were placed on Mons Bellus, the bishop's palace which was built at Birsay around this time (Anderson 1982: 73). For ten years or so thereafter there seems to have been relatively little friction between the bishopric and the tacksman. Henry Sinclair spent the last ten years of his life restoring islands devastated by famine (Thomson 1984).

Lord Henry Sinclair was killed at Flodden. From then until 1541, a period of almost thirty years, the tack of the *pro rege* lands remained in the Sinclair family in the person of Margaret Hepburn, Lord Henry's widow. The question of who drew the revenues and exercised the accompanying jurisdiction during these years is however more complicated and the family story is one of internecine strife between the Northern Isles and Caithness branches, culminating in the death of the earl of Caithness at the battle of Summerdale in 1529. This unrest came to an end with the brief emergence of Oliver Sinclair of Pitcairns, the last member of the family to enjoy anything like the old powers in Orkney and Shetland. His power was also leasehold, and it was short-lived, but he provides a definite link between the Sinclairs and the new Scottish families that were to appear in Orkney and Shetland. He represented the Ravenscraig/Roslin branch of the family, and as such was closely related to both sides at Summerdale. He was cousin to the late earl of Caithness, and to Henry and Sir William Sinclair.

Oliver Sinclair sought control of the tack — at first through the rehabilitation of the victor of the battle, James Sinclair of Brecks, and latterly in person. In June 1535 Sinclair of Brecks was legitimated, knighted, and received his rather curious charter of the islands of Sanday and Stronsay. He committed suicide barely a year later, but Oliver maintained support for his side in the dispute. In 1539 Brecks's chief companions at Summerdale were granted a respite, and when Oliver became tacksman one of these, James Sinclair's brother, Edward Sinclair of Strom, was one of his deputes. Just as in the case of Lord Henry's tack, the crown was favouring the Sinclairs purely as one element in a balanced system within the islands.

The rehabilitation of the Summerdale victors was not unconditional. Lady Sinclair had her tack renewed in 1536, the same year Kirkwall's status as a royal burgh was confirmed, and there was a grant in feudal form to James Irving of Sabay. And in 1540 an able bishop, Robert Reid, was appointed to the see of Orkney. James Sinclair's suicide however probably served as an invitation for Oliver Sinclair to become involved on his own account, though he did not become tacksman till 1541, after he had visited Orkney with the king. His ascendancy was short-lived; he fell with the humiliation at Solway Moss in 1542 and James V's subsequent death. But his appointment was significant in two ways. He was the first sheriff, as opposed to lawman or foud, and he was expected to pay a much more realistic tack duty for his privileges; 3000 merks was more than four times what his predecessors had paid, and a great deal more than the £1000 given as the value in the jointure of James V's first queen, Madeleine de Valois (Anderson 1982: 24-31). It also seems highly probably that he compiled the first estimate of the money income from Orkney and Shetland. This was given as £9750 per annum for Orkney, and £4210 for Shetland, indicating that from a royal point of view the earlier duties had indeed been modest. This total is just short of 21,000 merks, of which Oliver's duty would be one seventh (*ER*, xxi: 325-7).

Oliver Sinclair did not however profit from this arrangement. There now followed probably the most successful time of central rule in Orkney and Shetland during the whole of the period. From 1542 till about 1558, the royal and earldom lands — and probably the conquest lands as well — were ruled directly in the name of James V's widow Mary of Guise, who inherited them as her portion. Her governor, the obscure M. Bonot, received possession of Kirkwall Castle in 1543; he was still in control sixteen years or so later (Anderson 1982: 31). Though this period was a troubled one in Orkney and Shetland as a result of English and Highland invasions, it seems to have been administratively uneventful. It was brought to an end by the deaths of Robert Reid and the regent herself, and the scene was set for radical change.

For the years 1560-5, from the death of Mary of Guise to the first appearance of Robert Stewart, the revenues of the lands went directly to the crown. It was now in the bishopric that major changes in landholding in the north took place. Bishop Bothwell, under strong pressure from his relatives Gilbert Balfour of Westray and Sir John Bellenden of Auchnoull, feued off large chunks of the bishopric estates, both to them and to some lesser fry, including Sir John Bellenden's own brother Patrick. Adam Bothwell was the nephew of one Bellenden justice clerk, and the cousin of another. He was also stepson of Oliver Sinclair, the former tacksman. Both John Bellenden and Oliver Sinclair were major vassals of the commendator of Holyrood, Lord Robert Stewart. It is this Sinclair-Bellenden-Bothwell-Stewart connection which leads us from the Sinclairs, through their eclipse during the years of

178

Mary of Guise, to the Stewarts (Anderson 1982: 29-41). The Sinclairs were a spent force, though they still had one or two minor cards to play.

Robert Stewart first received a feu of the lands of Orkney and Shetland in December 1564, and he clearly felt that he would imminently be created earl. The royal favour had however been bought by subservience to Darnley, and the queen's disgust at her husband had its corresponding penalties for her brother. Robert was forced, in the aftermath of his sister's fall in 1567, to go to the north to seek to enforce his grant. In due course he realised his earldom ambition, but he had a far from restful career. Robert Stewart destroyed a Scottish policy with regard to the Northern Isles which was not to be resurrected for over 70 years. The 1472 annexation of the earldom and lordship had included a proviso that they were not to be alienated except to legitimate royal offspring, and since that time they had been treated as leasehold estates and as a widow's portion. Robert acquired them as a feu.

In the past there has been some indignation expressed at this apparent contravention of an act of parliament, that of 1567, by the privy council. This is a somewhat legalistic viewpoint. Parliament was free to object to the ignoring of its wishes; and anyone familiar with Scottish acts of parliament knows that they may be re-enacted again and again to keep them from desuetude. Robert himself may not have been legitimate, and his character may have left something to be desired, but he was of the blood royal. Moreover the acceptance of his right to a feu indicates a greater confidence on the part of the Scottish crown regarding its power in the islands — on the one hand its right to alienate what was undoubtedly a royal possession; on the other the assurance that the feuar had only one undoubted master, the king of Scots. Whether this confidence was justified is another matter, and it is noteworthy that among the allegations against Robert in 1575 was the charge that he had done homage to the king of Denmark — precisely the kind of thing that the old policy was designed to avoid (Anderson 1982: 84-5). But it is more important to ask whether this allegation was taken seriously. Robert certainly did try to open some sort of negotiation, but the Danes themselves were lukewarm. In fact, although Robert faced much opposition in his time, the charges against him were almost always about misrule. There was never any serious suggestion that the feu should be rescinded or, after 1581, the earldom abolished.

For Robert's first seven years or so in Orkney and Shetland, affairs in the south were too turbulent to interfere with his activities in the north. It was not until the regency of the earl of Morton that the voices of his enemies — in particular the Bellendens — were heard, and he was compelled to come south where he spent two years in ward, in Edinburgh and Linlithgow. The fall of Morton and the emergence of the young king as a force in his own right brought a recovery in Robert's fortunes and his advancement, nearly seventeen years after his first appearance on the scene, to a resurrected earldom of Orkney and lordship of Shetland. Only six years later however,

179

the Bellendens again found the ear of the central authorities. Robert was effectively removed from the earldom, replaced by his son, and forced to part with large sums of money (Anderson 1982: 112-117; 1992: 18-21).

What lay behind this? To discuss the aims of the Stewart earls in the context of the period from 1468 to 1615 it is necessary to go back again in time and trace the second of the themes which I mentioned at the beginning — the 'attempts by forces, within the islands and without, to counter the crown's intentions in order to bring power to themselves'. The Sinclairs may have been the strongest single element in the islands in the early part of our period, but as a family they were already riven. Earl William had had three sons by his two wives, and on his death about 1476 the family properties — in Caithness, in southern Scotland, and in the Northern Isles — were broken up between them. The Ravenscraig lands went to Oliver Sinclair of Roslin, and the earldom of Caithness went to Oliver's full brother, another William. In Orkney and Shetland the Sinclair estates — that is to say the conquest lands acquired by William Sinclair — went ultimately to his grandson, Henry, Lord Sinclair. He, in acquiring the *pro rege* lands as well, achieved control of the whole lands held by the last earl. In addition he wrested Ravenscraig from the Sinclairs of Roslin and was recognised as 'chief of that blude'. The Roslin and Caithness branches were nevertheless to continue to play a prominent role in what followed (Crawford 1985: 243-6).

Although on Henry's death his tack was inherited by his widow, his brother, Sir William Sinclair of Warsetter, 'to all intents and purposes stepped into his ... shoes' (Clouston 1932: 285). This was probably due to the youth of Henry's son William — he did not die until 57 years later. With Lord Henry's widow in nominal possession of the tack and actual control in the hands of Sir William Sinclair of Warsetter, matters were peaceful until some time after 1522, when the conflict flared up which led to the battle of Summerdale. The antagonists were the mature William, Lord Sinclair on the one hand, and on the other the sons of Sir William, the illegitimate James of Brecks and Edward of Strom, the legitimate Magnus Sinclair of Warsetter. The road to Summerdale begins when dissension between the two sides boiled over at Easter 1528, when Lord Sinclair was holding justice courts in Kirkwall Castle. Sinclair of Brecks and his brother of Strom broke in on the proceedings, killed three of their own nephews and seven of Lord William's servants, took him prisoner, and forced him to surrender the house. Lord Sinclair pursued his cousins before the council demanding return of the castle. The council permitted him to enlist the earl of Caithness's help in recovering it by force. On 7 June 1529 the pair tried to carry out this threat. Their expedition landed in Orphir, and made its way up over the hills into Stenness where it met the Orkney and Shetland Sinclairs at Summerdale. The result was utter rout. 30 Caithness men, including the earl, were killed on the field, 100 during the pursuit that followed, and 22 seamen were coldly butchered on the tide mark. By the time James and Edward Sinclair had

180

finished their extirpation, more than 300 had been killed in Orkney and Shetland (Anderson 1982: 21-5; Thomson 1987: 133-8).

What were they fighting about and why? Firstly the actual control of the lands held under Lady Sinclair's tack — the royal, earldom and lordship lands; secondly the conquest lands, independent of the others but in fact included with them in Lord Henry's rental. Lord William's mother held the tack continuously from the death of her husband till her own demise in the late 1530s, but after Summerdale there was an attempt to replace her with the stronger figure of the earl of Moray, suggesting that actual exercise of the tack was a contentious issue (Anderson 1982: 25). This failed, and we find James Sinclair of Brecks as 'Justice', holding the jurisdiction associated with the tack, which Lord Sinclair viewed as his right and had been seeking to exercise in Kirkwall in 1528. Regarding the conquest lands, it seems clear from the very title of the senior Orkney figure in the conflict, Sir William Sinclair of Warsetter, that he and his branch of the family had them in their possession. The estate of Warsetter does not appear in the early rentals as a unit in itself, but seems to have been created out of surrounding lands in order to provide a *bu*, or headfarm, for the conquest estates in Sanday (Marwick 1952: 17; Anderson 1992: 28). It was probably these estates which were referred to in the charter to James Sinclair of Brecks of the lands of Sanday and Stronsay. The Warsetter Sinclairs had sat down in the conquest lands, and the Caithness Sinclairs never forgot or forgave their loss.

The conquest lands are of great interest in charting the declining fortunes of the Sinclairs during the period. The tack of the royal lands was just that, a lease of lands which were indisputably the king's. The conquest lands were different. They were regarded by Lord Sinclair and his descendants as their rightful possession, and at any uncertain juncture in the course of Orkney and Shetland affairs, they saw an opportunity to press for their return. In 1541 when James V granted his tack of the islands to Oliver Sinclair of Pitcairns, Lord Sinclair secured a commission to him 'to tak cognition Quhat possessiouns landis and rowmes ... umquhile Henry Lord Sinclair, Sir David Sinclair and utheris had within the saids lordschippis of Orknay and Zeitland ...' In March 1567, when it was clear Robert Stewart was claiming a very broad infeftment of the lands of Orkney and Shetland, Lord Sinclair obtained another commission, though this 'be occasion of civil werris tuik not effect'. In November 1581, three months after Robert was created earl, another Henry, Lord Sinclair, son of William, petitioned parliament about his rights, narrating the whole sorry story. This came to nothing, and there was no further agitation on the topic (Crawford 1985: 252-3). There is no doubt that when George Sinclair, earl of Caithness, invaded Orkney in 1614, he had at the back of his mind the fate of his grandfather 85 years before (Anderson 1992: 118). But there is no evidence that he sought, even in the hour of his triumph, to press the old claims, probably because the conquest lands were by now inextricably bound up with the *pro rege* lands.

181

Caithness had, as we shall see, other irons in the Orkney fire. But the Sinclair claims on the conquest lands were dead.

At what point did they die? Some of the conquest lands do seem to have descended to branches of the Warsetter Sinclairs, including Warsetter itself. But in fact all the families which descend from Sir William Sinclair of Warsetter — Brecks, Strom, Brough, Ness, Essinquoy, Flotta etc. etc., seem to have been udallers in their own right, rather than the beneficiaries of successive divisions of the conquest lands. The greater part of the conquest lands seem to have become part of the *pro rege* lands, and I would surmise that this happened at the time of Oliver Sinclair of Pitcairns. The circumstances of his receipt of the tack of Orkney and Shetland are obscure, but they do point to grandiose aspirations. The greatly increased duty, much the same amount as that later paid by the Stewart earls, may have resulted from James V's view of how much Orkney at least was worth following his visit there. But it also suggests that it included all the land in Lord Henry's rental of 1500 — royal, earldom, lordship and conquest. Perhaps Oliver hoped ultimately for the resurrection of the Sinclair earldom, but his fall lost all for himself and the family as a whole. In 1544 he was in dispute with Lord Sinclair, over the latter's lands in Shetland (Anderson 1982: 30; Crawford 1978), which sound like the conquest lands amassed there by Sir David Sinclair of Sumburgh.

But Oliver Sinclair, though he had acute financial problems for much of the 1540s, was not finished yet. He arrived in Orkney again with bishop Bothwell, bringing with him echoes of all the old causes. His presence was noted by the Caithness Sinclairs, who concluded a contract with Magnus Halcro of Brough, chantor of Orkney, an ecclesiastical opponent of Adam Bothwell; the latter promised to assist any invasion by the earl of Caithness. Adam Bothwell in turn sought Oliver Sinclair's support. In part this may have been because of Sinclair's involvement in this whole Scottish carve-up of the bishopric lands. But it was also because the actual surviving Summerdale faction, the Sinclairs of Strom, were riven among themselves. This was ostensibly on the question of the reformation brought by Bothwell, though Bothwell himself saw the influence of Sir John Bellenden in the opposition towards him of the Sinclair of Strom sons, Henry and Robert. They had publicly humiliated him, and their father Edward, the Summerdale veteran, was not prepared to restrain them. The religious issue may be a red herring; Oliver himself was described by Knox as an 'enemy to God', which suggests that he would not have been favourable to Bothwell's reforms (Anderson 1982: 35-7).

But before we look at these later activities, it is as well to recapitulate on just what had happened to the lands of Orkney and Shetland on the eve of Adam Bothwell's arrival in 1560. In 1468, in the Orkney and Shetland game of monopoly, there were perhaps 7 types of square on the board. Very briefly, these were as follows: the crown estates, or *kingsland*; the earldom lands of Orkney; the lordship lands of Shetland; the conquest lands; the udal lands; the bishopric lands; and the kirklands. The story of the period 1468-1564 is that of the gradual simplification of this picture. The impignoration and subsequent appropriation of the earldom effectively united the royal, earldom and lordship lands. The conquest lands were also added to this, about 1540. Thus there were now only four types of territory — *pro rege*, bishopric or *pro episcopo*, udal, and kirkland. The story of the last fifty years or so of our period is that of the tension between the Stewart earls, whose clear intention was to simplify this picture still further, and the lesser landowners, who were seeking to carve their own smaller slices out of what was available, particularly in the bishopric and kirklands. The latters' activities made the picture complicated again.

Robert Stewart's intention was to obtain a feu of the *pro rege* lands, add to them control of the bishopric lands and such kirk and udal land as he could get hold of. This may sound too simple, implying a definite systematic programme. I do believe he had such a programme, and in fact he achieved quite a high proportion of this, though there were a number of complicating factors. The excambion with bishop Bothwell, whereby the latter parted with his temporalities in exchange for the estates of the abbey of Holyrood, is well-known; but it was not by any means the whole story. Robert Stewart arranged a further excambion with Sir John Bellenden, exchanging the lands of Birsay for the barony of the Kerse on the south bank of the Forth; but it became clear that Bellenden felt that he had been cheated, and the opposition of the family was to return to plague Robert twenty years later (Anderson 1982: 39-41; 1992: 18-20).

Robert was forced to fight off an invasion by Patrick Bellenden, and feu out further lands from the bishopric. The feuings of Bothwell and Robert Stewart created a whole new class of proprietors on the Orkney scene — feudal lairds on the Scottish pattern, who were to continue to flourish after the fall of the Stewarts — in some cases right down to the present century: the Balfours, the Bellendens, the Moodies, the Gordons of Cairston, the Hendersons of Holland, the Monteiths. Oliver Sinclair of Pitcairns was also prominent among the recipients of the Bothwell infeudation. He received lands in Eday, which he passed on to Edward Sinclair, his brother. However Edward Sinclair of Eday provides a continuing link with later events. In 1576, in financial straits, he granted a bond to the Edinburgh merchants Henry Hathaway and his wife Jonet Fockhart. This was bought up in 1601 by the earl of Caithness, who made the Eday Sinclairs his clients and used them as a stick with which to beat Patrick Stewart (Anderson 1992: 61).

By that time, the Sinclairs in Orkney had declined into a number of small udal families, mostly descended from Sir William Sinclair of Warsetter. In Shetland the situation was rather different. However obscure some of the branches there had become, they had not forgotten their exalted ancestry, nor how William Sinclair had built up estates in the Northern Isles independent of the crown. Two main figures attempted to amass large udal estates on their own account during the 1590s. These were Hugh Sinclair of Brough and the most significant of all the Scots who came in on the coat-tails of the Stewart earls — Laurence Bruce of Cultmalindie. Hugh Sinclair of Brough, son of Henry, grandson of Edward Sinclair of Strom, was the senior representative in Shetland of the Sinclairs who stood in direct line from the last Sinclair earl. In the year before his death he acquired no fewer than 15 grants of udal land, representing 25 or so separate lots, divided among his two families of sons, who on his death were each offered an embarrassment of assistance by both Patrick and the Bruces.

The other notable Sinclair line in Shetland is that which probably descended from a previous earl through Henry Sinclair of Havera and his son Ola. The two lines appear to have fallen out, in Shetland, in 1602. Matthew Sinclair of Ness, a great-great-grandson of William Sinclair of Warsetter, of the Orkney Campston line, was murdered at Dunrossness. The perpetrators were almost certainly Francis Sinclair of Uyea and Robert Sinclair of Ramnageo, but Earl Patrick was anxious to pin the crime on Adam Sinclair of Broo, one of their cousins through the Haveras. Broo was quick to seek 'ane conding essyse agreabill to his bluide and rank', a clear reference to his ancestry. Patrick appears to have incriminated Sinclair of Broo in order to enlist the support of the Uyea branch in his struggle to attain control over the whole Sinclair family in Shetland, a struggle he was waging against the Bruces of Cultmalindie and Symbister. The Shetland Sinclairs were still important and wealthy enough to excite the interest of Patrick Stewart, but two points indicate they were a spent force. The first is the sheer obscurity of the murder of Matthew Sinclair. Whatever use Patrick may have sought to make of it, it seems to have been a family squabble between the Orkney branch and an older Shetland branch represented by Francis Sinclair, a notorious wastrel. The second is the ill-luck the family had suffered in losing its senior members to early death (Anderson 1992: 67-76).

When Robert Stewart himself died, his position, at its zenith in 1581, had declined markedly. He had been forced to recognise the claims of the Bellendens; he had excited the discontent of Adam Bothwell, still pursuing him before the courts; and the king, probably on Bellenden advice, had effectively confiscated the earldom and granted it in fee to his son. Patrick spent his first seven years as earl, from 1593 to 1600, in a state of some uncertainty, partly because the king would not serve him heir to his father and partly because James wanted the income of the bishopric for his own purposes, notably that of the queen's maintenance. The 1590s, and in particular 1595, was a period in which the whole question of income from Orkney and Shetland was re-examined. Although at one point it was said that James was going to 'challenge' the earldom of Orkney, and Clerk Register Skene was hinting at increasing the duties, in the end Patrick was confirmed in his dominions, earldom and bishopric, in March 1600, apparently for no greater price than that of putting his affairs in order (Anderson 1992: 18-20, 46-59).

184

Patrick Stewart remained unchallenged only for five years. At the end of that time his notorious activities, coupled with the king's strong views on the virtues of episcopacy, resulted in the restoration of the bishopric. It was never James's intention to employ James Law as Andrew Pictoris had been — after a brief period in charge after Patrick's fall, he was superseded in his control of the crown lands — but it was intended that he at least try to influence Patrick. The earl had succeeded in falling out with all the major members of his two main groups of natural followers — his vassals of Orkney and the udallers of Shetland. He had quarrelled with members of his own family, and was ignoring the advice of Sir John Arnot and others, as well as the courts which were trying to bring him to book (Anderson 1992: 77-9). His rule shows no consciousness of the past, of the policies followed by his Scottish or Norwegian predecessors, of anything other than a desire to extend his power and wealth in Orkney and Shetland to the uttermost. Yet if he was not himself conscious of the power wielded by the Norse earls at the expense of their royal overlords, he nevertheless showed the continuing dangers for good government of a man of pretension in the area. It was for this reason that when he fell, the earldom disappeared for more than 70 years.

There were still those who sought an earldom in the north, most notably Patrick's brother John, and in a strange sense he found one — that curious dignity of Carrick, in Eday, the island which was the home of the greatest of the Orkney Sinclair opponents of Patrick (Anderson 1992: 143). But he had little influence on events; from the death of Patrick until the advent of the earls of Morton later in the century, government in Orkney and Shetland was in the hands of tacksmen and sheriffs.

Bibliography

Anderson, P.D., 1992: *Black Patie*. Edinburgh.
Anderson, P.D., 1982: *Robert Stewart, Earl of Orkney, Lord of Shetland*. Edinburgh.
Barry, J., 1805: *History of Orkney*. Edinburgh.
Clouston, J.S., 1932: *History of Orkney*. Kirkwall.
Crawford, B.E., 1976: 'The Fifteenth-century "Genealogy of the Earls of Orkney" and its Reflection of the Contemporary Political and Cultural Situation in the Earldom', *Medieval Scandinavia* 10, 163.
Crawford, B.E., 1978: 'David Sinclair of Sumburgh'. In: John Baldwin (ed.), *Scandinavian Shetland: An Ongoing Tradition*, Edinburgh, 1-11.
Crawford, B.E., 1985: 'William Sinclair, Earl of Orkney, and his Family: a Study in the Politics of Survival'. In: *Essays on the Nobility of Medieval Scotland*, Edinburgh.
The Exchequer Rolls of Scotland (Rotuli Scaccarii Regum Scotorum) Vol XXI, 1901: Edinburgh.
Smith, B., 1989: 'In the Tracks of Bishop Andrew Pictoris of Orkney and Henry Phankouth, Archdeacon of Orkney', *Innes Review* 40, no. 2, 91-105.
Thomson, W.P.L., 1987: *History of Orkney*. Edinburgh.
Thomson, W.P.L., 1984: 'Fifteenth Century Depression in Orkney; the Evidence of Lord Henry Sinclair's Rentals.' In: Barbara E. Crawford (ed.), *Essays in Shetland History*, Lerwick, 125-142.

PERCEPTIONS OF UDAL LAW IN ORKNEY AND SHETLAND

Michael R. H. Jones

On 23rd March 1990, a headline in *The Shetland Times* proclaimed: 'Udal Law buried by Crown Estate.' The article reported a ruling of the Court of Session that the seabed around Orkney and Shetland was owned by the Crown, as elsewhere in Scotland. A 'Special Case' had been raised by the Shetland Salmon Farmers' Association (SSFA) and Lerwick Harbour Trustees to test their claim that under 'old Norwegian laws, popularly known as Udal Law' (*Shetland Times* 18.3.1988) the Crown could not be the owner of the seabed around the Northern Isles.

The dispute arose after the Crown Estate Commissioners in 1986 announced a substantial increase in the seabed rental for salmon farmers. The SSFA argued that the Crown's right to the seabed off mainland Scotland was based on the feudal system. However, as Orkney and Shetland were originally udal, the SSFA maintained that feudal theory did not apply, and questioned whether the seabed around the Northern Isles really did belong to the Crown. If not, the Crown Estate Commissioners would not have the right to charge rentals. Lerwick Harbour Trustees wanted the question of udal law to be clarified in connection with land reclamation plans for the construction of a jetty at Dales Voe.

The Court of Session found that the Crown had the right of property on the territorial seabed from the low water mark out to the 12 mile limit. Hence the consent of the Crown Estate Commissioners is necessary for permanent fixtures on or over the seabed, and they have the right to charge rentals (*Shetland Times* 23.3.1990).

The claim that udal law was buried by this decision was contested in a letter to *The Shetland Times* of 30th March 1990 by T.M.Y. Manson. While he had never heard before of the claim that udal law might apply to the seabed, he pointed out that the Court of Session's decision did not affect udal rights on land above the low water mark.

In other words, udal law was still alive and kicking. It is in itself noteworthy that Norse cultural traditions have apparently persisted more than 500 years after the islands became Scottish. Despite the disappearance of the Norn language, certain rights and customs related to land holding still survive which are in marked contrast to the Scottish tradition. Orkney and Shetland thus provide an ideal case for examining the characteristics of cultural change and continuity in the meeting of two cultures over a long period of time.

I first heard about udal law from an uncle, who worked for the Ministry of Works in Edinburgh. My interest remained latent until I moved to Norway in 1973. My research into Norwegian land tenure gave me some points of reference. I spent the academic year 1985-86 in Scotland, when I began a study of geographical manifestations of udal tenure and undertook a month's field work in Orkney and Shetland.[1] This lecture recapitulates some of my work up until now. I will present preliminary answers to two questions:

— What are the characteristics of udal law as described in published literature on the topic?
— What are people's perceptions of the significance of udal law today?

What are the characteristics of udal law as described in the literature?

My approach is historical-geographical or cultural-historical rather then legal. As well as legal literature, I have looked at historical, geographical, topographical and popular literature.[2] As a frame of reference, I have compared the situation in Orkney and Shetland with that prevailing both in Norway and mainland Scotland.

In a broad sense, the term udal law is used to refer to the whole system of Norse law, based principally on the Magnus Code of 1274, in force when the islands were impignorated to the Scottish Crown in 1468 and 1469. In a narrow sense, udal law refers to certain survivals in the land-tenure system, sometimes referred to as udal tenure (Dobie 1936: 450, 455; Ryder 1989: 193, 196).

From the literature, I have identified ten main characteristics or aspects of udal law which still seem to have some relevance today. (The question of historical land measures and weights and measures will not be considered here.) Seven of these, relating directly to land tenure, are shown in Figure 1 in comparison with the situation in respectively Norway and mainland Scotland.

1) Absolute ownership of land (allodial tenure)

Unlike most land in Scotland, where feudal tenure dominates, udal land is allodial, i.e. the title does not emanate from the Crown and there is no feudal superior. A written title is not necessary under udal tenure, although it may be found convenient to take out one (Drever 1933: 323, 328-9; Dobie 1936: 451-3; Smith 1978: 197, 199; Ryder 1989: 201-2). This is similar to the situation in Norway, where there is no feudal superior to land. Although deeds have been registered in Norway since 1623 and a land register was established by decree of 1738, registration is not necessary for the acquisition of ownership to land (Imsen 1974: 344-5; Robberstad 1983: 59-60).

---

1. The study has been supported financially by grants from the Norwegian Research Council for Science and the Humanities (1985-86) and the Research Council of Norway (1993-94). Preliminary results of the study were presented in lectures given at meetings of the Traditional Cosmology Society and of the Scottish Society for Northern Studies in Edinburgh in November 1986.

2. Only a selection of the most central references will be presented in the following.

187

In the court case of 1963 concerning the treasure found on St. Ninian's Isle in Shetland, the finders claimed that, as the treasure was found on udal land with no feudal superior, it should be divided according to Magnus Law (Taranger 1915: 107): one-third should go to the finder, one-third to the landowner and one-third to the Crown. The Court of Session accepted that the land was held under allodial tenure, but ruled that the right of treasure nonetheless belonged to the Crown, not as feudal superior but as part of its sovereign rights (*Lord Advocate v. Aberdeen University and Budge* 1963 SC 533; Smith 1973: 149-51; Robberstad 1983: 64-5; Ryder 1989: 212-3).

Under Scots law, treasure belongs to the Crown if the proper owner cannot be ascertained (Smith 1973: 149; Ryder 1989: 212). We can note that in Norway, since 1905, treasure and other moveable antiquities older than 1537 belong automatically to the State when the rightful owner can no longer be traced[3] (Robberstad 1983: 64; *Kulturminneloven* 1978: 12-13).

2) Rights of kin

Udal land is held with an entail on the family. Land becomes udal if held unbroken in the family for a certain length of time: according to the Magnus Code, this was 60 years or four generations, or with immediate effect if it was a gift from the king. The principle was that if udal land was offered for sale, the kin had rights of prior purchase; or if the land had already been sold, they had rights of repurchase within a certain time (Taranger 1915: 98-100; Dobie 1936: 451-2; *NOU* 1972, 22: 7-8; Robberstad 1983: 60; Ryder 1989: 204-5).

This is still the essence of udal rights (*odelsrett*) in Norway today. Although an attempt was made to abolish udal rights in 1811, they were restored and enshrined in the Norwegian Constitution of 1814. Since 1857, land has become udal after 20 years. Since 1974, the family's right to repurchase sold land remains valid for two years, the owner being required to live on the farm and operate it (*NOU* 1972, 22: 9-11; Johannessen 1974: 240-1; *Odelslova* 1974: 7, 27, 40).

Evidence from the Orkney and Shetland Records and court cases indicates that the consent of kin (*roithman* or person with the nearest right) was often obtained on land sales until at least the beginning of the 17th century (Dobie 1936: 452; Ryder 1989: 205).

3) Partible inheritance

In the case of udal property, the principle is that all the immediate heirs share the inheritance. The Magnus Code gave the eldest son the right to take over the main house. It also stipulated that daughters should receive half the shares

---

3. However, the State can pay a reward, to be divided equally between the finder and the landowner, and in the case of gold and silver this is to be equal to at least the metal value plus 10%.

of sons. Partible inheritance tended to produce the sub-division of holdings, but only if the younger brothers and sisters could not be compensated in other property, moveables or shares in an undivided estate (Taranger 1915: 80-1; Dobie 1936: 453; Fenton 1978: 22; Robberstad 1983: 61; Ryder 1989: 204).

Partible inheritance of land contrasts with the Scottish feudal principle of primogeniture for male heirs, which was the main rule applied to heritage until 1964[4] (Smith 1958; Gloag & Henderson 1980: 647-54, 664; Walker 1983: 134-44).

However, in Norway, a decree of 1539 allowed the senior male heir to inherit land intact if he could buy out the other heirs or if he paid rent to them. This right (*åsetesrett*) was enshrined in the Norwegian Constitution of 1814. Since 1821, junior heirs have received their shares in the form of mortgage rights. Females have received full shares since 1854 (*NOU* 1972, 22: 14-15; Johannessen 1974: 376). From 1955, the sub-division of farm holdings has been forbidden without the consent of the agricultural authorities (*Jordlova* 1955: 55). The law was changed in 1974 to remove the distinction between males and females in the order of succession (*Odelslova* 1974: 12).

The last case recorded in the literature of udal land in the Northern Isles being sub-divided upon intestacy is the case of Hawick v. Hawick from 1893. The Sheriff Court upheld the law of udal succession, ordering the land to be divided equally among the heirs (two sons and two daughters, the latter receiving full shares) (Dickinson 1954: 159-60).[5]

4) Scat

In Norwegian, the general term for tax is *skatt*. In Orkney and Shetland, scat was a tax payable by udal landholders for government purposes. It was regarded as a tribute to the Crown or State, not as a feu duty, which in Scotland implied servitude to a feudal superior. Scat was payable to the Crown directly or to the Earl in the right of the Crown (Smith 1978: 198-9; Ryder 1989: 206-7).

An Act of 1812 allowed scats and other duties of the Earldom to be sold. During the 19th and 20th centuries, many — although not all — landowners redeemed scat upon the payment of a lump sum (Heddle & Johnston 1889: 14; MacGillivray 1986). According to the Scottish Office, 315 scats were still being paid in 1972 (265 in Orkney and 50 in Shetland).

---

4. The principal rule applied to intestate succession. Testamentary disposition of heritage was, however, permitted from 1868, while before this a landowner could before death dispose of heritage as he would, thus legally circumventing primogeniture. The Succession (Scotland) Act 1964 removed the distinction between males and females for the heirs of those dying after the Act came into force.

5. Shetland archivist Brian Smith has, however, been unable to find this case in the Sheriff Court records.

Since 1974, redemption has been compulsory on the sale of a holding. Since then, scat payments have become vestigial (Ryder 1989: 207).

In Norway, various land taxes were payable from at least the 12th century. Most were abolished in 1837. The remainder could be redeemed from then, and redemption was made compulsory in 1939 (Winge 1974: 143-4, 197-8, 199-201).

5) Scattalds

In its original meaning, a scattald was a territorial unit of landownership with several owners, apparently a unit for the payment of scat. Each owner possessed both privately owned arable land and a share in the undivided hill grazings, owned in common. The term scattald is apparently only found in Shetland, but the phenomenon appears to be similar to urislands in Orkney (Fenton 1978: 35-6; Smith 1984; Ryder 1989: 208-9).

By the 18th century, the term scattald came to be synonymous with commonties in mainland Scotland, i.e. hill grazings in which tenants have rights of pasture and peat-cutting. Scattalds may be divided among landowners under a Scottish Act of 1695 providing for Division of Commonty (Adams 1971: 1, 234-53; Knox 1985: 22, 199-234). The division of scattald among landowners and the apportionment of crofters' rights remain two distinct operations.

In Norway, it is still not unusual for hill pastures to be owned in common by several landowners, who as owner-occupiers have grazing rights. Common land could, however, be divided under ancient Norse laws, and from the 19th century by the Norwegian Enclosure Acts (Borgedal 1959: 135-6, 142-5, 155-62; Grendahl & Solberg 1959; Johannessen 1974: 361).

6) Foreshore

The ownership of udal land extends from the highest stone on the hill to the lowest of the ebb. This is often confirmed in title deeds, thus including the foreshore (to the low water mark at spring tide) in the adjoining holding. Possibly the earliest mention of this in Orkney is in a deed from 1480 and in Shetland from 1528. In Norway, the foreshore belongs to the adjoining landowner, in contrast to mainland Scotland, where the foreshore belongs to the Crown, although the right to property in the foreshore is alienable to individuals with the Crown as ultimate superior (Drever 1904: 10-16; Smith 1978: 200-1; Gloag & Henderson 1980: 593-4; Robberstad 1983: 65-6; Ryder 1989: 214).

Associated with foreshore ownership are rights to sand and shingle, and certain rights to build on the foreshore. Historically, proprietary rights included bait, sealing-places, seaweed, driftwood, whales and wrecks (Ryder 1989: 213-4). The right of tenants to seaweed etc. was not protected in Scotland until the Crofters Act of 1886.

Historically, landowners in Orkney and Shetland claimed a share of pilot or caaing whales driven up on to their shores. Under Scots law, landowners have no rights to whales. In the Northern Isles, the claims of landowners derived from somewhat complicated rules in the Magnus Code. These became in time modified so that one-third went to the captors, one-third to the landowners and one-third to the Crown. The Crown eventually ceased to exercise its right, but landowners' claims were upheld in court cases of 1831 and 1838. In the Hoswick whale case of 1890, however, the Court of Session declared this to be an unreasonable custom and the landowners were overruled. The decision was reached by a majority verdict, the dissenting judgement being that Scots law concerning the foreshore did not apply to udal land in Shetland (Taranger 1915: 158-60; *Bruce v. Smith* 1890 17 R 1000; Ryder 1989: 213).

In the Sinclair's Beach case, on the other hand, the Court of Session upheld the adjoining landowner's right to build on the foreshore on the basis of a udal title. A Crown grant to Lerwick Harbour Trustees was found not to be valid (*Smith v. Lerwick Harbour Trustees* 1903 5 F 680; Drever 1904: 4-5; 1933: 330; Ryder 1989: 214). A similar case in the Sheriff Court in 1950 was won by the Harbour Trustees, when the adjoining property was found to be feudal, not udal (*Shetland News* 7.12.1950; *Lerwick Harbour Trustees v. Moar* 1951 SLT (Sh Ct) 46; Ryder 1989: 214).

7) Rights to salmon-fishing

Salmon-fishing is a udal right belonging to riparian proprietors in Orkney and Shetland. In Norway, salmon-fishing rights have always belonged to the adjoining landowner, subject to the right of the State to regulate the equipment used (Robberstad 1983: 62; *Laksefiske- og innlandsfiskeloven* 1964: 43-56). Under Scots law, salmon-fishing belongs to the Crown as feudal superior, although alienable to individuals (Neish & Blades 1929).

In the Balfour case of 1907, it was found that a riparian owner in Orkney whose lands were held on a feudal title nonetheless possessed salmon-fishing rights. The Court of Session found that salmon-fishings do not constitute a separate feudal estate in Orkney and Shetland, but are part and pertinent of landownership. The right of salmon-fishing was never claimed by the Crown of Norway, and thus never conferred on the Crown of Scotland (*Lord Advocate v. Balfour* 1907 SC 1360; Drever 1933: 330-1; Smith 1978: 201-2; Ryder 1989: 315).

8) Ownership of the seabed

Udal rights to the seabed were not declared in the past until they were invoked in 1986 by salmon-farmers and others protesting against the decision of the Crown Estate Commissioners to raise rentals (*The Orcadian* 21.8.1986; 4.9.1986).[6]

In Scotland, the Crown regards itself as owner of the seabed. In Norway, private ownership rights extend as far out as the *marbakken*, i.e. where the coastal shallows end in a steep slope to deeper water. Where there is no clearly defined *marbakke*, private ownership rights extend to a depth of 2 m from the low water mark. Implicit in the Magnus Code, this was upheld by the Supreme Court in the 19th and 20th centuries. Within this boundary, the agreement of the shore-owner is necessary before a fish farm can be established (although subject to government rights of compulsory purchase). In 1985, the Supreme Court established that the rights of riparian owners — known as *strandrett* — extend even beyond this limit with regard to the taking of seaweed, sand and shingle, rights of infilling, building of piers and breakwaters, and the right of objecting to third-party use on aesthetic grounds. However, anyone can establish a fish farm beyond the private boundary. There is no question of paying a rental to the State (Austenå 1984: 4-21; Neergaard 1984: 317-9, 321-4; Belsheim 1987; Reiten 1987; Rogstad 1987; Ryder 1989: 218).[7]

In Shetland, the SSFA wanted to establish that the Crown had no property rights to the seabed. The SSFA was not, however, concerned with establishing competing ownership. Shetland Islands Council was worried that the defeat of the Crown Estate Commisioners would result in a multitude of proprietary claims from adjoining landowners (*Shetland Times* 11.3.1988). Counsel for the SSFA argued that there was a case for the seabed being seen as having some relationship to the land in general — which was udal in character — but without it belonging to particular holdings. There was no evidence that the Crown had rights to the seabed initially.[8]

Knut Robberstad (1983: 65-6) suggested that Norse law implying private ownership as far as to the *marbakke* may have become modified in Orkney and Shetland in the 15th and 16th centuries with the concept of ownership extending to the lowest of the ebb. It was argued by William Howarth (1988) that udal tenure ceases at the lowest water mark.

---

6. Thanks are due to William P. L. Thomson for drawing my attention to the discussion in the pages of *The Orcadian* in September 1986. In personal communications from James Moncrieff, Chief Executive of the SSFA in Lerwick, in October and November 1987, I was asked to assist in obtaining information regarding the status of the seabed in Norway and other Scandinavian countries in connection with the dispute between the SSFA and the Crown.

7. Information on the status of the seabed in Norway was obtained for the entry on 'Udal Law' in *The Laws of Scotland. Stair Memorial Encyclopaedia* (Ryder 1989) by the present author.

8. This argument was contained in a *Supplementary note for Shetland Salmon Farmers Association*, dated 9th June 1987, from Anderson & Goodlad, solicitors, Edinburgh. Thanks are due to James Moncrieff for making this document available to me.

The decision of the Court of Session in 1990 in favour of the Crown referred to the seabed within the limits of the territorial sea. As in the St. Ninian's Isle treasure case, the seabed was found to belong to the Crown as part of its sovereign rights, not its rights as feudal superior (*Shetland Salmon Farmers Association v. Crown Estate Commissioners* 1990 SCLR 483). The Crown might well have lost the latter argument in court.

9) Udaller class

The term udaller referred originally to any person possessing land under udal tenure. However, it is often used in the literature to refer to an intermediate class of small landowners holding udal property, and by implication descended from the original Norse landowners. It is not infrequently a romanticized concept: Walter Scott referred to 'the Norse inhabitants, the true Udallers of Zetland' ([1831] 1904: 9), while to David Balfour (1859: xxx, xxxv) the udaller was a 'peasant noble.'

In Norway, a udaller (*odelsbonde*) is a freehold farmer holding land with udal rights; 98% of Norwegian farms are owner-occupied, the majority small farms held under udal tenure.

10) Udal law as a symbol of Orkney and Shetland identity

Udal law was taken up by Orkney writers in the later 19th century, a period when the Norse connection experienced a cultural revival (Renwanz 1980: 9-10, 89-91; Cohen 1983: 316-91). David Balfour, in *Odal rights and feudal wrongs* (1860), associated udal rights with the opposition of landowners to the impositions of the Earls. Alfred Johnston idealized the Norwegian peasant democracy, and in 1886 founded the Udal League to campaign for Home Rule. The Udal League advocated land reform and the conversion of tenants to owner-occupiers, who would have their udal rights confirmed as protection against the feudal estate owners (Thomson 1985).

A hint of interest in udal law as a symbol of island identity is found in the Shetland Movement (Cohen 1983: 483) and, more markedly, in the Orkney Movement (*The Orcadian* 13.12.1979).

In Norway, udal rights were revived along with other Norwegian institutions after the split from Denmark in 1814. This was related to the power of agrarian interests and a developing Norwegian national consciousness (Tveite 1959: 112; *NOU* 1972, 22: 10-11; Østerud 1978: 79, 81, 240; MacGillivray 1986).

What are people's perceptions of the significance of udal law today?

My source material consists of interviews obtained through a network of contacts. During the spring of 1986, I talked to some 70 people about udal law — mostly in Orkney and Shetland, a few in Edinburgh. I asked them to

193

tell me what they understood by udal law and then to elaborate on particular aspects. The collected material varies from taped interviews (undertaken for the School of Scottish Studies) to notebook interviews as well as shorter chats and telephone conversations. I did not make a systematic sample survey. My informants were not representative in the statistical sense. My intention was to make an exploratory investigation to gain a general impression of present-day perceptions. The interview material allowed me to make a broad categorization into five groups according to the type of significance my informants attached to udal law. Besides interviews, I have undertaken supplementary archive investigations in the Shetland Archives and the Scottish Record Office.

1) The legal profession — solicitors

Solicitors practising in Lerwick, Kirkwall and Stromness (of whom I interviewed eight) are periodically confronted with questions concerning udal law. Their training is based on Scots law. Most lawyers regarded udal law as having little practical significance today. Udal law has been eroded, and exists only as survivals within Scots law.

The most important survivals are private ownership of the foreshore and of salmon-fishing rights, upheld in court cases this century. In practice, the foreshore is often a pertinent to both udal and feudal properties. Title deeds mention the lowest ebb or the tang ebbs. Landowners would also be able to claim ownership of the foreshore under the Scots law of prescription. In cases involving the Crown Estate Commissioners, the onus has been on the landowner to prove his title on the assumption that otherwise the foreshore belongs to the Crown. Commercial use of the foreshore (for example for sand and shingle extraction) is the right of the landowner. Crofters' rights to seaweed and driftwood from the foreshore are regulated by the Crofters Act.

An unclear area was whether crofters' traditional rights to fish for salmon and trout with fixed gill-nets was subject to prohibition under the Fisheries Act of 1951. Crofters prosecuted for poaching felt their udal rights were being infringed, but there has been no test case to clarify this. In Orkney, angling for salmon and trout is free for all, but legal opinion was that this is a local custom, unconnected with udal law.

Most udal properties have title deeds, but these are often defective. Feudal conveyancing is applied to udal properties, but titles in Orkney and Shetland differ somewhat from feudal titles elsewhere in Scotland.

Rights of kin and partible inheritance were regarded by most lawyers as historical curiosities they had not come across in practice.

Scat has largely been redeemed, but was still in 1986 — and in 1993 — being paid by some. I saw the scat ledger at one firm of solicitors in Lerwick.

As far as the seabed was concerned, most lawyers regarded this as belonging to the Crown, although some were in 1986 looking forward to a test case.

2) Townspeople — urban Shetlanders and Orcadians

I talked to about 30 townspeople in Lerwick, Kirkwall, Stromness and Scalloway. The majority appeared to regard udal law as largely unimportant. Many said they knew little about it. What they did know was largely anecdotal, referring for example to newspaper articles. Most knew it had something to do with the foreshore or with fishing-rights as a bone of contention.

Some had personal knowledge of disputes over foreshore ownership. In Stromness, the adjoining landowner's title had been accepted in one case but not in another in conflicts with the Harbour Authority, which claimed a title from the Crown. There has been no legal test case in Orkney, equivalent to the Sinclair's Beach case in Shetland.

Several mentioned that the seabed belonged to the Crown, but I heard two anecdotes suggesting traditions of private rights to adjoining water: in one case, they were said to extend as far out as one could wade, in the other as far as one could ride out on horseback until the sea touched the rider's scabbard.

Several of those with an academic education, including local historians, suggested that udal law was not properly understood by those making claims. As an example of a misconception, an Orkney Tourist Office brochure advertizing free angling for trout was cited, stating: 'no permits are required, thanks to ancient Norse law and Udal tradition.'

Some saw references to udal law as a hankering after a golden past, or as romanticism, while others saw it as a part of Norse tradition important for a feeling of Orkney or Shetland identity.

3) Landowners in the Scottish tradition

I had ten interviews with estate owners (lairds), proprietors of substantial areas of land and of owner-occupied farms, largely tracing their descent from Scots incomers, and with little or no tradition of udal practices.

Most felt that udal tenure had little significance other than that the foreshore belongs to the adjoining proprietor. For some, this was important for commercial sand and shingle operations. Historically, foreshore ownership had some significance for the kelp industry and for rights to a share in whales driven onto the beach. Several landowners referred to disagreements with the Crown Estate Commissioners over rights to piers on the foreshore; usually, but not invariably, these were accepted as belonging to the proprietor.

Some proprietors were aware that they owned salmon-fishing rights, but the main talking-point was the crofters' claims to traditional rights of netting salmon for their own use.

Some proprietors had title deeds indicating they owned a mixture of udal and feudal land. The land was invariably inherited by the Scottish law of

195

succession, although some made reference to land sub-division as a historical occurrence.

Relations with tenants are governed by the Crofters Act, which regulated crofters' rights to grazing and peat-cutting in the scattald, and to seaweed, shingle etc. for their own use from the foreshore. The right to cut peats commercially in the scattald belonged apparently to the landowner.

4) Crofters — tenants and owner-occupiers of recent date

Twenty crofters were interviewed. These were tenants or had been until relatively recently before purchasing their crofts.

On many of the smaller islands of Orkney, where the large estates had been broken up and crofters became owner-occupiers in the 1920s or later, I got the impression that there was little or no udal tradition, although it was accepted that landowners have rights to the foreshore.

An active member of the Orkney Movement claimed that udal law in its original sense was still valid, and that owner-occupied crofts could claim udal status after the requisite number of generations had passed. This would have implications for rights of kin and inheritance. It was claimed that udal landholders owe no allegiance to the Crown apart from the obligation to pay scat, and the government could not do away with udal law. Udal law was seen as a part of Orkney identity.

In Shetland, there appeared to be fairly strong awareness of udal law among several of the crofters I interviewed. Private ownership of the foreshore was generally mentioned. Several gave a wide interpretation of udal rights as including tenant crofters' traditional rights to take seaweed, sand and shingle from the foreshore, although this was less clearly expressed in the case of grazing and peat-cutting rights on the scattald.

The biggest source of contention was the claim that crofters have traditional rights to set salmon-nets off their own shores. I attended a meeting of the committee of the Shetland Crofters Fishing Rights Protection Society, formed in 1970 after a crofter was prosecuted for illegal fishing (Tirval 1986). The society aims to uphold crofters' traditional fishing rights, including the right to set standing nets, which was said to be handed down in the old udal laws. The use of gill nets is not allowed under Scots law. The local branch of the Crofters Union supported the right of crofters to set nets provided they used traditional methods, and the nets were set off their own shores (*Shetland Times* 11.7.86). According to the society, traditional methods meant the nets were not allowed to be attached to the shore, nor to block completely the mouth of a voe — the fish must be given a 'sporting chance.' The local interpretation was that crofters are allowed to set nets to catch 'one for the pot,' but not for commercial fishing.

The feeling was also expressed that crofters need to guard their foreshore rights against encroachment by Shetland Islands Council when the latter built roads and sewers.

196

The claim of the Crown Estate Commissioners for a rental from the seabed was seen as an anomaly, not in accordance with udal law.

Generally, udal law was regarded in a positive light, historically protecting the small farmer against the Crown and lairds. The Hoswick whale case of 1890 was seen not only as a victory for tenant rights, but also for udal rights: paradoxically, the lairds were seen as trying to stamp out udal law when demanding their right to a share of the whales!

5) The 'last udallers'

The term 'last udallers' might be applied to small udal proprietors whose land has apparently been inherited through the generations without becoming subservient to the lairds. Present owners may not always have a great deal of knowledge about udal law as such, but could tell of practices existing within living memory or recent generations which are clearly udal, such as partible inheritance and rights of kin. In some instances, however, the owners had made a special study of udal law, so that it was difficult to tell whether they were presenting book knowledge or oral tradition.

In Orkney, active udal traditions are to be found in Harray and Firth. People spoke of the 'Harray lairds.' Reference was made to property that could be traced back in the same family as far as the 16th century. It was observed that many do not have proper titles to their land when it has not been sold out of the family. Udal rights were held to include foreshore rights and rights to salmon-fishing as far as the horizon. It was said that genuine udallers only come to light when put under pressure. As an example was mentioned protests against the establishment of a Site of Special Scientific Interest (SSSI), which affected a large number of small udallers who regarded this as an infringement of their absolute rights of ownership.

Unclear ownership — farmers without title deeds — posed problems for the declaration of the SSSI. The dispute is documented in the pages of the local newspaper. Complexities of land tenure delayed the final notification of the West Mainland SSSI, first announced in 1983, until 1987. In all, 95 owners or occupiers had to be consulted. The Harray Commonty was divided into 166 strips (*The Orcadian* 19.2.1987). A group known as the Orkney Hill Users Association and Conservation Group objected to the SSSI on the grounds of 'ancient rights under Udal Law of Orkney' (*The Orcadian* 11.6.1987). There were incidents of heath-burning that were seen as a protest against the SSSI (*The Orcadian* 21.4.1988).

My attention was brought to the case of the Corrigall Farm Museum (also mentioned in MacGillivray 1986). An area of 0.26 acre was purchased in 1971 by Orkney County Council. The owner, who lived in South Africa, would not sell until the consent had been obtained of ten relatives — siblings and cousins, all grandchildren of the former owner, eight of them living in southern Africa. All signed the deed, apparently providing a recent example of the practice of rights of kin. An extract from the plan accompanying the deed, with the signatures, is shown in Figure 2.

A check in the Index of Sasines indicated that other branches of the Corrigall family appeared to be practising udal inheritance customs and rights of kin until the early 20th century. Property was inherited by all children equally, and later some brothers purchased the shares of others, including an instance where an elder brother bought back a share sold by a younger brother to someone in South Africa.

In Shetland, holdings with active or recent udal traditions and practices are found spread in different parts of the islands, including Yell and Mainland. At Clothan, West Yell, a will of 1842 divided a property equally among three sons, after smaller outlying parts had been set aside for three daughters. It was specified that if any brother wanted to sell, the first offer was to be made to the nearest brother, 'the brothers to have a preference to all others on equal terms.' Family members, who later got into debt, emigrated to Australia or otherwise left Clothan, sold or handed over their shares to remaining family members. The property is now reunited in the hands of one owner. A curious sasine from 1892 concerns the Free Church of West Yell at Clothan, where the trustees of the congregation disponed the church to themselves as 'udal proprietors ... without a written title.'[9]

At Fladdabister, in Cunningsburgh, is to be found a group of small proprietors known as 'peerie lairds' (see also Renwanz 1980: 128-33). They referred to their lands as free lands rather than udal lands. One related in detail how the original property, mentioned in a 17th century record, had been successively divided and now consisted of six holdings. Rights of family members who emigrated appear to have been taken over by those who remained. A check in the Sasine Register confirmed the sub-divisions. In several cases, one as late as 1928, daughters received half as much as sons. At the first sub-division in 1780 and again at a later one in 1880, it was stipulated that the property was not to be sold out of the family without being offered first to the other heirs. In 1972, one of the holdings was disponed equally to two sons, one of whom bought out the share of his brother in 1979. This example suggests that partible inheritance and rights of kin have been continuously practised until the present time.

Conclusion

Udal law survives in Orkney and Shetland today as certain peculiarities of land tenure in a dominating Scots context. The Scottish Court of Session has upheld the rights of landowners to foreshore and salmon-fishing, but not to rights of a share of whales nor of treasure, while the claim of salmon-farmers

---

9. Thanks are due to John Ballantyne for drawing my attention to the sasines in the Scottish Record Office and to other documents concerning Clothan among the papers of L.H. Mathewson (Shetland Archives D.13.47).

to a rental-free seabed was rejected. Scat exists as perhaps a thousand-year old survival of Norse administration[10], but is rapidly disappearing. Remnants of rights of kin and udal inheritance, paradoxically the poorest documented aspects of udal tenure in the present-day context, represent survivals of the essence of udal tenure, despite the forces ranged against them for 500 years.

The meaning and function of these udal survivals vary among different social groups. For landowners and crofters, where it has any significance at all, udal law has primarily an economic function related to the exploitation of the foreshore or fishing — either commercially or, still for crofters, within a household economy. In the seabed dispute, udal law was also of potential economic significance for salmon-farmers.

For townspeople, udal law is primarily a curiosity with little significance for everyday life. For some, it is part of a Viking heritage which can be used to promote tourism. Lawyers form a special sub-group with a professional interest, by and large, in the maintenance of the Scots law of their training, although some make a point of defending udal tenure where there is a chance that it can be legally upheld. For some politically active groups, heirs of the Norse revival of the late 19th century, udal law has a symbolic function as an element in a perceived local collective identity.

For the last udallers, or at least some of them, udal law may have an idealistic function, governing their conduct regarding perceived family land rights in matters of inheritance and sale. Perhaps we have here the vestiges of a collective memory with subconscious ethnic undertones.

Tradition and change in the context of Orkney and Shetland can be seen against the background of a cultural cross-pressure from Norse and Scots influences. In order to study how the significance of udal law has altered over time, it is necessary to place recent observations and present-day perceptions in historical perspective. Udal law is not a static phenomenon. Its significance has changed through time depending on the historical context. This requires further study.[11] As tradition, udal law is part of a collective memory of Norse origins, renewed through revived Norwegian contacts and the dissemination of written knowledge in the 19th and 20th centuries. As a cultural feature subject to change, udal law has undergone alterations under the pressures of Scots feudalism and later economic and social forces. Udal law has been continually reinterpreted within different historical contexts through time, and continues to be redefined within different social groups at the present time.

---

10. The payment of skatt or taxes from the Northern Islands to the Kings of Norway was mentioned in the sagas, although the connection between these payments and later scats may be somewhat tenuous (see Thomson 1987: 12, 37, 118-123).

11. A tentative sketch of the development of udal law through time was presented in the lecture, but this was omitted from the published version owing to lack of space.

Bibliography

Adams, Ian H. (ed.), 1971: *Directory of former Scottish commonties*. Scottish Record Society, New series 2, Edinburgh.

Austenå, Torgeir, 1984: *Eigedomsrett til og disposjonsrett over land og vatn i strandsona*. Konkurrerende bruk av kystsonen, Prosjektnotat nr. 5. Norsk institutt for vannforskning NIVA — Institutt for jordskifte og arealplanlegging, Norges Landbrukshøgskole, Ås-NLH.

Balfour, David, 1859: *Oppressions of the Sixteenth Century in the islands of Orkney and Shetland from original documents*. Maitland Club, Edinburgh.

Balfour, David, 1860: *Odal rights and feudal wrongs: a memorial for Orkney*. Edinburgh.

Belsheim, Kåre, 1987: 'Akvakultur, strandrett og oreigning,' *Kart og Plan* 47:4, 395-9.

Borgedal, Paul, 1959: 'Jordeiendommenes historie i Norge.' In: Torleif Grendahl (ed.), *Jordskifteverket gjennom 100 år 1859-1958*. Det kgl. Landbruksdepartement, Oslo, 9-166.

Cohen, Bronwen J., 1983: *Norse imagery in Shetland: an historical study of intellectuals and their use of the past in the construction of Shetland's identity, with particular reference to the period 1800-1914*. Ph.D. thesis, Faculty of Arts, University of Manchester (MS).

Dickinson, William Croft, 1954: 'Odal rights and feudal wrongs.' In: W. Douglas Simpson (ed.), *The Viking Congress, Lerwick, July 1950*, Oliver and Boyd, Edinburgh & London, 142-160.

Dobie, Wm. Jardine, 1936: 'Udal law.' In: *The Stair Society: an introductory survey of the sources and literature of Scots Law*, Edinburgh, 445-60.

Drever, W.P., 1904: 'Udal law and the foreshore,' *The Juridical Review* 16, 189-202.

Drever, W.P., 1933: 'Udal law.' In: *Encyclopaedia of the Laws of Scotland* XV, W. Green & Son Ltd., Edinburgh, 321-36.

Fenton, Alexander, 1978: *The Northern Isles: Orkney and Shetland*. John Donald Publishers Ltd., Edinburgh.

Gloag, W.M., & Henderson, R. Candlish, 1980: *Introduction to the Law of Scotland*, Eighth edition, eds. A.B. Wilkinson & W.A. Wilson. W. Green & Son Ltd., Edinburgh.

Grendahl, Torleif, & Solberg, Gunnar, 1959: 'Jordskiftelovene gjennom 100 år (1859-1958).' In: Torleif Grendahl (ed.), *Jordskifteverket gjennom 100 år 1859-1958*. Det kgl. Landbruksdepartement, Oslo, 167-304.

Heddle, J.G.Moodie, & Johnston, Alfred W., 1889: *Memorial for the Udal Rights Association*.

Howarth, William, 1988: 'A Norse saga: the salmon, the Crown Estate and the udal law.' *The Juridical Review* 1988, 91-116.

Imsen, Steinar, 1974: 'Tinglysing,' pp. 344-5. In: Rolf Fladby, Steinar Imsen & Harald Winge (eds.), *Norsk historisk leksikon*, J.W. Cappelens Forlag A.S., Oslo.

Johannessen, Knut, 1974: 'Odelsrett', pp. 240-1, 'Utskiftning,' p. 361, 'Åsetesrett', p. 376. In: Rolf Fladby, Steinar Imsen & Harald Winge (eds.), *Norsk historisk leksikon*, J.W. Cappelens Forlag A.S., Oslo.

Jordlova, 1955: Lov av 18. mars 1955 nr. 2 om tilskiping av jordbruk.

Knox, Susan A., 1985: *The making of the Shetland landscape*. John Donald Publishers Ltd, Edinburgh.

Kulturminneloven, 1978: Lov av 9. juni 1978 nr. 50 om kulturminner.

Laksefiske- og innlandsfiskeloven, 1964: Lov av 6. mars 1964 nr. 1 om laksefisket og innlandsfisket.

MacGillivray, Evan, 1985: 'Udal land tenure — myth or reality?' *The Orcadian* 18.4.1985, p. 4.

Neish, E.W., & Blades, D.P., 1929: 'Fishing.' In: *Encyclopaedia of the Laws of Scotland* VII. W. Green & Son Ltd., Edinburgh, 109-148.

NOU 1972, 22: Om odelsretten og åsetesretten. Norges offentlige utredninger 1972,22. Universitetsforlaget, Oslo.

Neergaard, Erik, 1984: 'Eiendomsrett i sjø — særlig i relasjon til akvakulturnæringen,' *Kart og Plan* 44:4, 317-24.

Odelslova, 1974: Lov av 28. juni 1974 nr. 58 om odelsrett og åsetesretten.

Orcadian, The, 13.12.1979: ' 'Orkney movement" seeks home rule.'

Orcadian, The, 21.8.1986: 'Salmon rents — Udal law implications.'

Orcadian, The, 4.9.1986: 'New rents would 'floor' prospects for land-based farms,' p. 1, & 'Courts unlikely to accept new Udal Law arguments,' p. 4.

Orcadian, The, 19.2.1987: 'West Mainland SSSI notified but there is still opposition.'

Orcadian, The, 11.6.1987: 'OIC asks for rethink on SSSI.'

Orcadian, The, 21.4.1987: 'Conservation grudge behind two heath fires?'

Reiten, Magne, 1987: 'Arealkonflikter i akvakulturnæringa,' *Kart og Plan* 47:6, 589-92.

Renwanz, Marsha Elizabeth, 1980: *From crofters to Shetlanders, the social history of a Shetland Island community's self image: 1872-1978.* Ph.D. thesis, Department of Anthropology, Stanford University. Printed 1983, University Microfilms International, Ann Arbor.

Rogstad, Daniel, 1987: ' 'Strandretten' — noen synspunkter,' *Kart og Plan* 47:6, 593-8.

Robberstad, Knut, 1983: 'Udal law.' In: Donald J. Withrington (ed.), *Shetland and the outside world 1469-1969,* Aberdeen University Studies Series No. 157, Oxford University Press, Oxford, 49-68.

Ryder, Jane, 1989: 'Udal law.' In: *The Laws of Scotland. Stair Memorial Encyclopaedia* 24, The Law Society of Scotland/Butterworths, Edinburgh, 193-219.

Scott, Sir Walter, [1831] 1904: *The Pirate.* Thomas Nelson and Son, London, Edinburgh & New York.

Shetland News, The, 7.12.1950: 'Ownership of harbour forelands. Sheriff's interlocutor in local iinterdict action. Verdict for Lerwick Harbour Trustees.'

Shetland Times, The, 11.7.1986: 'Crofters 'terror' in nets row.'

Shetland Times, The, 11.3.1988: 'Salmon farmers challenge the Crown' (Tom Morton).

*Shetland Times, Th*e, 18.3.1988: 'No county cash for test case.'

Shetland Times, The, 23.3.1990: 'Small salmon farms in strife — Udal Law buried by Crown Estate' (Phillip Hunter).

Shetland Times, The, 30.3.1990: 'Udal law confusion' (T.M.Y. Manson).

Smith, Brian, 1984: 'What is a scattald? Rural communities in Shetland, 1400-1900.' In: Barbara E. Crawford (ed.), *Essays in Shetland history,* The Shetland Times Ltd., Lerwick, 99-124.

Smith, David, 1978: 'Udal Law.' In: Kilbrandon, Lord (chairman), *The Shetland report: a constitutional study,* Nevis Institute, Edinburgh, 197-203.

Smith, J. Irvine, 1958: 'Succession.' In: *The Stair Society. An introduction to Scottish legal history* 20, Edinburgh, 208-221.

Smith, T.B., 1973: 'The law relating to the treasure.' In: Alan Small, Charles Thomas & David M. Wilson (eds.), *St. Ninian's Isle and its treasure* I, Aberdeen University Studies Series No. 152, Oxford University Press, Oxford, 149-166.

Taranger, Absalon (ed.), 1915: *Magnus Lagabøters landslov.* Cammermeyers Boghandel, Christiania.

Thomson, William P.L., 1985: 'The Udal League.' *The Orkney View* 2, 15-17.

Thomson, William P.L., 1987: *History of Orkney.* The Mercat Press, Edinburgh.

Tirval, 1986: 'The crofter and his net.' *The New Shetlander* 157, 12-13.

Tveite, Stein, 1959: *Jord og gjerning. Trekk av norsk landbruk i 150 år. Det kongelige selskap for Norges vel, 1809-1959.* A.s. Bøndenes Forlag, Kristiansand.

Walker, David M., 1983: *Principles of Scottish private law* Volume IV, Book VII: Law of succession, Third edition. Clarendon Press, Oxford.

Winge, Harald, 1974: 'Jordebokskatter,' pp. 143-4, 'Leidang,', pp. 199-201. In: Rolf Fladby, Steinar Imsen & Harald Winge (eds.), *Norsk historisk leksikon,* J.W. Cappelens Forlag A.S., Oslo.

Østerud, Øyvind, 1978. *Agrarian structure and peasant politics in Scandinavia. A comparative study of rural response to economic change.* Universitetsforlaget, Oslo-Bergen-Tromsø.

Legal cases:

Bruce v. Smith 1890 17 R 1000.

Smith v. Lerwick Harbour Trustees 1903 5 F 680.

Lord Advocate v. Balfour 1907 SC 1360.

Lerwick Harbour Trustees v. Moar 1951 SLT (Sh Ct) 46.

Lord Advocate v. University of Aberdeen and Budge 1963 SC 533.

Shetland Salmon Farmers Association v. Crown Estate Commissioners 1990 SCLR 483.

	NORWAY	ORKNEY & SHETLAND	SCOTLAND
Type of landownership	Allodial	Allodial & Feudal	Feudal
Rights of kin	*Odelsrett*	Udal survivals	None
System of land inheritance	Partible inheritance + *åsetesrett*	Primogeniture to 1964 + survivals of partible inheritance	Primogeniture to 1964
Land taxes and duties	Diverse land taxes to 1939	Scat + feu duty to 1974[1]	Feu duty to 1974[1]
Foreshore	Owned by adjoining landowner	Owned by adjoining landowner[2]	Owned by Crown
Rights to salmon fishing	Owned by adjoining landowner	Owned by adjoining landowner	Owned by Crown
Seabed	Owned by adjoining landowner to *marbakken*	Owned by Crown	Owned by Crown

Fig. 1. **Seven aspects of land tenure in Norway, Orkney and Shetland, and mainland Scotland.**

Notes:

1. Scat and feu duty were not entirely abolished in 1974: the Land Tenure Reform (Scotland) Act 1974 prohibited the creation of new feu duties or similar payments from land, and provided for their voluntary redemption, while making redemption compulsory upon the sale of land.

2. Court decisions have upheld ownership of the adjoining foreshore by landowners in the case of a udal title, but not necessarily in the case of a feudal title.

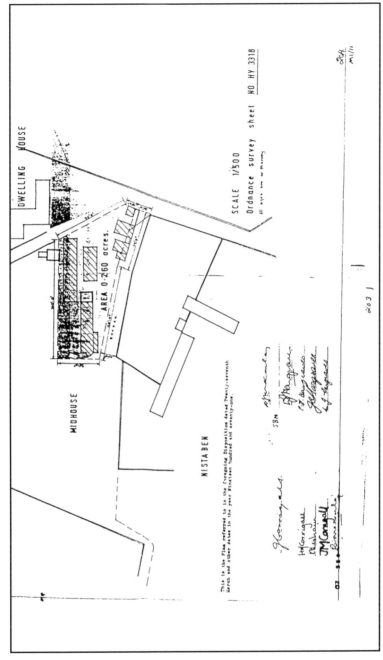

Fig. 2. Extract from the plan attached to the disposition of Corrigall Farm Museum to Orkney County Council in 1971, with signatures of kin giving consent to the sale.

HEAPS, HUMPS AND HOLLOWS
ON THE FOULA SKATTALD

John R. Baldwin

A historical framework

Foula is a small, remote, mountainous island west of the Shetland mainland. It is well-located with regard to once-rich fishing grounds, and lies close to the west-side seaway between Norway, north-west Scotland, the Hebrides and Ireland. Its hills provide good grazing; its seabird colonies were once harvested in considerable quantities; its eastern coastal strip contains some good, albeit limited arable land. It would have been attractive, therefore, to early settlers, and it is of little surprise that evidence of prehistoric settlement has periodically come to light. By far the most part of Foula's 'heaps, humps and hollows', however, belong to the last 200-300 years or so of life on the island; and they interrelate, more-or-less, with the overlordship of the Cheynes (c.1572-1696) and the Scotts (early 1700s-1893).

Foula, as part of the lands of Vaila and associated lands in Walls and Westside, formed part of estates in Norse Shetland that were maybe established c.1300, before passing to the Giske family. In 1490, they were apportioned to the Rosen family, following the death of the eldest sister of the last male Giske heir. The last Rosen heir — an heiress — was Fru Gorvel Fadersdatter, who died in Sweden in 1602. By 1572, however, she had not only appointed Robert Cheyne as manager of her lands in Shetland, but had formally leased him the lands. Fru Gorvel transferred her lands to the Danish crown in 1582 (in exchange for lands in Scandinavia); by 1664, through a labrynthine series of grants, charters and mortgages, and by successfully playing off the Danish crown against the Scottish crown, the whole of Foula (under Scots law at least) had been acquired by the Cheynes.

Foula's economy and lifestyle would seem to have changed but little during the overlordship of the Cheynes — though the cottar 'roumes and lands ther called Hamb and Ararer', first recorded in a sasine of 1698 (Vaila Papers, D.10/8/4 — J. Ballantyne/B. Smith pers. comm.), had seemingly been established sometime during the 17th century, if not earlier. By the later 17th century, however, the Cheynes were in financial trouble; they wadsetted heavily to James Mitchell of Girlsta, a Scalloway merchant, and by 1698 they were bankrupt. Mitchell's daughter and co-heir married John Scott of Gibbleston in Fife, grandson of Sir John Scott of Scotstarvet (who had been a member of the Privy Council in 1617, and Lord of Session in 1649); and the couple probably administered Foula from the early years of the 18th century. Along with a number of other Westside properties, including Vaila and Melby, Foula was formally made over to Mitchell's grandson in 1736. The

Scotts continued to hold tight rein on Foula until the estate was sold first to Herbert Anderton in 1893, and then to W. Ewing Gilmour. It was sold to the Holbourns in 1900 (Holbourn 1938: 114).

Nousts and skeos

During the 18th and 19th centuries in particular, Foula's economy focused so strongly on the sea that it is appropriate to make some reference to surviving features associated with sea-based activities before concentrating on the 'heaps, humps and hollows' on the skattald.

The fisherman had few needs — his boat, gear, clothing and food. He also required access to the shore, and winter shelter for his boat. On Foula, the only sheltered inlet is at Ham Voe (ON *höfn*, haven, harbour + *vágr*, creek, bay), and before the pier was built, small boats simply landed at the rocks or at the head of the Voe. The larger fishing boats that took away cattle to market tied up on the south side of the Voe, at the clett below the Orkneyman's Gait (J. Holbourn 1995). Although a small pier was built in 1914, extended in 1947-48, and reconstructed and further extended in 1989 and 1993 (when the Voe was blasted and deepened), for most of its known history Foula's small boats were overwintered in low hollows or nousts (ON *naustr*, boatshed), hugging the coast a little above high-water mark.

Fig.1. Nousts at the tun o' Ham, Foula. Before the building of the new pier in 1989/93, small boats were drawn up on the ayre during the summer; those remaining in the nousts year-round are old boats, no longer in use. The building just above the ayre once held equipment for the 'Advance' — the former mailboat, a converted sixern. Late 1950s.

206

Nousts

Nousts [Fig. 1] are simply boat-shaped hollows, rounded to something approaching a blunted point at the upper end and open at the lower end. Frequently — and particularly at the Riggs, the Ayre o' Ham and the Banks Ayre — the outline of the hollow has been raised by a loose stone dyke, especially at the upper end. These rough walls may be some 4/5 courses high. The atypical example at Ham, with walls apparently rising to as much as 2.3m on the upper side and 0.8m on the lower side, is not in fact a noust. A J. D. Rattar photograph shows it once roofed with an upturned boat and closed off with a wooden door. It housed the gear of the 'Advance', a converted sixern and the island's mailboat until c.1950; it no doubt served also as a store for fishing equipment, and was subsequently used as a saw pit (J. Holbourn 1995).

Fig. 2. Distribution Map: Nousts, Fishing Lodges and Skeos, Foula.

207

Nousts were scattered in five locations along the island's eastern shore: 7 at *da Riggs*, 5 at *Skeld*, 7 at *da Ayre o' Ham* (or *da Ham Ayre*), 1 at *Ham Little* and 12 at *da Banks Ayre* at the Hametoun — known variously as *da Hame Banks* or *da Doun Banks* [Fig. 2]. They are generally 4.5-7m long, 1.8-2.4m wide and 0.4-0.6m deep at the inner end — though on occasion they may extend to perhaps 8.2m long, or up to 2.7m wide and up to 1.4m deep.

Islanders recall that only fourerns (and smaller boats) were over-wintered in nousts; sixerns — though also beached in summer at the Riggs as well as at Ham — were beached for the winter at the head of the Voe where the gradient is but slight and the distance across the fine shingle relatively short (except on a low spring/neap tide when you could wade out to the 'most westerly moorings' in the voe: D. Gear 1973). The sixerns might be drawn up on the ayre itself, or above or west of the Ham doun yard; and on occasion they were even taken into the Ham yard (J. Holbourn 1995).

Surviving nousts feature the use of stone in a number of ways. Sometimes the slightly sloping inner sides of the hollow were lined with flattish stones [Fig. 3]; and stones, as well as pieces of timber, would be used underneath the boat to steady her and *shord* her up (ON *skorða*, to keep balanced, especially to put stays under a boat). Stones were placed inside the boat to weight her down; and the boat would be secured with ropes or heavy iron chains to a large anchor stone (or log, or lump of iron) at the head and foot of the noust (Gear 1983: 66). For it was vital to protect a boat against winter *flans* (Icel/Nor *flana*, to rush on blindly, to tumble) — roaring,

Fig. 3. Nousts at the Banks Ayre, Hametoun, Foula. 1969.

turbulent gales from the Atlantic which collide with the 155-368m high western cliffs of Foula. The winds shoot upwards under great pressure, burst over the top of the cliffs, nearly 3.5km in length, then race down the landward side, sometimes as whirlwinds, sometimes as near vertical gusts. Such winds take away and destroy anything not extremely well-secured — corn and hay stacks, sheds, roofs, wheelbarrows, boats (Mylne 1959: 13; L. A. Holbourn 1969; Gear 1983: 13, 66, 73, 144-5; J. Holbourn 1995).

Skeos

In addition to these boat-shaped hollows on the coastal fringe of the skattald, there are a number of other hollows or heaps of stone associated with the fisheries — two rock-cut rectangular 'tanks' where fish were washed, not far from the foundations of the factor's/merchant's Booth below the Haa and the former Shop; carefully-built fish drying 'beaches' of boulders close by the Grøps and Mogil; the remains of a mainland fishermen's summer lodge on the Head o' the Baa immediately south of the Voe (and possibly also at the Riggs, Nort Tuns); and the ruins of numerous *skeos* used to wind-dry those young saithe, haddocks and other small fish caught and eaten locally (ON *skjá*, shed; Nor *skjaa*, a drystone shed, drying hut; Icel *skja*, shelter). Because they were not salted down, they avoided obligatory sale to the owner's factor — part of the ill-favoured truck system.

Skeos were small drystone huts, loosely-built without mortar, with gaps or slits left in the walls through which the wind could pass. In other words, the insides were not 'clayed up'. They were roofed with pones (thin turves) and left unthatched (Mr & Mrs J. A. Gray 1970; R. & J. Isbister 1977). All surviving Foula skeos are highly ruinous, many having been built into the corners of a yard or garden dyke, far enough away from the main cluster of buildings for the wind to be unimpeded. Otherwise, skeos were built on exposed sites on the skattald, close to the low eastern cliffs, better to catch the salt-impregnated winds blown inland off the sea and also to minimise the smell — for 'Nothing can smell stronger than a number of these Skeos placed near one another' (Low 1879[1774]: 90)!

Whilst many houses, therefore, had a skeo close by, there was also a remarkable concentration at *da Skeos/Skoes o' da Ness* [Fig. 2] — one still referred to as *da Skeo o' Goteren*, after one of the medieval farms. The many scattered heaps of stones, formerly skeos, lie close to the cliff-top outside the Bankwell dyke, just south of the Hametoun Burn where it trickles over into the sea.

In former times (though much in decline by the 19th century), not only fish but unsalted meat could be wind-dried in skeos — whether sea birds, beef (*vivda*: ON *voðri*, muscle; Nor *vovde, vodve*, muscle), or mutton (*blawn* meat, *reestit* mutton). Furthermore, early 17th century lawsuits for elsewhere in Shetland show that butter, cheese and meal were stored within, and barrels of *blaand* (ON *blanda*, whey mixed with water) might be left there to mature/ferment (Fenton 1978: 160, 442-3, 451; Gear 1983: 82). Skeos, therefore, served as cold stores for dairy and other products, not simply as curing sheds; they could also be used for drying clothes (Jakobsen 1928-32). Their multi-purpose use closely resembled that of the Faroese *hjallur* — an outhouse for drying and storing, e.g. fish, meat and seabirds, where at least two of the sides were made of vertical, gapped wooden slats which let the salt-laden air blow through. Fish might still be wind-dried in a skeo into the early 20th century; when they became obsolete, however, they gradually fell into disrepair or were adapted to other uses.

Kros, buils and dykes

Most of Foula's heaps, humps and hollows have nothing to do with the sea. They are to be found well away from the coastline in association with land-based activities, and it is these features that form the main part of this paper.

Shelters out on the skattald were vital aspects of livestock husbandry on Foula. The stone-built *kro* or fank for rounding up sheep is found widely across the island; and only in the late 1980s was a new and large breeze-block fank built beside the road at Bloburn to replace sundry smaller and older facilities, and be easier of access to vehicular transport. All the kros have splayed stone dykes leading to an inner compartment that might be circular, semi-circular, square or rectangular, and older examples were called a *rett*. A *gripster*, by contrast, was a much smaller enclosure, in the cliffs, where just one or two sheep would be caught by hand.

The C-, T-, S- or Y- shaped *buil* or *snaa-buil* was also built of stone, but was intended more specifically as a place where sheep might shelter in bad weather — for instance, on the lower slope of the Noup, behind the Biggins. Natural hollows might fulfil a similar function, and the term *buil* can refer to anywhere an animal rests. *Da Kubel(s)* on the croft of the Gravins — latterly a squarish, once-cultivated field — was doubtless a one-time resting-place for cows (ON *kú*, cow + *ból*, resting place); *da Green Buils* lie between Harrier and Kruger.

Kros and buils have been examined in fuller detail elsewhere, as have lines of dykes across the South Ness built or re-used in association with the milking of ewes (Baldwin 1978: 97-127). By contrast, the (apparently rather insubstantial) dyke starting just outside of the Hametoun hill-dyke, running uphill behind the Baxter Chapel to the crest of Bodlifield and continuing to roughly the 250m contour, was said by Harry Gear of Mogil to be some 250 years old (first half of the 18th century). It was a *cooie-dyke*, built both to prevent Hametoun cattle from straying northwards and falling in the face of the Hamnafield, and to help lead them home again for milking. This is probably SMR site 2284. The Lammus o' da Wilse is almost on the line of it (W. G. Simpson 1971: pers. comm.).

210

Given the nature of Foula's terrain, there are numerous other such dykes built to keep cattle out of the cliffs. Some were built of stone, some of turf, others just earth with a ditch. The earth and ditch dyke at the southern (Kame) end of the Nort Bank is particularly massive; whilst the longest dyke stretches from the Sneck o' da Smallie at the western end of the Daal, up to and above *da Hus a Borri* (Seim 1938)/*da Hooses o' da Borri*. This area of the Ufshins — precipitous and extremely rough slopes ending at the cliff-top edge of the Muckleberg — is a progression of natural hollows and passages with rock fissures which have been blocked off with short lengths of rough dyke.

Such dykes were frequently of turf, or turf on a footing of stone; though with the reorganisation of the infields in the earlier 19th century, the more important — mainly hill-dykes — were built entirely of stone. The most notable stone dyke on Foula is that around the Hametoun. It was built by men by the name of Abernethy from Walls in the 1880s — the south/south-west sections being fashioned with stone, reputedly quarried in large part from the prehistoric site on the South Ness (J. A. Gray 1977, 1988). Lengths of earlier, older hill-dyke survive on the infield, however, both as fossil features on the ground and on the Six Inch Ordnance Survey map for 1900 (surveyed 1877).

Some such earlier dykes undoubtedly suggest pre-enclosure loanings for the movement of stock from byres to hill grazings — notably at the Biggins, Norderhus, Goteren and Kwenister, but with an emerging *closs* at the Brekkans also. They represent an earlier interface between the infield and the skattald. Apart from a further partial *closs* at North Harrier, and a 'very old' dyke partly visible in the same area and running from Bloburn over Skiordar towards the Nort Tuns (J. Gear 1993; J. & I. Holbourn 1989, 1995), known hill-dykes north from the Hametoun are almost all likely to be 19th century in date. Burns and Loch were not in existence in 1860, and Mornington — close by Hamnabrek — was possibly not broken out until 1885-6 (J. A. Gray 1974). Burns is the smallest croft on the island, and perhaps the last, since Peter Gray said that he was 'no longer young' when he and his father finished cutting the peat that created the large rig south of his house (J. Holbourn 1995).

Not all stone dykes were solid like the Hametoun hill-dyke. Loose and untidy-looking single-thickness dykes were favoured by the late Peter Manson of Bloburn, for instance — the carefully-planned gaps between the stones, bridged by larger single stones, allowing easier passage of the strong winds and flans that would have damaged a more substantial dyke in these particular parts of the island (Fenton 1978: 97). Furthermore, many hill-dykes north of the Hametoun (eg at Sloag) were simply old peat banks. The area where peat had been removed, as at Burns and Ham for example, became either new rigs or *ootrun*, bounded by the edge of the peat bank (J. Holbourn 1995).

Hill-dykes apart, other surviving dykes lie within the present-day infield, enclosing a number of specific features — gardens, kailyards and

211

punds. But just as sections of the older hill-dyke at the Hametoun appear to have been kept in a reasonable state of repair to act as a *cooie-dyke* — to keep cattle on the rough infield grazing or *ootrun* away from the unfenced arable land — so also were shorter dykes used not only to enclose particular fields and yards to keep stock out, but also to enclose particular areas of land within the infield to keep stock in (eg SMR 2273, 2274 — just west of Punds). What survives today of the several *punds* is a low stone footing; at one time they were perhaps heightened by the use of turf in the manner of those *krubs* at the tun o' Ham recorded in 1902 (Baldwin 1984: 47-50; see also Fig. 6 below).

Krubs

Like punds, yards and skeos, krubs went with individual houses and families, rather than representing wider community resources. The term *krub* appears

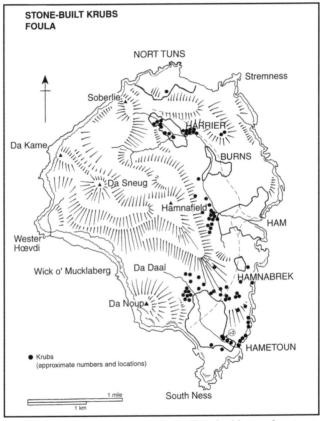

Fig. 4. Distribution Map: Krubs on Foula. (Based, with amendments, on the Ordnance Survey 6 Inch Map, Sheet LIV, revised edition 1900).

212

Fig. 5. Krub cultivated by Edith Gray, Dykes, Foula. Wire-netting helps keep out sheep; the bits of cloth tied to a rope slung across the krub help keep out birds. Tiny kail seedlings have appeared by August. 1969.

to equate with Nor/Swed/Far *krubba*, a crib or box for holding fodder, or possibly with Icel *kro*/Gael *cro̍*, an enclosure, fold (particularly for sheep). On Foula [Fig. 4], as in many other parts of Shetland, it refers to a small enclosure where kail was sown in July/August, and overwintered as seedlings before transplanting the following April/May into the kailyard. (It is old Shetland kail, particularly good at surviving salt spray, that continues to be grown on Foula). A substantial load of manure is given at transplanting time, but very little, if any, when the seeds are sown as this would bring them on too fast to survive the winter.

Foula *krubs* (the term *plantikrub* was not widely used), are circular almost without exception, and where they are rectangular they appear to represent the re-use of an earlier structure. More generally in Shetland, krubs may be circular, rectangular or square, often within the same district. Shape appears to have been of no significance, unless it reflected simply the nature of the available stone or the skills and/or preferences of the builders.

The single-thickness walls were sometimes built as tightly as possible to try to keep out rabbits. Many, however, were built of evenly-sized stones with gaps between, so as to let the winds blow through without creating a back-draught which would blast the growing seedlings (Fenton 1978: 97). On occasion the choice must have been difficult — but either way they provided a sheltered environment for young and tender plants.

Most Foula krubs [Fig. 5] are single, with an inner diameter of 3-4m and an overall diameter of up to 4.9m — though the largest extends to some

213

5.6m internal diameter and 6.4m overall. External height averages 0.9-1.4m, on occasion reaching 1.7m according to the lie of the land. If necessary, little surface drains were dug around the outer sides of a krub to prevent it getting waterlogged within. Internally, the application of muild and manure, as well as turf stripped off the skattald and chopped up with a *dellin spade* over a considerable number of years, has raised ground level to give an average internal height of 0.6-1.2m — on occasion over 1.5m. In other words, internal ground level may be 15-30cm or so higher than that outside.

Since brassicas exhaust the soil in a very short time, kail or cabbage roots had to be pulled up each year to prevent re-sprouting, and on Fetlar the old chopped-up turf and earth was to be removed every two or three years from the krubs and new turf added — the old turf being returned to the skattald to replace the newly-cut turf. In practice, this does not seem to have happened — fresh turf and black muild, as well as byre manure simply being added to the krub as required (Fenton 1978: 103-4, 281). Nowadays, no special preparation is necessary on Foula according to Edith Gray (1969), since the soil/muild is already there. She simply adds a very little dung before sowing the seed, and peat ash was also commonly added (J. Holbourn 1995).

Very much the exception is the double krub, where (as beside the Crooked Burn below Harrier) a 'three-quarter' circular krub is built onto the first. Eppie's krub (towards the Doun Banks, close to the Hametoun nousts) is another — originally single but later extended (J. A. Gray 1993). Equally rare is a step built through the wall either side to allow easier access (in another krub close to the Crooked Burn). You normally expected to climb over — or take down a part of the wall.

Stakes were frequently jammed into the cracks towards the top of the wall, protruding outwards and slightly upwards. Strings (or more recently wire netting) were then tied from post to post to discourage sheep and rabbits. Another length of rope, with bits of rag attached at intervals, was often slung across the middle of the krub to scare away birds — though in other parts of Shetland, as now also on Foula, a piece of old fishing net is draped over the whole krub. This is particularly useful in keeping out the *maalies* (fulmars) which, once inside and unable to get out, completely destroy the plants (J. Holbourn 1995).

Surviving krubs are built entirely of stone. Evidence survives, however, of a different kind of building tradition — in stone and turf. For around the tun o' Ham, close to the meeting of the New Tun o' Ham and the back of the Gravins dyke, an early 20th century photograph [Fig. 6] shows only the footings to be of stone: the rest was a *fealie-dyke*, carefully constructed of layers of turf or *feals* cut from the surrounding skattald and weighted down on the wall head with stones.

Turf krubs were the exception, however. They required a lot of maintenance and were only worthwhile on crofts some distance away from a suitable supply of stone (J. Holbourn 1995). Kail needed the minerals from the clay that underlies the peat, so turf (like stone) krubs were frequently found only where the turf and peat had already been scalped. The stone footings and the infill of muild and chopped-up turf raised the seed bed a little above the surrounding scalped land, providing natural drainage. As with stone-built krubs, these krubs too were topped by wooden stakes, inserted towards the outer edge of the uppermost layer of turf at some 46cm intervals, and angled outwards by about 10°. Three lines of rope tied between the stakes helped keep out unwanted animals. Such turf krubs have not existed on Foula for some considerable time, and they have left virtually no trace in the landscape. For at some point after they became obsolete, the turf walls and well-worked tilth within would likely have been removed to enrich a garden or kailyard (passing first, perhaps, through a byre).

There is no evidence that krubs were in use at an early date; in fact they appear to have developed very much as a response to increasing population and pressure on limited cultivable land in the 18th — early 20th centuries. It would seem that tenants could build and use as many as they wished, and that there was no restriction on their location on the skattald. Eppie's krub, for

Fig. 6. Krubs built of 'feals' or turf, on stone footings. Back of the Gravins dyke, close by its junction with the Ham New Tun, Foula. E.C. Curwen Collection. 1902.

215

instance, was built by James Andrew Gray's great-grandmother — his mother's grandmother, Eppie Isbister — four generations ago (J. A. Gray 1993). That some Foula krubs, notably at the Hametoun, are within the big stone hill-dyke rather than outside, suggests that they may have been in existence before the reorganisation or planking of the township in the 1830s — though their location on the *ootrun*, close to the inside of this hill-dyke, may simply reflect the continuing need to keep the plants secure from stock grazing *innadykes*. Some krubs within the hill-dyke, however, undoubtedly post-date the abandonment of certain crofts in the late 19th-early 20th century. On the old Bankwell land, for instance (only taken in as a croft c.1873-5, and abandoned early), new krubs were built by the Isbisters and the Ratters in the first decades of the 20th century (J. A. Gray 1974, 1993).

As the indigenous population has died or moved away, most krubs on Foula have been abandoned. Where traditional methods are still in use, however, even though fragmentarily, a few krubs have continued to be dug over and planted. The Mansons of Bloburn used a krub just east of Muckle-grind until 1950; it was taken over by Alastair Holbourn until 1960 and by John and Isobel Holbourn until 1989. One close to Ham was still worked by the late Andrew Umphray of Lerabakk in 1971; and on the skattald close to the eastern edge of the Hametoun, from Kru Kaitrin south to Bankwell, certain members of the Isbister, Gray and Ratter families still work the occasional krub.

Roogs and peat cutting

Krubs represent only one form of building or structure found on the skattald. Others are associated with the intensive use of top turf and peat.

Sometimes over 3.1m deep, peat extends over the whole of the eastern lowland of Foula. It extends up the Daal and also up to and around Overfandel and the Fleck. Being an isolated island, difficult of access and with a still-abundant supply of peat, peat cutting continues to be a regular seasonal activity. Peat banks are generally 'hereditary' until the peat runs out — though if left uncut for more than two years you lost your right to that bank (R. & J. Isbister 1974). New peat banks were allocated by the laird or his factor/ground officer, and the key to selecting a good bank lay in the grass. Short rich grass on top usually indicated better quality; if there were knots of 'horse-flesh' in the peat (a brown/black mass of vegetation), the peat would simply sag and break under the *tuskar* (P. Gray 1974).

Once the ground was dry enough in March, the top turf was (as it still is) flayed off and the feals turned on their edges and left to dry. This made them lighter and cleaner to handle. It was usual to employ an ordinary dellin' spade, generally without a foot-peg and worked horizontally like a breast spade (J. Gear 1969; R. Isbister 1969). The top of the bank was then cleaned, but only just in advance of casting — for if done earlier it would begin to harden over and make it difficult for the peat spade to penetrate. The peat was, and is, cast or cut with the *tuskar* (ON *torfskeri*, peat spade) — generally two or three peats deep and with stepped 'ledges'. This allowed more than one man to work the bank at the same time, and lessened the chance of the face collapsing. The peats can be laid flat on the ground both above and below the bank, or set in gapped 'dykes', three or more rows high on top of the bank, where they are left to dry for about two or three weeks. Once sufficiently dry, they are raised into small conical stooks (some four or five peats, capped with a single peat), or set on edge, herring-bone fashion, each resting along a line of peats laid long edge to the ground. When dry, the peats are either taken directly back to the house, or built in a stack or *roog* on the moor.

Although but temporary in nature, these *roogs* (ON *hrúga*, a heap) were constructed with great care in order to keep the peats dry [Fig. 7]. The bluish-

Fig. 7. Peat 'roog' north of the tun o' Ham, below the Hamnafield, Foula. 1960s.

217

black peats, generally from the third layer down in the peat bank, dry first and will decay if they get wet again. If not taken home immediately (difficult in the fine days of summer when time was at a premium), they were put into the centre of the roog and protected on the outside by a wall of the larger, more fibrous peats from the upper layer, built with their damper sides outwards (Miss E. Gray 1969). When the outermost peats were dry, they were then all ready to be transported back to the house where they were piled up inside one of the outbuildings or rebuilt carefully as an outdoor stack.

The secret of building roogs or stacks of peats — generally sub-rectangular, with a flattish top — was to have gently tapering sides, which were not so tapering as to cause the bottom to slip away sideways. The peats in the outer skin, morever, should all stand at the same angle, and the corners were rounded to minimise wind resistance. Rounded corners also allowed best use of the more irregular, wedge-shaped peats which had come from the eroded outer face of the previous year's cutting. Once completed, the top was covered with turves so placed as to allow the rain to trickle down the outside of the roog, rather than penetrate to the hard blue-black peats within (Miss E. Gray 1969; Nicolson 1978: 93-4). These covering turves could be secured with large stones laid on top, though nowadays the ubiquitous nylon fishing net has once again replaced the natural material.

Scalping and muildikusses

Above the peat, however, was the turf — which had first to be stripped away to get at the more heavily compacted vegetation. Best practice required these thick divots not to be removed for use as a building material or chopped up in a krub, but to be placed in neat and regular order in the bottom of the peat bank. Here they would grow back in and thereby continue to provide maximum grazing and avoid the spread of large expanses of black boggy wasteland. In practice, this frequently did not happen.

Turf off the skattald

In the early years of the 20th century, *feals* or sods/turves were still cut to build not just all but the lowest courses of *krubs*, but the *upperhooses* of water mills, *møldikusses* and parts of dykes, sheephouses, henhouses and byres (P. Gray 1974). No doubt they were also used for duck-houses, gable infills and other similar minor building works. Surviving oral evidence suggest that turf was used more at the tun o' Ham than at the Hametoun or further north — the result of an absence of suitable building stone (either poor quality or difficult to obtain) in an area of deep peat that would have been combed clean for ballast for fishing sixerns based in the Voe. Indeed, except for Mogil and the upper corner of Lerabakk, there is no sandstone in the tun o' Ham. Once abandoned, turf buildings would break down under the impact of frosts, wind and rain, and they tend not to survive in the landscape in the way that ruinous stone buildings can. However, it was even more likely that obsolete old turf walls close to the house would simply have been broken down and carried off — perhaps to provide earth for a kailyard or krub, but more frequently into the byres. Most old folk kept a cow for as long as they could, and in more recent times at least (when more of the younger islanders had left), if not also formerly, it was much easier to take dry turf from an old building than to cut, 'hurl or carry it from a piece away' (J. Holbourn 1995). Little evidence would be left on the ground, therefore, except perhaps for occasional grassy or heathery humps following the now-concealed footings of a building or krub.

Feals for building dykes and walls were quite distinct, however, from *pones* used in roofing. Pones (ON *spánn*, shingle for thatching; Nor. dial. *panna*, roof tile) were much thinner than feals. They were roughly rectangular strips of green top turf taken where possible from dry, shallow, clay ground. They were often small, 23cm x 18cm x 5cm thick, though sometimes they could be up to 90cm x 47cm x 7.6cm thick at the centre, thinner at the edges, before drying out (Mrs A. Gray 1970). A flaughter spade such as that owned by Scott Umphray, South Harrier, in the 1950s-1960s, and referred to on Foula as a *muckle shovel*, might be used to pare off the turf; more generally it was the ordinary Shetland delling or digging spade. Just as for a peat bank, the tough upper surface of the moor was first notched with a *ripper* — a 25-30cm iron blade, set roughly at right angles into the end of a 1.2m long wooden shaft and sharpened on the outer edge. According to Peter Gray, the *ripper* was first introduced to Foula sometime between the 1870s and the 1890s; his own was made by Thomas Isbister, probably in the 1930s (J. Gear 1969; R. Isbister 1969; Miss K. Manson 1969; P. Gray 1974).

Scraping off the muild

In John Holbourn's youth, turf and sludge from field drains would be collected in *roogs* and left to rot before being spread on the rigs. This was a very different process, however, from *scalping* or stripping the surface off the skattald — whether the top turf alone, or the additional practice of scraping off the upper layers of fibrous peat, sphagnum or light mossy earth, once this had dried out following the removal of the top turf and, where appropriate, before peat-cutting.

On Foula, scraping muild was carried out with a *shul* (L Sc. *shool*, shovel) [Fig. 8]. Modern examples, referred to simply as *scrapers*, have a rectangular board nailed at right angles to the end of a long shaft; with earlier versions the board, with cut-off upper corners, was attached obliquely at approximately 45° and could have a bevelled edge. In design this is very similar to the *møldin-klubb, møldinklog,* or *mildin-stump/-stick* used variously in different parts of Shetland to smooth down the top soil after sowing (ON *mylda*, to cover with; Far/Nor, to smooth the muild). And it is not dissimilar to the Faroese *klárur*, used to pound rather than smooth the

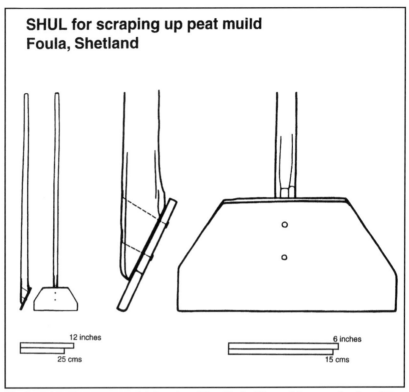

SHUL for scraping up peat muild
Foula, Shetland

12 inches
25 cms

6 inches
15 cms

Fig. 8: A 'shul' to scrape up dried peat muild on Foula. The muild was used as byre litter, then added to the midden for spreading on krubs, yards or rigs. 1971.

muild (Williamson 1948: 208, 210) — though it is the bottom, outer edge of the *shul* that is used for scraping, not the flat face. Pushed away from you, the *shul* could also be used for spreading manure (R. & J. Isbister 1974). Traditionally blades, like shafts, are of wood, though a metal head was noted in 1969.

An area of skattald thus scraped for byre muild was known on Foula as a *møldiblett* (ON *møld*, earth; Far./Icel. *blettur*, spot) or a *møldigrøp* (ON *gróp*, pit, hollow) — whence the house name *da Grøps* (=Magdala) in the tun o' Ham (R. & J. Isbister 1974). (*Mosiblett*, by contrast, is a mossy spot on Taing Head, east of the Sloag: Seim 1938). Gathered in the summer, the granulated peat or muild was intended as winter bedding for livestock, in order to save precious straw for fodder. In the process it absorbed urine and was used to bulk out the manure. In John Holbourn's time it all went into the midden — either every day, or every few days depending on the number of kye and the amount of storage in the byre.

In earlier times, when corn for meal was the most important crop, great care was taken with the middens; and although also dug fresh into the land in spring, seaweed was often added in layers to rot in the midden. There were, however, two kinds of midden. The winter middens were the ones furthest away from the byres — folk had time enough to spare then, and these middens were normally covered with feals to prevent leaching. Excess fish, by contrast, might well end up in the summer middens, nearest the byres. These old middens, then, could be some distance from the buildings, convenient for spreading in the spring (perhaps with an added creelful of coarse sand from the shore). They created definite hollows in the landscape, amongst the rigs (Gear 1983: 138; J. Holbourn 1995).

STONE-BUILT MUILDIKUSSES
FOULA

NORT TUNS

Stremness

Soberlie

HARRIER

Da Kame

BURNS

Da Sneug

Hamnafield

HAM

Wester
Hœvdi

Wick o' Mucklaberg   Da Daal

HAMNABREK

Da Noup

HAMETOUN

● Ruinous Muildikus (stone-built)

1 mile
1 km

South Ness

Fig. 9. Distribution Map: Stone-Built Muildikusses. Foula.

Storing the muild

Muild could be taken direct to the croft in a *kessi* or creel carried on the back by a rope around the shoulders, and it was stored in a special corner of the byre. Alternatively, and since gathering muild was a summer activity when time was at a premium, it could first be piled up on the skattald and protected from the elements in a *møldikus* (ON **møldar*, earth, muild + ON *kos*, heap).

A low circular wall was built on the *møldigrøp;* the scraped-off dried top peat (or sphagnum moss) was piled inside, and the conical structure roofed. In more sheltered parts of the island, and generally where peat was being cut concurrently for fuel (notably, in recent times, between Ham and Harrier), wall and roof were built of *feals* — often secured since the late 1960s with bits of old seine net weighted down with stones. In more exposed places, one family in particular opted for stone-built structures, and it is these examples, abandoned by a rapidly declining indigenous population, that have survived, atypically, and been mistaken for some kind of cairn (Simpson 1968: 315-6). Whilst turf-built muildikusses seem to have been erected amongst the peat banks during and beyond the 1970s, by their very nature they are impermanent. They were in use for just a year or so, whilst a particular piece of skattald was being cut and scalped; then, thereafter, just like turf-built krubs and other turf-built structures, they began to disintegrate. They disappeared altogether once the peat underneath them was cut.

Identifiable, albeit heavily decayed stone-built muildikusses survive east of the road between the Baxter Chapel and the southern edge of the tun o' Ham. Other likely sites are at Overfandel, Netherfandel and in the Daal, but the best examples are at the North End, on the Skiordar ridge and — exceptionally — on the tail of Soberlie where the peat cover is thin and lying on rock [Fig. 9]. Examples on Skiordar and Soberlie [Fig. 10] are some 2.7-3.8m diameter, to an overall height of up to 2m. Actual wall height varies between 0.5-1.8m according to the angle of slope; and the inner wall of carefully constucted courses of stone 0.5-0.6m thick is reinforced by an outer wall of large, long and narrow, flat stones laid upright at an angle against it. This 'reinforcement' appears to echo a building tradition characteristic of some turf-built muildikusses (or small roogs), where photographs from the 1960s show that feals in the lowest course were sometimes stacked upright on the short edge. This would help protect the heaps both from collapsing outwards and from being dislodged by livestock or by flans. On occasion, some of these stone-built muildikusses apparently incorporated a narrow entrance way; others are a complete circle, all the muild being put in from the top. In all cases the conical structure was roofed with flattish, roughly overlapping pieces of stone [Fig. 11]. To extract the muild, therefore, the stone roof and part of the sides would be dismantled — to be rebuilt only if the muildikuss were to be re-used.

According to the late Alastair Holbourn, the stone muildikusses around Hamnabrekk were built by Georgesons and Mansons, relatives of the

222

Mansons of Bloburn. Peter Manson of Bloburn, helped by his sister, the late Katie Manson, built the Soberlie muildikus not long before his death c.1960. It was the last stone-built muildikus to be built on Foula (Miss K. Manson 1969), and between 1969 and 1993 suffered significant deterioration and partial collapse. In another 10 or 20 years it may well be a fairly shapeless and largely unrecognisable rickle of stones, even more easily misinterpreted as some indeterminate 'cairn'. In earlier times, however, like peat roogs and fealie krubs, it would likely not have survived at all, except perhaps as a slightly raised piece of ground surrounded by the remains of a circle of stones. For once the natural resource was exhausted, its purpose became obsolete, and another muildikus would be built on a suitable area of skattald nearby.

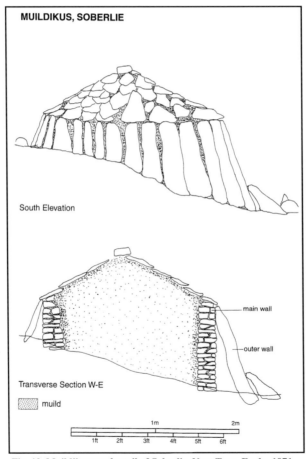

MUILDIKUS, SOBERLIE

South Elevation

main wall

outer wall

Transverse Section W-E

muild

1m   2m

1ft 2ft 3ft 4ft 5ft 6ft

Fig. 10. Muildikus on the tail of Soberlie, Nort Tuns, Foula. 1971.

Fig. 11. Decaying muildikus on Skiordar, Nort Tuns, Foula. The covering stones have begun to fall away, revealing the friable muild stored within but long abandoned. 1969.

Fig. 12. Muildikus on Skiordar, Foula, surrounded by artificially bleak, boulder-strewn moorland. Scalped land on the tail of Soberlie is also clearly visible. 1969.

The introduction and impact of scalping

Scalping was not popular with landowners or visitors to Foula. For once too much of the overlying peat had been removed and the bedrock exposed (as along the slopes of the Daal, or outside the Hametoun dyke, or on the Skiordar/Soberlie ridge), serious soil and gully erosion took place, further removing peat, soil and pasture [Fig. 12]. One account refers to 'the bleak moor, a veritable picture of desolation, owing to the wanton scalping, and dotted with the ugly little mouldie heaps. Here too is death where once all was green and fair' (Holbourn 1938: 180). Other landowners thought similarly. Long ago the Scotts tried to forbid the practice — albeit to no effect — when the entire population of the Hametoun reputedly received a subsequently unenforced notice to quit (*ibid*: 180). Made illegal under late 19th century crofting legislation, and an offence for which a crofter could be evicted (L. A. Holbourn 1972), scalping has continued through to modern times. That bare areas are now beginning slowly to grow over again is undoubtedly welcome, and some re-colonisation is by non-peat-forming plant communities — although invasion by crowberry perhaps suggests a reversion to peat in the very long term (J. Holbourn 1995). Meantime, it may be that in certain places, and over the medium to long term, scalping — however unintentionally or unscientifically — could have brought about an 'improvement' in the potential vegetation. Regeneration owes as much to reduced trampling by cattle, however, as it does to reduced scalping (J. Gray 1988), and reflects the terminal decline in traditional crofting life. Reintroductions of stock at the South Biggins apart (and the grazing there of first a few goats, later of a cow, has been restricted to the infield), the last four cows were removed from Foula in 1974.

The lands on Foula laid waste by peat-cutting, turf-cutting and scalping are clear to see [Fig. 13]. The distribution of those lands, morever, reinforces the view that the Hametoun was the primary centre for settlement (Baldwin 1985: 33-64). At one time, according to James Andrew Gray, you could have rolled an egg from the top of the Noup to the back of the Goteren dyke! Gradually the skattald surrounding the Hametoun, up the Daal and along the sides of the Noup was stripped, exhausted and degraded (with the exception only of a small area left around Kru Kaitrin), and the inhabitants of the Hametoun had to look to the skattald around and north of the tun o' Ham for fuel, turf and muild.

At Kru Kaitrin, by contrast, the land was left unscalped, reflecting island traditions that it was once inhabited by one Katherine Killyoch or Kirlyoch (R. Isbister 1974) — otherwise referred to as Karioch/Kurioch/Kirkyoch (A. Umphray 1974), but also as Asmundder by Mrs Mima Gear and by Professor Holbourn (1938: 45-55), who suggested she was born in 1568. She was supposedly descended directly from the old Norse families — Foula's last Norse heiress and the 'last Queen of Foula'. Whether the land was left unscalped by order of the landowners or out of respect is unclear. The

225

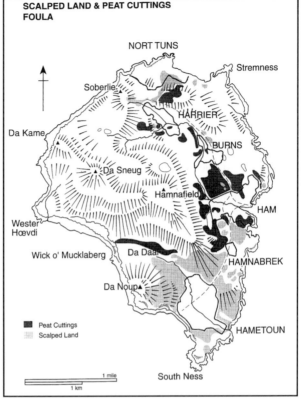

Fig. 13. Distribution Map: Peat Cuttings and Scalped Lands, Foula. 1969.

old people, however, told James Andrew Gray not to go and dig there (J. A. Gray 1974, 1993), and the Royal Commission noted that ashes and a number of bits of pottery had been found in the small enclosure some years previous to 1930 (RCAHMS 1946: 153, site 1687).

As with krubs, there is no early evidence for scraping muild on Foula. According to island tradition, it coincided with the arrival of (H)ellen/Ellie Walterson. She was a great-great-great-grandmother of the late Bobbie Isbister, and reputedly descended from one or two Faroese who had drifted ashore on the Westside in bad weather and ended up in Walls. From Dale, Westside, so the story goes, she came to Foula to marry one Peter Jamieson who lived in the Brekkans/the Grind (Hametoun) before moving to Breidfit. This might put her arrival on the island as late 1700s/early 1800s. She was said to be a wise woman, by some a witch (Holbourn 1938: 95-7; J. Gray 1977, 1993; R. Isbister 1974) — perhaps because she retained words no

226

longer understood in Shetland? By this time — 100 years on from when the Scotts first acquired Foula — the haaf fisheries were well-developed, the population had increased substantially and the lands had been much divided to accommodate the fishermen and their families. Her husband, it is said, died early leaving her with five small children to feed, so that whether or not she introduced to Foula the practice of scalping muild, and whether or not she later remarried (she is said later to have married Andrew Jamieson, but is also referred to as Mrs Peterson), it is evident that a widow with five children would have had to maximise her land resources — for she could hardly go off to the fishing. She would have had every reason to scalp the skattald.

At the same time, we must remember that the arable heartland on Foula had always been limited, and that from at least the mid/later 18th century, the amount of land available to each family, particularly bere land, was much too small. Bere, therefore, was always grown in the same place, and the same land dug over each year. It was never rested and required a good deal of manure each year — hence the growing dependence on scalping. Fresh muild was added in the byre each night and was cleared out every 3-4 days. In addition, feals were cut and placed under the cows' hind feet, and these too were taken out and added to the midden every few days. Given that the muild was well-impregnated with byre manure, it is hardly surprising that scalping was generally accepted as producing much better crops; and it is hardly surprising that families each had maybe seven substantial muildikusses (J. A. Gray 1977; R. Isbister 1977).

Conclusion

The landscape of humps, heaps and hollows as we see it today, therefore, is largely a legacy of the Scotts, superimposed upon a frequently indeterminate blend of fragmentary prehistoric and medieval features — notably burial cairns, burnt mounds, ecclesiastical sites and other earlier landuse and settlement features. To generate substantial income from their properties — primarily through developing the commercial fisheries — the Scotts needed fishermen. They allowed the sub-division of the earlier farms; they imported new families (mainly from their other Westside properties); and they encouraged the breaking out of new small-holdings on the skattald, particularly in areas outside and to the north of the Hametoun. It would appear that they were 'in great wrath', nonetheless, when they discovered that the Nort Tuns had been broken out; and they unsuccessfully sought to get the people to break out land in *da Green Buils* instead — an area of relatively sheltered skattald between Harrier and Kruger, where sheep naturally gathered and had improved its fertility (Baldwin 1978: 117). Ironically, the Nort Tuns never did prove particularly successful, on account of the salt blast (J. Holbourn 1995).

In due course, mainly in the early 19th century, the Scotts reorganised the townships to give small consolidated holdings to a population far in excess of what the island could realistically support from the land; and it is this landscape, now largely uncultivated and fossilized, that survives to the present-day. Because none of the 18th-19th century tenants were in any position to increase their holdings, or to take advantage of the improved agricultural methods and equipment increasingly favoured on larger farms elsewhere, they were entirely dependent upon traditional subsistence practices which, perforce, were further refined and extended under the pressure of a greatly increased population. Thus it would be that — although krubs and scalping would seem to be essentially 18th century developments — they are rooted somewhat deeper perhaps in the island's Norse past.

The essentially detrimental impact of these later practices is clear for all to see. The responsibility for environmental degradation does not lie directly with the ordinary people of Foula, however, who had little option but to skin the land in order to survive; rather does it lie with those proprietors, merchants and factors who sought to exploit the resources of the sea — as they did the island's human population — in such a way and to such a degree that the quality of life and environment on Foula declined in proportion perhaps to the increased wealth that accrued to themselves.

Acknowledgement

Yet again I am grateful to those on or of Foula who have taken an interest in my research and contributed so willingly over the years. In particular, I would like to thank the Gears, Grays, Holbourns, Isbisters, Mansons, Ratters and Umphrays — notably those who once lived, and in a few instances still live at the Biggins, Bloburn, Breidfit, Burns, Dykes, Freyers, Grøps, Ham, Lera-bakk, Mogil, Mucklegrind, Nigarts and the former Schoolhouse.

Many others have helped in so many ways: Brian Smith and John Ballantyne for bringing a number of obscure but fascinating references to my attention; the late Einar Seim and his family in Norway, who have made available material that he collected in the 1930s; and those leaders and members of Brathay Exploration Group expeditons to Foula who gathered much valuable data in the 1960s and 1970s — in particular Donald Brownrigg, Gavin Simpson and Ian Tulip, and members of those expeditons that I also have led.

John and Isobel Holbourn very kindly read the draft text and offered numerous invaluable suggestions, as did Val Turner of the Shetland Amenity Trust for the archaeological material (most of which has had to be set aside to await publication on a future occasion!). I am grateful to Kerry Houstoun for redrawing the distribution maps, and to Helen Jackson for drawing Figure 8. Other illustrations are reproduced by courtesy of Chistopher Mylne (Fig. 1); the Scottish Ethnological Archive, National Museums of Scotland (Fig. 6); and the Brathay Exploration Group (Figs. 7, 10). Remaining photographs were taken by the author.

Bibliography

Baldwin, J.R., 1978: 'Norse Influences in Sheep Husbandry on Foula, Shetland'. In: J.R. Baldwin (ed.), *Scandinavian Shetland: An Ongoing Tradition?*. Edinburgh.

Baldwin, J.R., 1984: 'Hogin and Hametoun: Thoughts on the Stratification of a Foula *Tun*.' In: B.E. Crawford (ed.), *Essays in Shetland History*. Lerwick.

Gear, S., 1983: *Foula: Island West of the Sun*. London.

Fenton, A., 1978: *The Northern Isles: Orkney and Shetland*. Edinburgh.

Haugen, E., 1965: *Norsk-Engelsk Ordbok*. Oslo.

Holbourn, I.B.S., 1938: *The Isle of Foula*. London.

Jacobsen, M.A. & Matras, C., 1961: *Førosyk-Donsk Orðabók*. (+ supplement 1974). Tórshavn.

Jakobsen, J., 1928-32: *An Etymological Dictionary of the Norn Language in Shetland*. 2 vols. London/Copenhagen.

Jakobsen, J., 1936: *The Place-Names of Shetland*. London/Copenhagen.

Low, G., 1879: *A Tour through the Islands of Orkney and Schetland* [1774]. Kirkwall.

Mylne, C., 1959: 'Home on the Edge of the World'. In: *Scotland's Magazine*. September.

Nicolson, J.R., 1978: *Traditional Life in Shetland*. London.

Ordnance Survey, 1900: *Six Inch Map of Zetland Sheet LIV* [1877].

Ordnance Survey, 1896: *Six Inch Name Book of the Island of Foula*. ms

Ordnance Survey, 1986.

RCAHMS, 1946: *Inventory of Shetland*. vol. 3. Edinburgh.

Reid, J. T., 1869: *Art Rambles in Shetland*. Edinburgh.

Seim, E., 1938: *Place Name Map of Foula*. ms.

Shirreff, J., 1814: *The Agriculture of Shetland*. Edinburgh.

Sibbald, R., 1711: *A Description of the Isles of Orknay and Zetland*. Edinburgh.

Simpson, G., 1968: 'A Preliminary Survey of the Archaeology of Foula'. In: *Brathay Exploration Group Annual Report and Account of Expeditions*. Ambleside.

av Skarði, J., 1984: *Ensk-Føroysk Orðabók*.. Tórshavn.

Smith, S., 1949: 'Foula: The Ultimate Isle'. In: *Scotland's Magazine*. March.

SMR, 1989: *Shetland Archaeological Sites and Monuments Record — Foula*. ms. [update].

Stewart, J., 1970: 'Place-Names of Foula'. In: *Fróðskaparrit, vol. 18*. Tórshavn.

Stewart, J., 1987: *Shetland Place-Names*. Lerwick.

Thomson, D., 1792: 'Parish of Walls and Sandness'. In: *Old Statistical Account, vol XX*. Edinburgh.

Tudor, J.R., 1883: *The Orkneys and Shetland: Their Past and Present State*. London.

Williamson, K., 1948: *The Atlantic Islands*. London.

Zoëga, G.T., 1910: *A Concise Dictionary of Old Icelandic*.Oxford.

THREE RIFTED OR FOUR TOPPED
NINETEENTH CENTURY LUG MARKS
FROM NORTH YELL

Alexander Fenton

Introduction

Identification marks are well known amongst many peoples in Europe, Asia and Africa as a means of attributing ownership under conditions of nomadism or of community existence where stock grazes in common. The phenomenon is most usual now in relation to sheep in this country, but other animals can also be lug-marked. An example is the reindeer herds held by the Lapps.

In a recent study from Norway, Johs. Falkenberg outlined the results of a survey he carried out in 1962 amongst the Rørøs Lapps, and made a number of points that have general relevance for lug-marking systems. At a technical level, the forms of the marks used were conditioned by being made with a small knife, or sometimes a pair of shears, so that slits, slices, nicks and angled cuts and openings prevailed (Fig. 1). At a community level, the animals were the personal property of individuals — husband, wife, daughter, son — and each had an individual mark, though the marks were often linked by common features that indicated family relationships. There was, therefore, a close connection between the marks used, the individuals within families, and the families within their communities.

A glimpse of the ear of a reindeer even in a fast moving group might immediately identify some major feature of a mark that pointed to a handful of owners for whom this was shared, whilst closer examination of the supporting features of the marks then tied the reindeer in with a family and with an individual within the family. It could be possible even to establish family relationships from the lug-mark code. In this way, lug-marks and other identification marks are capable of giving insight into the socio-economic relationships within communities. At a further level, broad regional variations in the form and composition of marks is also evident, so that territorial attribution can be added to the other criteria. And since marks could be inherited, sometimes over several generations, there is also a historical dimension. Where a mark was sold or given away, which was also possible, the historical sequence was, of course, broken. Finally, it appears that there has been in more recent times a reduction in the range and complexity of reindeer marks, which points in turn to less cohesion in the older well-knit forms of community existence.[1]

This example from a distant land highlights a number of the aspects of the system of sheep's lug-marks in Shetland (and Orkney). The present paper

---

1. Falkenberg, Johs, 1979: 'Om öremerking av rein hos Rørøs-samene', *Kultur på karrig jord*, Oslo, 37-76. (Also in *By og Bygd*, 1977. Norsk Folkemuseums årbok XXVI).

concentrates on the lug-marks from North Yell, about which a good deal of evidence is available in the Irvine of Midbrake papers,[2] and makes a preliminary analysis of them.

In the Northern Isles, identification marks were used on cattle and horses, as well as on sheep.[3] Records of marking the ears of cattle go back to the early seventeenth century in Shetland. The term 'cattle marks' is used every so often in the Irvine of Midbrake papers, though it appears that this is

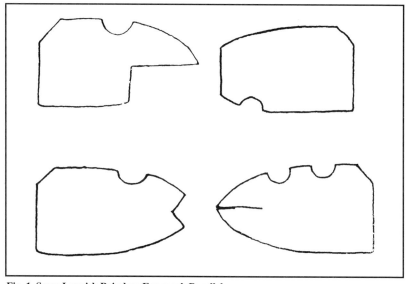

Fig. 1. Some Lappish Reindeer Ear-mark Parallels
1. **Half out** (*skaavhte*); **bit** (*dable* or *tjiehkie* — the former is bigger)
2. **Shear or shule** (*skaarja*, cf Norwegian *skar*); **bit**
3. **Stued, piece off** (*namhpe*); **bit**
4. **Rift** (*sloeptje*); **two bits**
(After Falkenberg, pages 52, 54, 58, 65. Numbered from the top down).

---

2. The Irvine of Midbrake Papers, now in the Shetland Islands Council Archives, were formerly in the Library of the Society of Antiquaries of Scotland (National Museums of Scotland), under the following references:

  MS 395/1, bearing dates ranging between 1802 and 1805.
  MS 395/2, diagrams (cut-outs) of lug-marks.
  MS 395/3, *'Register of Marks'*, listed mainly alphabetically, with dates ranging from
      1833 to 1872.
  MS 395/4/1, description of a lug-mark dated March 1781.
  MS 395/4/2, extract from the *'Register of Marks'*
  MS 395/6, 'A General List of All The Cattle Marks in the Parish of North Yell',
      compiled from a list drawn up in 1785. Dates given in the body of the text range
      from 1816 to 1824.

3.   An initial survey of Shetland lug-marks was made in Fenton, A., 1978: *The Northern Isles: Orkney and Shetland*. Edinburgh, 475-476.

used generically for 'stock' and primarily for sheep, but the fact that entries sometimes specify the word 'cattle' may indicate use of the marks on bovids:

'Jerom Anderson in Basta 1 Cattle mark viz the Right Lug half away before, the Left Shulled and a bitt out before and no more' (MS 395/6, p 3).

Lug-marks for horses are specifically referred to. Examples are:

'Bain George Cullivoe Right Lug Rifted & a Bit on each side in the Left Lug the same Given to him by his aunt Molly (?) Bain who brought it from Fetlar where it had been used as a horse Mark. Registered 1860' (MS 395/3 p 3).

'Clark James — Horse Mark Rt. Lug *half behind* two Bits before Left Lug *half before* — Sheep Mark Rt. Lug *Half behind* — *Rift before* Left Do. *Half before*. Magnus Clark Mid Yell his Son has both these Marks in use — Febry. 1851' (MS 395/3 p 4).

'Danielson Alexr. Horse Mark — A Bit before each Lug & a hole on the Right. May 2nd. 1857' (MS 395/3 p 5).

'Irvine, Mr. Thos. of Midbrake Right Lug a hole & a bit before, Left Lug Rifted. This is called the Horse-mark .... 2 Bits behind the Left Lug & a Bit behind the Right Lug, is the mark on the Mare bought Augt. 1855 from Mr. Henry of Burraster' (MS 395/3 p 11).

'Robert Robertson or Johnson Otterswick — E. Yell A Horse Mark — A bit behind each Lug and a hole on the Left. June 4th 1858' (MS 395/3 p 25).

Descriptions of horse marks are few as compared with those for sheep. They appear to be of a relatively simple form, consisting in the examples quoted of slits and notches on the edges of the ears, and holes in the centres. The James Clark example quoted above shows that on occasion there were only minor differences between the marks of horses and sheep in the same ownership. The situation with sheep, however, was in general much more complicated. Nevertheless, the range of marks for North Yell was less than that of the total recorded for Shetland and Orkney as a whole, the implication being that this was a smaller area with a set of communities and families that did not require to utilise all the technical possibilities (Fig. 2). The total number of owners of sheep in the three lists comes to about 150.

Terminology and description of North Yell lug marks

Bit. A bit can be half round or V-shaped, and can be positioned anywhere round the edges of the ear, e.g. a 'bit behind' or a 'bit before'. There is one occurrence of 'a bitt behind at the Root of the Lug' (Thos. Robertson, Sellafirth, MS 395/6, p 2), and of 'a bit off the top', the latter in combination with a 'half behind' (Peter Gray, Basta, MS 395/3, p 11). There was also 'a bit off the top of the fore half' (Jerom Anderson, Basta, MS 395/3, p 1), described in the Register as an 'Old mark'.

232

A bit could readily be added to existing marks, as when a lug-mark changed hands, as a distinction.

'Robertson Gilbert, West the firth, Right Lug Stued Left Lug rifted. Decr. 6 1852 — Granted to his granddaughter Margt. Robertson with the addition of a bit behind the Left Lug' (MS 395/3, p 11).

Such an additional distinguishing mark, not always a bit, was known as an 'obright' (MS 395/3, preliminary note), otherwise known in Shetland as an 'afbreg(d)' or 'obregd'.

Crook. In the *Register of Marks*, entry No. 18 is:

'Davidson Janet, Kongnaseter. Right Lug sheered, Left Lug Knaed behind & a Crook or bit' (MS 395/3, p 5).

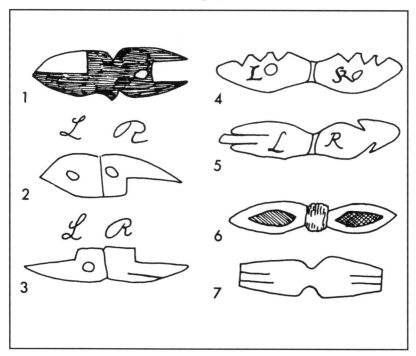

Fig. 2. North Yell Lug-marks from the Midbrake Papers.
1. James Moar, Jr., Gloup: Right — middled, a hole; Left — half out before, a bit behind.
2. George Moar, Gloup: Right — half out behind, a hole; Left — knead, a hole.
3. Andrew Manson, Kirkabister: Right - half out before, rift behind; Left — half out before, a hole.
4. Alexander Fordyce, Unst: Both lugs — three bits before, a hole.
5. Andrew Fordyce, Montulie: Right — crook before and behind; Left — two rifts or three topped.
6. Samuel Johnson: Both lugs — heart out.
7. William Nesbit, Kongnaseter: Both lugs — top off, two rifts or three topped.

This clearly equates a crook with a bit, and in MS 395/6, p 1, there is a diagram showing one of two marks of Andrew Fordyce, Mont(h)ulie, with ' a crook before and a crook behind'. It is a slightly elongated notch, like an extended bit (Fig. 2,5).

That this also brings it into line in some degree with a rift is indicated by a mark on a lamb given by Mr. Thomas Irvine of Midbrake to Laurence Smith 'in halvers', in Sept 1843:

'Right Lug full House mark — Left Lug One crooks or rifts upward & One Do. downwards on each side of the Ear' (MS 395/3, p 11).

A crook, therefore, like a rift, could be cut upwards or downwards, though the majority were cut downwards.

Feathered. A feather is a thin slice off the side of the ear. In the Midbrake Papers, the word never occurs as a noun, but always in the verbal form. It is a reasonably common mark, usually in combination with a bit, hole or rift, and it can be on one or both sides of the ear:

'William Sutherland Tail 1 Merk viz: The Right lugg Feathered before & behind with a holl on it, the left lugg half away before & a rift behind' (MS 395/1, p 4).

There is one example where both ears are treated in this way:

'Laur. Gray there (Basta) 1 Merk viz: The Right lugg Feather'd on both sides (sic), the left lugg Feather'd on both Sides' (MS 395/1, p 10).

The term is equivalent to *Strawdrawn*, which appears to have begun to replace 'feathered' after about 1850.

Half (out) before or *behind.* This represents the removal of the front or back half of the ear, using a cut made downwards from the top and then at right angles at the appropriate side. It is an easily recognisable and frequent mark, sometimes alternating fore and aft on the right and left ears (Fig. 2, 1-3):

'Thos. Robertson in Sellafirth 1 Mark viz the Right Lug half before & a rift behind, the Left Lug half behind and a bitt behind at the Root of the Lug' (MS 395/6, p 2).

Heart out. This mark is not common. It involves taking a section in the form of an elongated oval from the heart of the ear, leaving a complete surround:

'Johnson Samuel — The heart of both Lugs cut out leaving the Sides and top standing as below June 16th 1856' (MS 395/3, p 14) (Fig. 2, 6).

The fact that it was illustrated in the Register further suggests that it was unusual. There are, however, two other occurrences. In one, the term used is 'hearted downward':

'Arthur Williamson Burraness 1 mark viz Both Lugs hearted downward & no more' (MS 395/6, p 7).

The other term is 'heart hole':

'Anderson Marble Kellister Right Lug Rifted Left Lug a Heart hole. Augt. 12 1835' (MS 395/3, p 2).

This mark had been listed as the second mark of John Sutherland, West the firth, but had been claimed by Marble Anderson and was given to her by the authority of the Registrar of Marks in 1835 (MS 395/3, p 26).

The remaining example is:

'Moar David, (Son of George) Basta, Right Feathered, Left Lug a Hart hole. May 21st. 1833' (MS 395/3, p 19).

If this mark is rare in Shetland, it appears from the available evidence that it is quite unknown in Iceland and in the Faroes. It looks as if it would be rather easy for the ear to be caught on a stalk of heather, so that it might become torn.

Hole. A hole in the ear, in various positions, and in general use (Fig 2, 1-4).

Knead. A 'knee' (only the verbal forms appear in these lists) is a slanting cut off the side of the ear, starting at the top. It is illustrated in the lists along with the description of one specific mark:

'George Moar Gloup 1 Mark viz. the Right Lug half behind & a hol on it the Left Lug knead & a hol on it & no more...'.(MS 395/6, p 3) (Fig. 2,2).

An ear could also be 'knaed round', which presumably means that the cut was made on both sides of it:

'Danielson Jas. Cullivoe. Right Lug a bit behind & a bit before. Left Lug Knaed round & a hole. This mark was assigned to Daniel Williamson, Cullivoe, in 1837' (MS 395/3, p 5).

'Flaws Magnus Sellafirth — Right Lug a Crook behind & a Rift in top — Left Lug Knead round & a hole' (MS 395/3. p 7).

Another related term is 'half knead':

'Chirsten Johnsdaughter in midseat viz the Right Lug half Knead behind and a holl, the Left Lug Stoued and no more' (MS 396/6, p 6)

'Manson Barbara Neep — Right Lug half away before & a hole — Left Lug Knaed behind — Given to her by George Moar in Goodseter; her grandfather' (MS 395/3. p 29).

Middled. A rectangular cut from the top towards the middle of the ear. An example is illustrated:

'Jas. Moar Junr. Gloup 1 Mark [viz the] Right Lug Midled with a holl on it the Left Lug half [out before] a bit out behind' (MS 395/6, p 3) (Fig. 2,1).

That this is an old mark is not in doubt. It goes back at least to the seventeenth century as a Midbrake mark:

'Irvine Mr. Thos. of Midbrake

1st Both Lugs Middled a hole & a bit before on the Right Lug

N.B. The original Record of this mark was Kept in the House of Midbrake among the Title Deeds in the little old Oak Charter Chest. It was dated 16 hundred & odds, but I do not remember the exact year, and came to Midbrake along with Some of the Land (4 Ms [merks] of the Garths (I think)) from the original Udaler & held as an heirloom — Hence the mark is always called the *House Mark*. The said Record was lodged in the Sheriff Court at Lerwick in 1804 or 1805 on occasion of a Process 'twixt my father & some men in West Yell about sheep' (MS 395/4/2, copied by Thomas Irvine of Midbrake from MS 395/3, p 11).

The widespread nature of the mark is shown by the parallel forms and terms in Iceland, *mið-hlutað*, and in the Faroes, *midt ûr hajlun* (1780s), *miðjulutað*. 'Middled' may well be a form of the Norse expression, though influenced from English.

Middle standing. This refers to the situation, noted once in the lists, in which the sides and top are cut away, leaving a rectangular piece standing. It is the reverse of middled:

'Robertson Peter, Mid Yell, Right Lug, a third part away behind & before, the Middle standing & the top off, Left Lug Rifted' (MS 395/3, p 25).

This mark is known in Iceland as *hamrað*, *hamarskorið*, and in the Faroes as *hamarsmerki*.

Piece off the top. This mark refers to the removal of the tip of the ear. It is found only once in the lists:

'Hay Basil Junr. Burrabrake, Right Lug Stued & a Shule in it, Left Lug a piece off the top & a hole. Jany. 11th. 1833' (MS 395/3, p 10).

It seems certain that a 'piece off the top' is similar to a 'stoo', since the same mark is referred to again, but as a 'half stoo', which presumably was not as substantial as a stoo proper:

'Sutherland John West the firth, Right Lug Stued & a shule in it, Left Lug half Stued & a hole. N.B. Given to Basil Hay Jr. Burrabrake Jany 11th. 1833' (MS 395/3, pp 10 and 26).

Rift. A narrow slit downwards from the tip of the ear, or from the outer edges of the tip if another mark (a shear, shuil or half away) had already been made in the tip, or from the middle down if a stoo had been made. If two rifts were made in the whole ear or in the stooed ear, the mark was then called two- or three rifted or three- or four topped (Fig. 2, 3 and 5):

'Robertson David, Sellafirth. Right Lug rifted in the top, two bits before & two behind, Left Lug half away behind' (MS 395/3, p 25).

'Robertson Thos., Sellafirth, Right Lug half away before & a rift behind, Left Lug half away behind & a bit under' (MS 395/3, p 25).

'Sinclair John, Virdick, Both Lugs Sheered in the top a Rift on each side & a hole on the Left Lug. 1860 Used by Wm. John Hay as a halvers mark' (MS 395/3, p 28).

'Moar Wm. Backhouse, Right Lug Shuled the Left Lug shuled in the top & a rift on each side a hole & a bit behind' (MS 395/3, p 17).

236

'Manson Andw. Papil, Right Lug half Stued a rift in the Stue & a bit before, Left Lug Knaed, a hole & a bit behind' (MS 395/3, p 20).

'Moar Janet, Junr. Right Lug half Stued & two Rifts in the Stue, Left Lug Feathered & a hole' (MS 395/3. p 18).

'Nisbit William Kongnaster The top off Both Lugs and two rifts in the cut of each thus May 11th. 1869' (MS 395/3, p 22) (Fig. 2, 7).

'Alexander Spence there (Breaken) 1 merk viz: The Right lugg Stowed the left lugg three Rifted or four Toped & a holl on it' (MS 395/1, p 3).

All of these variations are also known in Iceland: *heil-rifað, tvírifað í heilt, þrírifað í heilt, stúf-rifað, tvírifað í stúf*, etc., and there are Faroese equivalents, *riving, rivað heilt, rivað stúv*, etc., but there seems to be no evidence for the use of the three rifted or four topped mark there.

Sheared. This mark involves cutting a V-shaped notch in the tip of the ear (cf Fig. 1,2). It does not occur very often in the lists, seemingly because it was the same as the much more frequently used term, *shuled*. One entry, in fact, glosses sheered as shuled:

'Anderson Andrew Basta. Right Lug Sheered (Shuled) & a Hole, Left Lug a Bit before & a Bit behind' (MS 395/3, p 1).

It happens also that the same entry occurs in two of the lists, one using sheered and one using shuled. Both are given here because they also show how the description of the same mark can be varied:

(a) 'Jas Leisk in Basta 1 Cattle mark viz the Right lug sheered in the top with a holl & a bit before & Do. behind, the Left lug two rifted or three toped with a bitt before and Ditto behind & no more' (MS 395/6, p 4).

(b) 'Leisk Jas. Basta, Right Lug Shuled a bit on each side & a hole, Left Lug two rifts or three toped & a bit on each side' (MS 395/3, p 15).

Shear, which is simply the English word, may represent a stage in the anglicisation of a good native word of Norse origins (see *Shuled*).

Shuled. This is the same as sheared. It is known from at least the late eighteenth century:

'At Cullavoe 24 March 1781 Compeared Andrew Moar in Mursetter and presented the following Cattle merk viz: The Right Lugg Shulled with a Rift on each side of the lugg Cut downward, the left lugg Shulled with a Rift on each side of the lugg Cut downward & a holl on said lugg, which merk he Desired to have and the said merk was published in the presents of the Parish being met at said Place, no objections made, therefore the same is granted to him, as his lugg merk, to be used by him on his Cattle, and by Virtue of Powers Invested in me by the Sheriff Substitute of Shetland I hereby warrandize said merk to him which is Recorded and Extracted from the same by Desire of Alex Irvine' (MS 395/4/1).

The term and shape are the same as for Icelandic and Faroese *sylt*.

Slit. There is only one example of this mark:

'Fraser George Brae — One Slit upward & one Slit downwards on each side of each Ear, & a hole on the Left ear. — 1843' (MS 395/3, p 7).

It seems to be like the Icelandic mark, *andfjaðrað*, two slits half way down the ear that start from two different points and run towards each other, or *oddfjaðrað*, where the two slits start from the same point and run away from each other

As used here, it may represent an anglicisation of rift, though no other examples of rifts taking this upward and downward form have been found. A possible parallel may be found under *Crook*.

Stooed. With this mark, the tip of the ear is cut off. The term 'half stooed' also occurs and seems to indicate that a smaller piece was removed; it could be found on both ears.

'Jas. Anderson in Cirkabister 1 Mark The Right Lug feathered behind and a Rift before, the Left Lug stoued' (MS 395/6, p 2).

'Elizabeth Leisk Basta 1 Mark viz. the Right Lug Rifted the Left Lug half Stoued & one hole on it' (MS 395/6, p 3).

'Mr John Spence Mercht. Stonganess 1 Mark viz: The Right lugg half stowed & two Riftes in it, the left Lugg half stowed & two Riftes in it' (MS 395/1, p 3).

The Icelandic equivalent is *styft*, and the Faroese *styv*. *Styft* is also the name in Sweden (Öland).[4] The term and shape are, therefore, in wide use.

Straw drawn. This is a thin slice cut off along the full length of the ear, equivalent to *Feathered*, as is specifically stated in the description of one mark. The mark might also alternate in position on each ear:

'Smith Jas. Both Lugs straw drawn on each side (feathered) and a hole on each — Old Mark' (MS 395/3, p 23).

'Williamson Peter John — Right Ear Straw-drawn before and a bit out behind — Left Ear a Bit out of each side — The above mark was presented by Peter Jn. Wm.Son a year or two back for Sheep in halvers with Mr. Pole Cullivoe — Entered in this Register Feby. 23d. 1852' (MS 395/3, p 30).

'Moar Bruce — Lingarth Rt. Lug Strawdrawn before & a bit behind — Left Lug Strawdrawn behind and bit before — March 31st 1866' (MS 395/3, p 29).

There is one example of the form 'strawn':

'Also May 28th. 1856 — The same Thos. Moar Junr. (Konnaster) presented the following Mark — Right Lug Strawn on both sides — the Left Lug Knaed and bit behind' (MS 395/3, p 16).

---

4. Comparative evidence for the forms and terminology of Scandinavian marks is taken from: Berg, Gösta, 1966/67: 'Johannes Galejas märkebok och andra öländska märkeböcker', *Kalmar läns fornminnesförenings årsbok*, 23-34; H Pálsson, 1958: 'Fjármörk', *Freyr*, Nr. 7-9, 132-137; *Almanak hins íslenzka þjóðvinafélags um árið 1912*, Reykjavík 1911, 80-81; *Seyðamark*, serprent úr Álmanakkum, Tórshavn 1964, 3-7.

Topped. Occurring in the phrases 'three tops' or 'four toped', seemingly as a Yell speciality. See *Rift*.

Top off. The mark for William Nesbit, Kongnaster, quoted under *Rift*, shows in the illustration that this is equivalent to being stooed (Fig. 2, 7).

Lug marks and the community

Lug-marks were, in effect, like legal documents that established an owner's claim. They had to be publicly accepted before they could be officially granted to an owner, to ensure that they did not duplicate those of another man, and that they did not have too close a resemblance to any other. They were listed in Registers of Marks by the local registrar, whose authority to do so came, as Alexander Irvine noted, from the Sheriff Substitute of Shetland (MS 395/4/1). In this way they had both a legal basis, and a basis of joint agreement amongst the stock owners of the various districts, in this case North Yell. There was also a registration fee of 6d in the mid nineteenth century, for example on change in ownership of a mark:

'Gilbertson Charles — residing in Halsingarth — presented the following Sheep Mark viz. A hole & a Bit behind & a Bit before on each Lug — descinded from Molly Jameson from Buster wife of Gilbt. Anderson Out Harra — Registered accordingly & Extract given dated Agt. 9th 1851 — fee 6d paid' (MS 395/3, p 8).

The keepers of the registers were men of responsibility, who had to be scrupulously careful in order to avoid disputes. A note written by Thomas Irvine in the *Register of Marks* shows that the succession of keepers, probably from the late eighteenth century, was Mr John Spence of Stonganess, then Mr Gilbert William Irvine of Midbrake, then Thomas Irvine, also of Midbrake. A note by Thomas's nephew, also called Thomas, states:

'The above Mr. Thos. Irvine was the last official Registrar of Sheep Marks for the Island of Yell. My Father Gilbt. Will. Irvine held it before him and His father My grandfather James Irvine of Midbrake before him again I had the Bladder bag Containing the bundle of cut shapes of Ear Marks but lost this. Thos. Irvine' (MS 395/3).

The 'bladder bag' gives some insight into the way in which the actual outlines of the marks could be kept, cut out in paper, as a complement to the written descriptions in the registers.

Within the community, various activities could take place in relation to marks. A mark could fall into disuse, perhaps through the sale of an owner's flock when he died or became too ill to look after them, and had no direct descendants in the area. A mark that had belonged to Edward Fraser in 1781 was 'renewed' to Thomas Anderson, Brough, in 1833 (MS 395/3, p 1), and in 1824, a mark given up by the heirs of Olla Gray Junior in Basta was given by the registrar to Helen(?) Skollay in Buraness (MS 395/6, p 4).

The giving of marks was common. Andrew Fordyce, Monthulie, gave a mark to his grandson, Geo. Jameson, and Christan Fraser to Basil Moar,

Colvister (MS 395/3, p 7). David Moar, Kolvister, gave one to his son Andrew (MS 395/3, p 18), Magnus Nesbit Senr., Bixter, to his daughter Janet in Kirkabister, and Peter Nesbit, Senr., Kirkabister to his youngest son Robert in 1849 (MS 395/3. p 21). The mark of John Sutherland, West the firth was given to Basil Hay Jr., Burrabrake, on 11 Jan 1833 (MS 395/3, p 26), and that of Gilbert Scollay, Kongnaseter, to his grandson, Gilbert Scollay Nesbit, though in this case a bit off the top of the left lug was added as a distinction (MS 395/3, p 26). George Moar in Goodster gave a mark to his grand-daughter, Barbara Manson in Neep (MS 395/3, p 29).

From these examples, it appears that the giving of marks between members of the same family was frequent, and that grandchildren tended to be especially favoured. Youngest sons also came into the reckoning, as the following examples emphasise:

(a) 'Nesbit Peter, Senr., Kirkabister. Right Lug half before & a bit under. Left Lug half behind. Extract given May 16th 1849 to Robt. Nesbit youngest son of the above & fee of 6d paid'.

(b) 'Nesbit Peter Junr. (Son of the above) Right Lug two holes Left Lug a hole & bit behind. N.B. This was Mr Scott of Greenwell's mark in N. Yell Allowed to Thos. his 3rd son untill Robt. the youngest child requires it (meaning P.N.'s children)' (MS 395/3, p 21).

Marks could also be sold:

'Danielson Lodwick, Lingarth, Both Ears half Stued and a Bit behind each, a Hole on the Left Ear and a Rift in the Right. This Mark is sold to him by Miss B.B. Irvine of Midbrake to whom it belonged' (MS 395/3, p 6).

Miss Irvine, in fact, acquired the mark from Mr William Henderson of Petester (formerly in Gloup), who in turn got it when he bought the stock of Charles Simpson in Vigon (MS 395/3, p 11).

A second example is:

'Nesbit Thos. presents the following Mark sold to him by Janet Peggie Irvine daughter of Hannah Anderson Right Lug Rift behind Left Lug stued bought for Peter Jas. Nesbit his son -' (MS 395/3, p 22).

From these records, it is clear that women as well as men could have their own marks, and also children, and this is in line with the reindeer owning situation among the Rörös Lapps.

A further point that relates to aspects of community life is the existence of halvers marks. At Midbrake in 1863, a halvers sheep was held with A(n)drina Moar, servant there. Another sheep was in halvers with Jane Spence (possibly also a servant), and a lamb bearing the house mark was given to Laurence Smith in halvers in Sept. 1843 (MS 395/3, p 11). Mr Gilbert William Irvine had a sheep in halvers with Daniel Smith, and in March 1863 a mark was given as a halvers mark between Susan Irvine and Louisa Katharine Fraser (MS 395/3, p 15). John Sinclair of Virdick's mark was used as a halvers mark in 1860 by William John Hay (MS 395/3, p 28), and Peter John Williamson's mark was presented in mid century for sheep in halvers with Mr Pole, Cullivoe (MS 395/3, p 30).

From this evidence, it looks as if the big house was in the habit of having sheep in halvers with servants, perhaps as part of their wages, but flocks might also run together under a shared mark.

Conclusion

This initial analysis of North Yell lug marks refers only to the situation in the first two-thirds of the nineteenth century. Logically, it should be followed by analysis of later evidence, right up to the present day. In itself, it could also be taken much further, for example by listing the various communities in North Yell, noting the names of the individuals (and their families) associated with them, and relating the forms of the marks to them. That there are possible associations seems to be beyond doubt; for instance, George Moar, Basta, and Basil Moar and Andrew Moar, both of Colvester, had the right ears of their sheep stooed and a half out before on the left ears, though there were also minor differentiating marks. Of course, such associations can become obscured by changes over time, but careful examination is very likely to give further pointers, so that these identification marks can be more clearly seen as the indicators of community life that they are.

SAND, INNERSAND AND GARDERHOUSE
PLACE-NAMES IN USE

Doreen J. Waugh

Introduction

As a Shetlander, now living in Edinburgh, I was keen to promote a conference in Shetland during my presidency of the Scottish Society for Northern Studies. The year 1993 marked the twenty-fifth anniversary of the Society which, as its constitution states, exists '...to provide a Scottish meeting-ground for papers and informal discussion on subjects in various fields concerned with Scandinavian and related cultures...' and it, therefore, seemed most fitting to celebrate the Society's twenty-five years in existence with a return visit to Shetland which was one of the earliest conference venues chosen by the Society shortly after its formation in 1968. The proceedings of that first Shetland conference are now sold out but are still available in libraries and merit reference (Baldwin 1978).

The Society's planned visit to Shetland in 1993 fortuitously coincided, almost to the day, with the centenary of the arrival of the philologist Jakob Jakobsen in Shetland from Faroe at the start of his intensive three-year period of place-name and dialect field work. Not surprisingly, plans were already afoot in Shetland to honour the centenary and the Scottish Society for Northern Studies was very happy to cooperate with the Shetland-based Jakob Jakobsen Centenary Committee in jointly commemorating a great 'Faroeman and scholar', as he is described by Professor Michael Barnes earlier in this volume. Many Society members were particularly pleased to be present at the launch of the reprint of Jakobsen's work on Shetland place-names (Jakobsen 1936; reprinted 1993) and to note that Dr Gillian Fellows-Jensen of the University of Copenhagen — distinguished name-scholar and Society member — had been asked to provide its new introduction and to launch it as a publication.

The original 1936 English-language version of Jakobsen's work on place-names has been unobtainable for many years and its scarcity is tribute to the fascination of its topic for Shetlanders in Shetland and elsewhere. It is of place-names that I wish to write in this post-conference article.[1] During the conference, I had the pleasure of hearing (or reading) talks by Michael Barnes, Laurence Graham, Gunnel Melchers[2] and Brian Smith, all of whom

---

1.   I should like to thank Ronald Cant, Gillian Fellows-Jensen and Brian Smith for reading and commenting on this paper. In addition, Brian Smith supplied several references from the Shetland Archives.

2.   Gunnel Melchers was unable to attend the conference due to ill health but she submitted a paper which was made available to conference members at the time and which is now printed in this volume.

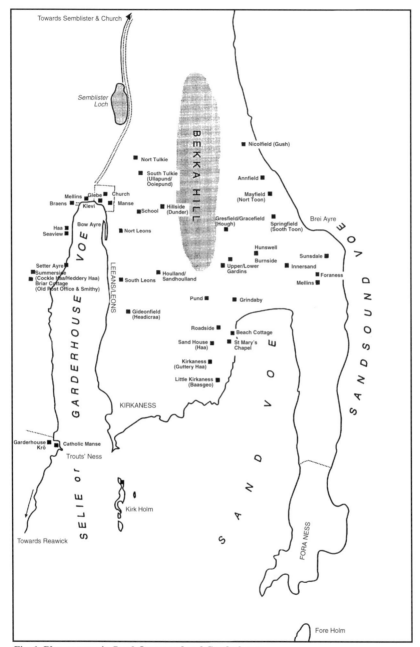

Fig. 1. Place-names in Sand, Innersand and Garderhouse.

243

spoke about aspects of Shetland's linguistic heritage in such a way as to draw attention to the living, working Shetland dialect and, as a result, I began to think more closely about the place-names in use in the village of Sand on the west side of Shetland where I grew up in the schoolhouse as daughter of the teacher, Williamina Laurenson. The influence of Laurence Graham and his brother, John, has, in fact, been with me since my secondary school years when I was privileged to be their pupil and, therefore, to learn to appreciate the riches of the Shetland dialect while still at school. John Graham is well known for his efforts to raise the status of Shetland dialect in public perception and his dictionary of dialect words played an important part in his campaign. I use Graham's spellings for dialect words throughout this article, and if an item is not recorded in Graham's dictionary I have modelled my spelling on his usage (Graham 1979). The spellings of place-names recorded from maps are taken from the 6 inch Ordnance Survey, Second Edition, 1902, unless otherwise specified. Hitherto unrecorded place-names are either modelled on Graham or are modelled on Jakobsen's spellings in those instances where he records other similar place-names elsewhere in Shetland.

Discussion of place-names

Until I read Shetland dialect poems and discussed dialect words in the classroom, I doubt if I had thought of the words I spoke as anything other than a means towards the end of immediate, and fairly utilitarian, communication and the same can be said of Shetland place-names, although the 'classroom' for these was the School of Scottish Studies at the University of Edinburgh. Along with the bulk of the population in Sand, Innersand and Garderhouse, I certainly did not pause to consider whether or not I 'understood' the place-names I used as a child because, as W. F. H. Nicolaisen has pointed out, there is no need to understand a name in order to use it (Nicolaisen 1979-80: 106). In recent years, when studying place-names, I have accepted the commonly-held view of Shetland place-names, as expressed by Jakobsen in the introduction to his book:

> While the Norn dialect itself as such is now lost beyond recall, the predominant part of the place-names, on the other hand, is Norn, i.e. in Norn dialect; a number of original Norn names or compounds ... have been, so to speak, translated into Lowland Scottish. ... A number of names of a later date are in L. Sc. dialect, and in more recent times some names (of houses) occur in the English language (Jakobsen 1936: 2).

Jakobsen uses 'dialect' where one would expect 'language' here, but it seems reasonable to suggest that he is implying that the majority of Shetland place-names are repositories of words from the Norn language which are no longer used or understood in the everyday Scots-based dialect speech of Shetlanders.

There is, of course, truth in what Jakobsen says but, judging from the specific sample of place-names from Sand, Innersand and Garderhouse, one

244

could take minor issue with his statement on two counts and suggest some qualification of the claim he makes. Firstly, the Norn place-names which have survived in use are not necessarily in a 'dialect' which is 'lost beyond recall' because many of them have survived precisely because their constituent elements are understood, either in whole, because they are still used as words in the dialect, or in part, because the people who use them understand how to apply them, although understanding of a place-name in this latter sense differs from understanding of a lexical item in being impressionistic rather than clearly defined. Locals might, for instance, find it difficult to say exactly what some place-names mean in lexical terms but they would be certain where and how, in the landscape, they could or could not be used. Secondly, it is an exaggeration — at least at village level — to say that 'the predominant part of the place-names is Norn'. A very large number of the place-names which were in use in Sand, Innersand and Garderhouse in the 1950s and -60s were, in fact, of Scots origin and arose from the period when the common land was being divided up into portions for crofting purposes. The picture which emerges from a detailed study of all the place-names of an area such as Sand, Innersand and Garderhouse is of a community which uses its Scots speech in the creation of its nomenclature. Shetland dialect does, of course, have many Norn words in its vocabulary, as Gunnel Melchers points out in her contribution to this volume, but these have not been 'translated' into Scots; they are simply used as Norn words in the Shetland dialect, which is a dialect of Scots.

Some of the local place-names do contain Norn words which are now obscure, and it would be nonsensical to argue otherwise, but such place-names are in the minority in the settlement which is spread around the two arms of the sea known as Selievoe — or, as it is sometimes known, Garderhouse Voe[3] — and Sand Voe. It is, of course, fortuitous that the name Sand, itself, can be so readily understood because it derives from Old Norse *sandr* which happens to be a word which is common to all Germanic languages, including English. Many early village names elsewhere in Shetland are obscure and have survived in spite of their opacity because they have been in regular use since the time of the initial Norse settlement. Jakobsen records the following information about Sand: '... the main village, *Sand*, after which the parish (Sandsting) is named, is mentioned in a charter of 14 April 1355 (D.N. III, 1): a sande [á sandi]' (Jakobsen 1936: 125). Sand also occurs in several 16th century documents and is sometimes accompanied by reference to Garderhouse, as in the following extract: '...1½ marks land in Sand, 3 marks land in Garthishous...' (Ballantyne & Smith 1994: 67).

The original Norse settlement of Sand probably skirted the edges of Sand Voe, as the name suggests, and could have extended across the

---

3. Selievoe often appears in older documents as Sandselivoe, presumably to distinguish it from the other Seli Voe further west near Gruting. Probably for the same reason, Selievoe is now often referred to as Garderhouse Voe.

intervening low-lying hill to Selievoe or Garderhouse Voe. The name which has survived as the present-day parish name — Sandsting — clearly points to Norse social organisation in the area (Jakobsen 1936: 94, 125; Andersen 1984: 30; Stewart 1987: 300). The beach of fine white sand at Sand Voe would have attracted the Norse who had sailed past Fore Holm and in along Fora Ness (ON *for-hólmr* 'fore-island'; *fornes* 'a promontory') to establish settlement. Their curiosity might also have been aroused by seeing signs of building on the small island now known as Kirk Holm (ON *kirkja* 'a church' + *hólmr* 'an island') at the point of the other promontory — Kirka Ness — which bounds Sand Voe. Dating and identification of these buildings, however, is problematic. There may have been a pre-Norse monastic presence on the island Kirk Holm (Lamb 1974: 81-2) but the *kirk* which is referred to in the names Kirka Ness and Kirk Holm is more probably the medieval St Mary's Chapel which, like other churches associated with late Norse settlements, stands at the head of Sand Voe but 'just round to one side, so as not to occupy prime economic locations' (Ritchie 1985: 91). Kirk Holm has many legends attached to it, including the persistent local belief that a Spanish Armada ship was wrecked on the island having been driven north by gales after defeat at sea in 1588 and that the surviving Spaniards reached land at Innersand and sought sanctuary in St Mary's Chapel. Memory of pre-Reformation times is also preserved in the name — Da Catholic Manse — which was used by locals of a ruin to the south of Garderhouse, lying directly across the voe from Kirkholm.[4]

It is oddly difficult to define where, on the ground, Sand ends and Innersand begins, in present oral usage. The name Innersand is of considerable age, appearing in written records dating from 1597 (Ballantyne & Smith 1994: 118) and, no doubt, having been in oral use for some time before that date, just as Sand would have been. Perception of the point at which Innersand begins depends, very logically, on where one lives in Sand. People who live at the side of Selievoe (as I did) think of the watershed between Selievoe and Sand Voe as the point at which Innersand starts; and people who live on the other side of the watershed think of Innersand as a particular cluster of houses in the innermost part of their community. The former perception, however, is closer to the original application of the name because the township of Sand was valued as 36 merks of land (a big Shetland township), and was equally divided into 18 merks land of Innersand and 18 merks land of Outersand.[5] The latter is recorded as Utir Sand in 1589 and

---

4. John Arthur Morrison of Seaview, Garderhouse, kindly provided this information and much more relating to Garderhouse and Sand.

5. There is some evidence that the two halves had different 'pertinents' attached to them: in 1673 Laurence Umphray of Sand conveyed to Patrick Umphray the 18 merks land of Innersand and the ness thereto belonging called 'Bearer', running northward from the town to the 'air' of Saltnes (SRO, RS.45/5, f.813r.); and in 1702 Patrick Umphray of Sand sold to John Mitchell of Westshore 18 merks land in Uttersand, with the holms called Kirkholme and Foirholme and the 6 merks land of Sandshoul (SRO, RS.45/5 f.535r.).

Uttersand in 1606 (Ballantyne & Smith: 61, 198), but the name is no longer used and the opposition is now between Sand and Innersand. The distinction between Outer and Inner Sand was still remembered at the end of the 19th century when a document, dated 1871, concerning land owned by Joseph Leask, records: 'My room and lands of Sand and Innersand, otherwise called Outer and Inner Sand.' (Shetland Archives: SC. 12/53/14 fol. 96).

Garderhouse is the name which refers to the part of the community which clings to the side of the hill to the west of Selievoe (ON *selr* 'seal' + *vágr* 'voe or inlet of the sea'). The name contains ON *garðr* 'a yard, enclosure' which is one of the most popular Norse habitative terms in use in Shetland. Stewart records five examples of the compound Garderhouse from various parts of Shetland. The earliest recorded forms of the Sandsting name date from the 16th century when the name appears as: Gardishous and Gardshouss 1507; Garthishous 1524; Gardyshous 1544 (Stewart 1987: 167). The second element in the compound is ON *hús* 'a house' which, being common Germanic, is even more widespread and very difficult to identify as being Norse in origin rather than Scots except, as in this case, when compounded with another unquestionably Norse element. Old Norse *garðr* is no longer understood and the survival of the name suggests uninterrupted habitation and/or regular passage through Garderhouse from neighbouring Semblister to Reawick on foot or on horseback.

A sketch map of the commonty of Semblister and Sand, dated 1858 (SRO: RHP 3912), identifies Garderhouse as the property adjacent to the Glebe of Selievoe[6] and places the house along the side of the voe rather than at its head, seeming to indicate the ruined building known as Da Haa o Garderhouse or 'The Hall of Garderhouse' — *haa* being a Scots term which is often used with reference to the house of the local laird or other dignitary and, in this case, reputedly built for a Captain Cumming who was the son of a Sandsting minister. The croft-house beside this old ruin was also known until recently as Da Haa but it has now been de-crofted (i.e. the land is now being farmed by someone else and the house has been bought by its present occupants) and renamed Seaview. Da Haa o Garderhouse is not, of course, a building from the Norse period but, like its more recent equivalent at the side of Sand Voe, it could have replaced an earlier building or a series of buildings on the same site or it could have been built alongside existing buildings. Sand House, or Da Haa o Sand as it is known locally, is the laird's house, built in 1754 for the Mitchell family on the site of a previous building which was also occupied by the local laird.[7] Da Haa o Sand is situated on the side of the hill above St Mary's Chapel.

---

6. Selievoe and Garderhouse often paid scat together but in c.1600 half of it was retained by the minister for his glebe (SRO, E.41/7).

7. The present laird, Mr Peter Hick, kindly provided me with the information about Sand House.

The name of the settlement of Semblister (Samlesetter 1605; Samlsetter 1607; Semblesetter 1609) (Ballantyne & Smith 1994: 187; 207; 240) mentioned above, which lies to the north of Garderhouse, is also of Norse origin and its meaning is obscure to present-day Shetlanders who turn to Jakobsen for its interpretation (Jakobsen 1936: 153, 115). Semblister — although now recognised as a separate settlement — is only about one mile distant from Sand[8] and when St Mary's Chapel in Sand fell into disuse in 1780 (Cant: forthcoming publication on the Churches and Chapels of Shetland), a new church was built by the shore at Semblister where it could be reached by boat and, therefore, serve a wider congregation. People could approach it from Sand and Garderhouse by foot along the side of the Loch of Semblister, or by boat from Innersand and Tresta. As they walked past the Mill Burn at the north end of the Loch of Semblister, church-goers would have seen three water-mills at regular intervals along its length; possibly one for each of the townships of Innersand, Sand and Garderhouse. The church at Semblister was in use until the early 1950s, but not for evening worship because there was no lighting.[9] A small house, situated next to the church and inhabited latterly by an elderly impoverished lady, was referred to as Da Pauper's Hoose and was in use until the early 1900s.

The church at Semblister was, in turn, supplemented in 1911 — and replaced some forty years later — by one at the head of Selievoe (Cant: forthcoming). This was built on the plot of ground where the old manse of Sand had been situated and a new manse was built adjacent to, but not adjoining, the church. It was often the case in the medieval period in Shetland that the manse and glebe, or portion of land assigned to a parish minister in addition to his stipend, were at some distance from the church itself and that was the case in Sandsting, with the church of St Mary's beside Sand Voe and the manse and glebe beside Selievoe. 'The vicarage of Sandsting' is noted in a document from 1580 (Ballantyne & Smith 1994: 2). The current farmhouse known as Da Glebe is a very old building and parts of it are believed to date back to the early 1600s. Da Glebe is still the major farm in the area, occupying prime agricultural land.

On the opposite side of Selievoe from Garderhouse, the name Da Leeans, sometimes spelt Leons (ON *hlíð* 'a hillside, slope'), is used to refer to the crofted section of the sloping hill which runs along the side of the voe. Unlike Garderhouse, however, Da Leeans is not now used as a village name in its own right. It is a description of a particular part of Sand and although local people would not be able to define its meaning precisely, they would

8. As an ancient settlement, Sand paid scat; however, Semblister did not and as a result paid a 'tulbert scat' of £2 Scots to the proprietors of Sand (SRO, RS.45/4, f.478v.).

9. I owe this information to Bertie Deyell who now lives at Semblister in a house built in 1860, sometimes called the Old Baptist Manse. Bertie has a huge fund of local knowledge which he generously shared with me when I was preparing this article.

consider it appropriate that it should be used with reference to sloping, cultivated ground and not of any other type of ground. Jakobsen does not record the Sand example but he mentions similar names elsewhere in Shetland, one of them being 'de Liens' in Sandwick, Unst (Jakobsen 1936: 78). Stewart records the Sand name as follows: 'Leeons 1821-60; Leeans 1860; Leons 1869-1954' (Stewart 1987: 134). Similarly, at the head of Selievoe, the flat ground at the top of the beach across which people walk from Sand to Garderhouse is known as Da Mellins, sometimes spelt Maillands (ON *melr* 'sand'), and locals would be aware that such a name should properly refer to the grass-covered, sandy soil at a beach head. For example, one of the croft houses on the side of the hill at Fora Ness is known as Da Mellins/Maillands and a local informant, clearly considering it to be unusual as a house name, explained that this is because the land allocated to the croft abuts on the sandy beach.[10] The croft is recorded in a transaction of 1705 when Patrick Umphray sold to James Mitchell of Girlsta '18 merks of land in Innersand, with the piece of land called the Maill lands next adjacent' (SRO, RS.45/6/2, fol. 641).

Da Mellins is not recorded as a place-name on the 6 inch Ordnance Survey map of Sand and neither is Da Klevi (ON *kleif* 'a ridge of cliffs or shelves in a mountainside') which is the steep path or *klevi* (Jakobsen 1928 (reprinted 1985): 430) leading up from Da Mellins towards a group of houses in Garderhouse known as Da Braens. The houses are named on the map but the path which leads towards them does not merit having its sections identified by name and it is unfortunate that these minor names are not recorded because, in my opinion, they are important evidence of the way in which the Scots language was sufficiently elastic to use Norn words when they fitted the situation more precisely than Scots equivalents. In his place-name volume, Jakobsen refers to other examples of the name 'de Klev' or 'de Klevi' in Shetland but does not record the Sand example (Jakobsen 1936: 66).

The use of *da*[11] — the Shetland dialect form of the English definite article *the* — with all of these names, implies that the dialect speakers who employed these descriptive terms as names were using the Norn words as part of their own dialect of Scots just as, for example, a current Gaelic speaker does not hesitate to say, 'A bheil *an càr* agad dubh?', fully incorporating the useful English word *car* into his own language and preceding it with the correct form of the Gaelic definite article. When thinking of inflected languages, such as Gaelic and Norse, it is interesting to note the common Shetland place-name ending which appears variously as *-ins/-ens/-ns*, as in

---

10. Patricia Alderson (née Fraser), who lives at Gracefield in Innersand, provided this comment and many others and I owe a great deal to her extensive local knowledge and to her willingness to conduct some local research on my behalf.

11. I have followed Graham (1979) in using the spelling *da*, rather than *de* which is favoured by Jakobsen (1936).

Da Mellins and Da Braens. In the case of examples of Mellens from elsewhere in Shetland, Jakobsen notes three possible meanings: '... *Mellens* may ... be either a "*meðal-heimar" or pl. of "*meðal-land", or ... def. pl. of "melr" (sand)[12]...' (Jakobsen 1936: 58), which latter possibility suggests that the same Norse inflectional ending has been added to the Scots word *brae* 'a slope' in the formation of the place-name Da Braens. The linguistic situation is, of course, further complicated by the fact that the final -s, in all names of this type, is the Scots/English plural ending which has been added to the earlier Norse plural ending.

Survival of obscure Norse elements in place-names which can be partly understood because the other elements in the names are current in the Shetland dialect can be noted in Grindaby and Da Bowayre (the first element of the latter name being pronounced [bu]). Grind (ON *grind*) and ayre (ON *eyrr*) are still commonly used for 'gate' and 'gravelly tongue of land running into the sea' respectively and it seems possible, although lack of early references inhibits precise identification, that the -by of Grindaby and Bow- of Bowayre may have the same origin in ON *boer (býr)* 'a farm'. Jakobsen records a number of Shetland farm-names ending in -by and also mentions the use of '*Bø*' in fisherman's tabu-language for certain villages which could not be named at sea, such as '*Kjorkabi* [*kirkju-bœr]' (i.e. 'church farm') (Jakobsen 1936: 32, 164). Grindaby is situated at a short distance from the gates of Da Haa o Sand and Da Bowayre is situated across the voe from Da Haa o Garderhouse on a spit of land which has a fisherman's booth or *böd* on it. This spit of land runs in along the voe towards the present church and glebe which are situated at the head of the voe on the same side as Da Bowayre. It is very likely that the situation of the priest's manse and glebe at the head of the voe gave rise to the name Da Bowayre in the medieval period.

Before leaving names which contain Norse elements, I should mention some further place-names from Sand and Innersand. Firstly, there is a croft named Houlland on the watershed between the two parts of the community. Houlland is a very common Shetland place-name, ultimately of Norse origin (ON *hó(há)-land* (referring to elevated situation)) (Jakobsen 1936: 77), and because of its common occurrence the name is usually identified more specifically on maps or in documents as Sandhoulland (Stewart 1987: 198). Secondly, there are two examples of the commonly occurring Norse place-name, Gardins, prefixed by English Upper and Lower. Jakobsen notes that Gardins derives from ON *gerði* 'a fenced patch of ground' and is frequently in the plural form with preserved definite article, as is the case in Innersand (Jakobsen 1936: 45). Thirdly, the field-name Hunswell refers to the rounded side of the hill above the crofts of Innersand. Neither Jakobsen nor Stewart records this name and early references are not available for a field which is not particularly productive. The likelihood is, however, that it contains the

---

12. Def. pl. of *melr*: *Melarnir* (nominative); *melunum* (dative).

ON elements *hundr* 'a dog' and *völlr* 'a field'. Gillian Fellows-Jensen comments, with reference to the street-name 'Hungate' that when *hundr* is used in place-names it is likely to indicate that the locality in question was 'insignificant' (Fellows-Jensen 1979: 45-46) and Hunswell would have been one of the least desirable of the surrounding fields, being on the brow of the hill. Finally, I should mention Baasgeo, which is an example of a croft being named after rocks in the sea before it. Both of the elements in this name are frequently used in Shetland dialect and the precise reference is to sunken rocks or *baas* in a steep-sided inlet of the sea or *geo*. The name of the croft is sometimes given as Little Kirkaness but it is never thus known locally. The 6 inch OS map records neither of these two names.

The place-names in the next group which I should like to discuss are largely of Scots origin and, like Baasgeo, they function as local alternatives to the place-names recorded on maps. This group of names is particularly fascinating because, if one extrapolates from the local situation in Sand, a picture of 'bilingualism' in Shetland place-naming emerges. Just as there is a Little Kirkaness on the map, locally known as Baasgeo, so is there a larger property, now vacant, officially called Kirkaness but never known as such. When the property was occupied, in the earlier years of this century, it was known either as Maggie Sandison's — after its occupant — or, more frequently, by the wonderfully evocative Scots expression Da Guttery Haa or 'The Muddy Hall'. The house was adjacent to Da Haa o Sand and local people seldom missed an opportunity to debunk. In similar vein, although less pejorative in reference, one finds Da Cockle Haa in Garderhouse, which appears on the map as Summerside. It is tempting, given the situation of Summerside on the upper edge of the community and on higher, less fertile ground, to suggest that the English name, Summerside, may hark back to an earlier Norse *sætr* 'shieling' which was used during the summer for the pasturing of animals, but there is no written evidence to support the suggestion. There is, however, some support from a hitherto unrecorded coastal name, Setter Ayre (ON *setr/sætr* 'a shieling or hill farm'+ *eyrr* 'a gravelly bank'), which is used of the stretch of beach below Summerside. A link between the beach and the house would explain the reference to shellfish in Da Cockle Haa.

Other crofts which have alternative names are Gideonfield (known as Headicraa 'somersault/head-over-heels', perhaps because of the steepness of the fields); Newhouse — as it was recorded in the 1851 Census — or Hillside (known as Dunder 'a sound like thunder', often used with reference to wind noise)[13]; Nicolfield (known either as Bekka[14] — from the hill named Bekka on

---

13. The croft was established in the 19th century and, therefore, I have suggested the Scots word *dunder* but it should be noted that *Dunder-* also occurs as the specific in some Norwegian place-names (Rygh 1905: 16, 146).

14. A name of Norse origin for which Jakobsen suggests ON *bekkr* in the sense of 'rounded hill' (Jakobsen 1936: 33). The top of Bekka is now known locally by the biblical name Pisgah.

251

the slopes of which it stood — or Gush — by the people of Sandsound who, according to local lore, saw a clifftop loch at Nicolfield cascade into the sea in the early twentieth century); Mayfield (known as Nort Toon) and Springfield (known as Sooth Toon); and, finally, Gresfield/Gracefield (known as Da Hoch/Hough — possibly Scots *haugh* 'river-meadow land', an interpretation which is supported by the spelling *Gres-* which suggests abundance of 'grass', although the specific could equally well be the personal name *Grace*, paralleling some of the other local names in *-field*, such as Annfield, Gideonfield and Nicolfield). It would seem from these examples that there was a degree of resistance to the English names which were allocated to crofts at the time of division of the commonty. For some reason, the croft named Annfield survived with its name intact.

Sometimes, of course, documents record a croft by the occupant's name and the place-name thus created is often as evanescent as the occupant if, indeed, it was ever used other than as a map or estate-plan reference. For example, one of the crofts opposite Sandsound is identified as Magnustown in the 1851 census but it is now known as Sunsdale, a name which Stewart records in 1580 as Soundsdale (Stewart 1987: 75) and for which Jakobsen suggests derivation from 'ON *sund* 'a sound' + *deild* 'a deal or portion', used commonly in Shetland as the generic in place-names in the sense of: 'patch of ground; part of field' (Jakobsen 1936: 34). The name is also recorded as Sounsdaill in a document dated 1691 (SRO, RS.45/4, fol. 488r.). One suspects that the patch of cultivated land beside the sound has been thus known since it was broken in from the hill at a time when Norn was the speech of the district and that the people farming the land, then as now, knew their stretch of beach as Da Brei Ayre (ON *breiðr* 'broad' + *eyrr* 'gravelly bank'),[15] although the name is not recorded on the 6 inch map.

Other dialect terms used in the place-nomenclature tell us about the daily activities of people in a crofting community who, for instance, put their cattle out to graze in summer in Semblister and named the park where the cows lay Da Coo Böls — *böl* being a word commonly used in Shetland dialect for a resting-place for cattle (ON *ból* 'a lying place of beasts or cattle'). The crofters also required to pen their animals from time to time, as recorded in place-names containing the Scots word *pund* 'an enclosure for animals'. There are two such names, one of which is no longer used and which has, therefore, been forgotten by almost all the inhabitants of Sand, although it is faintly remembered by a few who suggest spellings such as Ulla- or Ullipund. One of my informants, however, was able to dip into his aural memory and tell me that South Tulkie — an interesting name in its own right — was earlier known as Da Ooie Pund, which indicates that the *pund* or enclosure was used for penning sheep when they needed to be *rooed* or to

---

15. For another example see the Shetland village name, Brae, which Jakobsen derives from ON *breiðr* + *eið* 'an isthmus, neck of land' (Jakobsen 1936: 36).

have their *oo* (i.e. wool) plucked. The language of origin of the name Tulkie is debatable but the fact that it is used to describe two outlying crofts, one of which was situated by an earlier sheep-pen, points to Scots rather than Norn.

The other example of Scots *pund* occurs in the simplex place-name, Da Pund, which is close to Da Haa o Sand and which was, according to local tradition, a place where ponies were penned. An earlier name for another house close to Da Haa also points to ownership of horses. According to my informant, Bertie Deyell, the small house close to the gates of the laird's house once functioned as stables and was known as such, but that name in turn has been replaced by a twentieth-century English name, Roadside, which must be one of the most common house-names in Scotland. The name indicates the increasing importance of access by road to the community of people living in Innersand and Sand who, in earlier centuries, were much more dependent on the sea for their supplies, as the situation of Da Aald Shop by the sea at Sand Voe indicates. Da New Shop by the road at Grindaby, in turn, has been superseded in the process of constant change and renewal which characterises village life. Shops are now considerably more distant and assume car-ownership. Other local facilities have also disappeared, leaving nothing other than a memory of a name. I am thinking both of the school in Sand, which I attended as a child, and of Da Smiddy (now known as Briar Cottage) which was situated beside Summerside in Garderhouse and where the horses from Innersand, Sand, Garderhouse and Semblister would have been shod.

Conclusion

I think what I, personally, find so fascinating about many of the place-names mentioned above is the fact that they are so obviously living entities and should not merely be revered as icons of the dead Norn language. The overall picture is one of onomastic change and renewal in response to the changing nature of the community. The place-names discussed here also point to the necessity of consulting local people, as well as maps in the library, when conducting research, because it has been shown that the latter may not always reflect the reality of place-names in use. I have to say that, once I began to study the area in detail, I was surprised at the extent to which maps and local usage differed in the case of Sand, Innersand and Garderhouse and I have been impressed by the strength of the oral tradition in naming. Many of the place-names listed above have never been recorded on maps or in documents.

Collection of such oral material presents a challenge to the onomastician but the rewards are great, particularly when one encounters a piece of oral evidence which suddenly opens up a whole new field of possibility in terms of interpretation of place-names and what they can tell us about the present and past life of the community being studied. Lack of space has meant that I have omitted many topographical place-names and also some of the most recent names created for new houses which have been built within the last decade, but I hope that I have conveyed a reasonably full picture of Sand, Innersand and Garderhouse, as seen through place-names.

Bibliography

Andersen, Per Sveaas, 1984: 'Peter Andreas Munch and the Beginning of Shetland Place-name Research'. In: Barbara Crawford (ed.), *Essays in Shetland History*, Lerwick, 18-32.

Baldwin, J.R. (ed.), 1978: *Scandinavian Shetland an Ongoing Tradition*. Scottish Society for Northern Studies. Edinburgh.

Ballantyne, John H. and Smith, Brian (eds.), 1994: *Shetland Documents 1580 - 1611*. Lerwick.

Cant, Ronald, (forthcoming): *The Churches and Chapels of Shetland*. Lerwick.

Cleasby, Vigfusson, Craigie, 1874: *An Icelandic-English Dictionary*. Oxford. (Reprinted in 1982).

Fellows-Jensen, G., 1979: 'Hungate. Some observations on a Common Street-Name', *Ortnamnssällskapets i Uppsala Årsskrift*, Uppsala, 44-51.

Graham, John J., 1979: *The Shetland Dictionary*. Lewis.

Jakobsen, Jakob, 1928: *An Etymological Dictionary of the Norn Language in Shetland*. Copenhagen. (Reprinted in Lerwick, 1985).

Jakobsen, Jakob, 1936: *The Place-Names of Shetland*. London and Copenhagen. (Reprinted in Orkney, 1993).

Lamb, R.G., 1974: 'Coastal Settlements of the North', *Scottish Archaeological Forum 5*, Edinburgh, 76-98.

Nicolaisen, W.F.H., 1979-80: 'Early Scandinavian Naming in the Northern and Western Isles', *Northern Scotland 3*, No.2, Aberdeen, 105-121.

Ritchie, Anna, 1985: *Exploring Scotland's Heritage. Orkney and Shetland*. Royal Commission on the Ancient and Historical Monuments of Scotland. Edinburgh.

Rygh, O., 1897-1936: *Norske Gaardnavne*. Kristiania.

Stewart, John, 1987: *Shetland Place-Names*. Lerwick.